# A GAME FOR HOOLIGANS
## The History of Rugby Union

Huw Richards has been the *Financial Times* rugby correspondent since 1995. He is the author of *Dragons and All Blacks*, which was shortlisted for the William Hill Sports Book of the Year, and co-author of two acclaimed volumes of essays on Welsh heroes, *Heart and Soul* and *More Heart and Soul*. He has covered all six World Cups and reported on nearly three hundred rugby internationals.

### ALSO BY HUW RICHARDS:

*The Bloody Circus: The Daily Herald and the British Left* (1997)

*Dragons and All Blacks: Wales v. New Zealand – 1953
and a Century of Rivalry* (2004)

*Raising the Dragon: A Clarion Call to Welsh Rugby*
– with Robert Jones (2001)

*Heart and Soul: The Character of Welsh Rugby*
– edited with Peter Stead and Gareth Williams (1998)

*More Heart and Soul: The Character of Welsh Rugby*
– edited with Peter Stead and Gareth Williams (1999)

*For Club and Country: Welsh Football Greats*
– edited with Peter Stead (2000)

# A GAME FOR HOOLIGANS

## The History of Rugby Union

# HUW RICHARDS

MAINSTREAM
PUBLISHING

EDINBURGH AND LONDON

First published in Great Britain in 2006 by
MAINSTREAM PUBLISHING COMPANY
(EDINBURGH) LTD
7 Albany Street
Edinburgh EH1 3UG

ISBN 9781845962555

A catalogue record for this book is available
from the British Library

The author has tried to clear all copyright permissions,
but where this has not been possible and amendments
are required, the publisher will be pleased to make any
necessary arrangements at the earliest opportunity

Typeset in Gill Sans and New Baskerville

Printed in Great Britain by
Clays Ltd, St Ives plc

9 10

To my brother John and to the memory of his partner
Ruth Sophia Cohen (1964–2006)

# Acknowledgements

This book would not have been possible without the help of others. Particular thanks are due to Gareth Williams, Huw Bowen, David Scott and Rob Steen, who read the manuscript as it was being written and, in ploughing through large amounts of rough-edged text and offering insights, prompts and notification of howlers, provided assistance far beyond the usual demands of friendship. The same goes for Kate Green, still no more interested in rugby than the last time she read one of my books, who proofread the entire text.

Museums on opposite sides of the world provided essential assistance, at the same time offering the warm welcome that makes such a difference to the itinerant researcher's existence. Bob Luxford and all at the New Zealand Museum of Rugby, Palmerston North, provide a home from home for any visiting researcher and guidance on what best to extract from their archives within the time constraints of a visit. Particular thanks to Bob for his assistance in finding photographs for this book. The Museum supplied the pictures of Billy Wallace, Jim Parker, the Swansea v. All Blacks match of 1935, Peter Jones, Colin Meads, Gareth Edwards and the Eden Park aviator of 1981. Thanks are due to the *New Zealand Herald* for permission to reproduce the Jones and 1981 pictures and to the *Dominion Post* for the Edwards picture. Jed Smith and the staff of the RFU's Museum of Rugby achieved the minor miracle of making a Welshman feel completely at home at Twickenham, not only tolerating but apparently welcoming my presence in their excellent library for several weeks during the spring of 2006.

Any researcher in this field not only stands on the shoulders of predecessors but is indebted to contemporaries for suggestions and, in some cases, the loan of books and papers. Thanks here are due to Phil Dine, John Jenkins, Adrian Smith, Tony Collins, Jed Smith, Charles Little, John Hollyman, Frankie Deges, Greg Ryan, Gareth Williams, Peter Stead, Bob Luxford, Richard Holt, Brian Harrison and Mark Curthoys.

Thanks to the New Zealand Rugby Union (with specific thanks for assistance to Joslyn Titus and Mark Vivian) for permission to reproduce the photographs of Jonah Lomu and Richie McCaw. Special thanks are also due to Frederic Humbert (www.rugby-pioneers.com) and John Hood (www.ovalballs.com) for their generosity in lending items from their own collections. Thanks also to *L'Equipe* and its UK agents, Offside, for permission to reproduce the pictures of Jean Prat and Martin Johnson.

My main employers as a freelance writer – Charles Morris of the *Financial Times*, Mandy Garner of the *Times Higher Education Supplement*, Jonathan McConnell and Paul McFarland of scrum.com and Peter Berlin of the *International Herald Tribune* – were all tolerant of the grumpiness and unreliability almost inevitable in someone who's writing a book (at least that's my excuse and I'm sticking to it). Help both practical and moral came from many friends – Simon Targett and Alison Brace, James and Margaret Belich, Mary Scott, Paul Melly, Ian Lewis, Paul Geradine, Bill and Fiona Dinning, Rob Steen, Steve Pinder, Jane and Roy Elvin, Mike Marqusee and Liz Davies, Peter and Bethan Charles, Len and Frances Scott, David Ballheimer, Eva Melly, Ron and Helen Hollick, Michael Fitzpatrick and Agnes Briand, Kate, Andrew and Christopher Green, Mark McDonald and Melinda Wittstock. Thanks too to Apartamentos de Sevilla for providing an ideally tranquil environment for much of the writing.

John Pawsey again showed himself everything one might wish for in an agent, while Graeme Blaikie, Kevin O'Brien, Emily Bland, Lee Fullarton, Korena Hillier and the remainder of the team at Mainstream Publishing once more showed that combination of patience, firmness and professionalism that any author needs from his publisher.

It almost goes without saying that my parents, Stan and Sheila Richards, have been a constant source of support, affection and encouragement. I probably do not say it enough. This book, though, is dedicated to my brother John – who is hereby publicly forgiven for having both annexed the entire family inheritance of sporting ability and, at an early age, chosen English roots over Welsh in his allegiances while I was doing the opposite – and to the memory of his late partner Ruth Cohen. That he stuck with this choice throughout England's serial failures of the 1970s and 1980s was an early indication of the commitment and integrity later shown in the much more significant sphere of his relationship with Ruth, who died suddenly in March 2006 after enduring multiple sclerosis with great courage and much humour.

Being the dedicatee of a rugby book would have tickled that sense of humour, since she swore never to go to a match again after being soaked to the skin on both her visits to Murrayfield. That she never got the chance to change her mind is cause for profound and lasting regret.

*Huw Richards,*
*Seville and Walthamstow*

# Contents

# Contents

# INTRODUCTION

# Contesting Possession

'A sport that is strange, singular, complex and undoubtedly perverse in its inextricable and existential mix of violence and intelligence, power and shrewdness, of the exercise of force and mastery of technique; difficult to understand for the layman – and at times the initiate'

Jean-Pierre Bodis (1993)

'Homoerotic wrestling on the run'

Louis Nowra (2003)

We all have our own year zero. As with all childhood memories, the problem is to disentangle what one truly saw from what one has been told, or maybe read, subsequently. The basic details, though, of that first match, seen on 30 December 1967 as an eight year old on the annual post-Christmas visit to grandparents, remain clear. Swansea beat Neath 11–9 at St Helen's. Clive Rowlands captained Swansea, and Doug Rees kicked the match-winning conversion from near the touch-line.

It was a brief, in-the-flesh exposure to the game but enough to establish both a taste and an allegiance pursued via match reports heard over crackling airwaves on Radio Wales's *Sports Medley* and intensive weekly perusal of the playing records of rugby clubs printed in *The Guardian*.

That first match also supplied heroes. Delight when Rees was selected to play for Wales turned to disappointment when he missed a vital kick and disbelief when he was subsequently left out in favour of a medical student from London Welsh called John Williams – initials as yet superfluous. It was similarly disappointing when

13

Rowlands retired at the end of the season and seemed to disappear from sight. Little did I know.

It is sobering to look back four decades and see how much has changed. Swansea v. Neath was, incongruous as the word is in the context of a South Wales derby, a friendly match. At the time, there was no other type, apart from the Floodlit Alliance, a still novel activity carried out after dark in midweek. There were no leagues, not even a merit table as yet, and no knockout cup, although the regularity with which Wales's leading clubs played each other, plus the unofficial tables in the *Western Mail*, meant that pecking orders were well understood. Fixtures were settled years in advance by club secretaries – a threat to cut them off was the ultimate sanction and insult. The season had a familiar rhythm, punctuated by seasonal exotica such as Watsonians (whatever they were) and UAU at Christmas and the Harlequins and Barbarians at Easter.

The players were still amateur. No doubt, they benefited from what Gareth Williams has termed 'blindside remuneration' – Welsh rugby club treasurers grasped creative accounting well ahead of the City of London – but they still had jobs. Rowlands was a teacher, Rees a tinplate worker. They trained together two nights a week. They were essentially local heroes, mostly graduates of the tough schooling provided by the suburban and village clubs of the West Wales Rugby Union.

Welsh club rugby was as good as it got – a belief supported by results against the leading English clubs. Only the historic quartet of Cardiff, Swansea, Llanelli and Newport got to play against the All Blacks, Australia and South Africa as individual clubs – and Swansea had beaten them all by 1935 – whereas the English and Scots fielded regional teams and the Irish their provinces. That Swansea might one day amalgamate with Neath to try to keep pace with Leicester (whom they routinely beat), Wasps (who were not thought worth playing), Irish provinces and French clubs would have been considered preposterous.

St Helen's itself was an international ground still in abeyance, the grievance that after several decades of alternation all of Wales's matches since 1954 had been played in Cardiff a live one, even if it was evident that the Welsh Rugby Union (WRU) was not pouring money into the capital city's National Stadium in order to play games anywhere else.

The game itself has changed profoundly over the decades. A try in 1967 was worth three points, the same as a penalty or drop goal. It was possible to kick directly to touch from anywhere. Rowlands was notorious for precisely this tactic and had used it so relentlessly against Scotland at Murrayfield in 1963 that there were 111 lineouts and Wales's outside-half David Watkins touched the ball five times. Memory insists that Rowlands confined the Neath game to a narrow strip in front of the St Helen's grandstand, but this recollection may have become confused with Gareth Edwards' virtuoso kicking performance in his 50th international at Twickenham in 1978 or even stories of Cliff Morgan's similar feats in the lee of the Arms Park stand in the 1950s.

The game was on the verge of great change – much of it touching upon, or touched by, Rowlands. He would shortly become Welsh national coach – not the first person to hold that office, but the first to impinge on national consciousness as his team performed in a dazzling style diametrically opposed to his own. His gifts as tactician and rhetorician would be applied to a group of players whose attacking talents have rarely been matched in any country at any time, aided by new limits on touch-kicking which, while not attributable solely to his influence – New Zealand and Australia were pressing for them before he was born – were certainly helped along by his *reductio ad absurdum* of unlimited kicking at Murrayfield.

Rowlands would be manager of Wales at the first rugby World Cup in 1987 and president of the WRU two years later, as the issues of the era – the malign influence of South African apartheid and the inexorable forces driving an unwilling game towards professionalism – were juxtaposed to devastating effect. As broadcaster and commentator, he was around to see both the final acceptance of professionalism in 1995 and its convulsive after-effects, leading to the final downfall of the Welsh clubs in 2003 with the introduction of regional franchises.

Of course, 1967 was only year zero in a narrowly personal sense. Rugby union is, and always has been, subject to change and development. It always will be, since the alternative is to stagnate and die. The previous decade had seen significant change – New Zealand, Australia and South Africa were granted equal representation on the International Rugby Board (IRB) in 1958, although France was still waiting for admission. (NB: Although the IRB has changed its name at least twice during its history, it will be called the IRB throughout this book to avoid confusion.) The same year had brought a law amendment as liberating as limited kicking would be: removing the requirement to play the ball with the foot before picking up after a tackle. Touring teams had made British fans aware of rugby in far-off and previously unsuspected countries like Canada (1962) and Fiji (1964), although the closer-at-hand Romanians were still held at arm's length. In an age wont to fret over thin ends of wedges – although most rugby officials would have assumed that counter-culture was something to do with shops – some changes were nevertheless being admitted, with the WRU reluctantly accepting the Floodlit Alliance in 1964 and appointing Ray Williams as national coaching adviser in 1967.

In those processes of change, one of the most important drivers is, paradoxically enough, an unchanging element: that rugby is not, and never has been, a simple game. Seven varieties of football emerged from the common origin of pre-modern folk games. There are Association Football, two varieties of rugby and two North American mutations thereof, plus the creations born of Irish and Australian cultural resistance to British games.

Each competes with others for players, fans, publicity, money and cultural space. Each has qualities proclaimed by its adherents to make it superior to all others. It is no coincidence that an Australian football anthology and a rugby league magazine share the title *The Greatest Game*. Preferences are personal and cultural. Most of us feel happiest with the game we grew up with and played (however incompetently) and assess the others, sympathetically or otherwise, in terms of our own. Rugby union's distinctiveness is complexity rooted in a single fact: that the contest for possession remains integral rather than, as in the other handling games, simply a means of restarting the game.

And the wide range of contests for possession makes rugby union at its best a game of subtle variety. It enables the multiplicity of specialist skills, favouring different physical attributes, that in theory at least enables participation by all shapes and sizes. The aficionado can thrill to a soaring lineout artist like John Eales, a back rower like Richie McCaw winning his battles of inches at the breakdown or the dynamic power of Munster's pack driving inexorably forward, as much as to the brilliance of great attacking backs. Great rugby comes not only as free-flowing spectacle but in battles of wits between teams of different strengths and styles, each attempting to impose its virtues on the other.

It is at the same time the game's great weakness – a barrier to comprehension and enjoyment for non-devotees epitomised by my grandfather, a West Country man whose real passion was Somerset cricket. He was wont to say, 'I like it when they're running with the ball and passing, but I don't understand it when they all stick their heads down in those scrums.' Complexity and that interdependent multiplicity of phases offer copious opportunities for disruption, discontinuity and negativity and for those whose first aim is, rather than playing themselves, to stop their opponents playing.

The process of law-making is one of dialectical exchange between legislators and players. Describing one of the earliest sets of laws in 1846 as 'a set of decisions on certain disputed points' acknowledged a pattern maintained ever since. The legislators of the past set out with one purpose: to ensure a fair contest for possession. (This battle has been lost in the scrummage, but is still fiercely contested elsewhere.) The intention has survived into the present, but with greater emphasis on creating and maintaining a flowing spectacle attractive to spectators. Players and coaches rapidly work out how to negate or subvert that intention. To be any sort of games player is to instinctively test the limits and weaknesses of the laws under which one plays.

Contests for possession are not confined to the field. The ownership of the game itself has been disputed since alumni of Rugby School started to debate rules with university students from other schools in the 1830s and 1840s. Rugby's pattern of diffusion has been that of most sports: down the social scale and from rich, powerful countries to those with less wealth and influence.

The process has had a strongly British accent. Just as Wilfred Wooller could joke that 'if it had been left to Scotland, handling might never have been legalised', if it had been left to the British, rugby would be almost entirely English-speaking. It was the French, the main linguistic exception, who drove development in Continental Europe.

One consequence of this pattern of diffusion is the game's engaging inversion of conventional geopolitics, with Germany, Japan and the United States as likeable underdogs and New Zealand as a ruthless imperial superpower. A less happy outcome was that rugby was more susceptible than other sports to the poison released by South African apartheid.

Uniformity has been sought but rarely attained. Each community, society and nation which took to rugby followed adoption with adaptation. The rules and the name of the game may have been the same, but the forms of rugby played by Malay house-servants in Cape Town, Catalan clerks in Perpignan, dairy workers in New Zealand, pitmen, policemen and clergymen in Wales, millhands in Yorkshire or medical students in Argentina differed from each other as they differed from the game played by suburban and old boys' clubs in London. Each suffused the game with its own attitudes, preferences and priorities. Each wanted to play the game in its own way and treat its players according to local conditions and mores.

Those desires – whether they be the leading northern English clubs wanting to compensate players for time off work, New Zealand's commitment to its detached wing-forward and seven-man scrummage, the southern hemisphere unions' desire for a formal voice in ruling councils or their subsequent push for the creation of a World Cup – have been both a source of conflict between centre and periphery and a driving force in change.

Rugby is by its nature violent, a quality beautifully caught, via the agency of his creation Bertie Wooster, by P.G. Wodehouse, a committed fan until his post-war exile in the United States:

> The normal scheme is to work the ball down the field somehow and deposit it over the line at the other end, and in order to squelch this programme each side is allowed to put in a certain amount of assault and battery and do things to its fellow man which, if done elsewhere, would result in fourteen days without the option, with some strong remarks from the bench.

David Kirk, the thoughtful, highly intelligent man who led New Zealand to its 1987 World Cup triumph, has acknowledged the importance of intimidation via legitimised violence. He described the rucking techniques developed in Otago then adopted in modified form by the All Blacks as 'a discovery that applied violence, legally, to great effect. It was a way of clearing the ball away from a tackle quickly, legally, demoralising and hurting the opposition at the same time.' Violence underpins the description of rugby as 'a game for hooligans played by gentlemen'.

There was also a strong and unattractive element of social condescension in the accompanying description of soccer as 'a game for gentlemen played by hooligans'. In certain times and places – most notoriously in apartheid-era South Africa but also in parts of England and Scotland – rugby has been exclusive in the literal sense of excluding those who are 'not like us'. Yet it never was the poshest people's game. Many schools for Britain's upper classes, such as Eton and Harrow, played soccer. Eric Dunning and Kenneth Sheard have speculated that soccer's less fundamentalist response to professionalism was precisely because its rulers were so exalted socially that they felt unthreatened. In some places, rugby could claim, in a limited way, to have been an agent of social mixing. The Marxist historian Gwyn Alf Williams called it 'the only field on which it was possible to be simultaneously Welsh and a gentleman (normally a difficult undertaking), where doctor and lawyer could ruck happily together, shoulder to shoulder with miner'.

Rugby has been accused of propagating mindless male machismo, yet the women's game has enjoyed vigorous growth over the past two decades. The sport was condemned as an instrument of diabolism by a celebrant in the last great Welsh religious revival, Jenkin Thomas, erupting from Evan Roberts's congregation in Kenfig Hill to announce 'I used to be full-back for the devil, but now I am forward for God', and it was denounced – unanswerably – by a late nineteenth-century clergyman as 'twin sister of the drinking system'.

It has been wont to declare itself non-political, most frequently as an excuse for its engagement with that most politicised of societies, apartheid-era South Africa. Yet its adherence to amateurism had the rootedly ideological persistence of the Soviet Union's commitment to Marxist-Leninism. Rugby has its politics, and these have tended to the right. All Black scrum-half Chris Laidlaw wrote in *Mud in Your Eye* in 1973 that it is:

Universally an establishment activity ... normally played and administered by the conservative elements in society. The rugger-buggers of today are far from radical; rugby's traditions would hardly survive if they were. They are acquiring reputations as thundering bores with short hair and a suspicion of 'lefties'. Today's players are, by and large, tomorrow's Tories.

If Tony Collins has been able to equate rugby league with Yiddish – never the language of a ruling class – union's affinity has been with Latin, an instrument of power and exclusivity.

Yet there are conspicuous and important exceptions. Amédée Domenech argued that French rugby tended to 'vote to the left', while the most famous Argentinian rugby player of all time was not Hugo Porta but a half-back of more limited talents – in sporting terms, at least – called Ernesto Guevara. Che's first-published writings were on rugby rather than revolution, and his biographer Jorge Castañeda argues that playing scrum-half helped develop his strategic sense.

Irish politicians, particularly those involved directly in the struggle for independence, might be expected to favour Gaelic codes over a 'garrison game' like rugby. Yet Eamon de Valera, most influential and certainly most enduring of that generation, had been a reserve for Munster and argued heretically that rugby suited the Irish temperament better.

Rugby is not generally associated with literature. J.E Morpurgo asserted – rather disconcertingly, as he was introducing an anthology on the game – that 'Rugby football is too rapid for the contemplative, too cooperative for those who seek symbolism and too vigorous for aesthetic delight.' Welsh novelist Gwyn Thomas complained that 'the game, with its magnets of remembrance, has drained off much of the ardour which might have gone into a more sedulous cultivation of the arts'.

Yet Wodehouse, arguably the greatest of British literary humourists, wrote to a friend in the mid 1930s: 'Isn't it amazing that you and I, old buffers of about fifty-five with civilisation about to crash, can worry about school football. It is really about the only thing I do worry about.' John Mulgan, creator of a defining New Zealand literary archetype, the 'Man Alone', wrote brilliantly about the game's appeal. In France, publisher Gaston Gallimard and

Alain-Fournier, author of *Le Grand Meaulnes*, helped found a group of rugby-minded literati in 1913. Bob Dwyer, coach of Australia's World Cup winners in 1991, has argued for the game as an extension of the arts: 'the spirit of the *William Tell Overture* in the power of a scrum, the beauty of a Rodin sculpture in the sweeping movement of a back line'.

At the 2006 Heineken Cup final between Munster and Biarritz, actor Peter O'Toole reminisced about the enthusiasm for playing and watching the game he shared with screen and stage contemporaries Richard Burton and Richard Harris and spoke of his awe at meeting Bleddyn Williams. The French comedian Jacques Tati's Monsieur Hulot could trace his descent to the mimicry of players and referees performed by the young Tatischeff for Racing Club de France teammates after matches. Too bad none of them ever performed in All Black trialist Greg McGee's *Foreskin's Lament*, a landmark in New Zealand theatre, or John Breen's *Alone It Stands*, recreating the previous greatest day in Munster history: the victory over New Zealand in 1978.

Whether or not rugby union is inimical to the arts, it has been careless with its history. It has enshrined its dubious myth of foundation in naming its World Cup trophy after William Webb Ellis. Its wealth of whiskery anecdotage has led Stephen Jones, the most influential current British chronicler, to promise violence if ever again subjected to the story about 'Good old Catchy or Wakers adding a penny for the toilet to his train fare so his expenses rounded up to three pounds'.

Undoubtedly the most influential historical work on the game has been *Football: The Rugby Union Game* (1892), edited by the Revd Frank Marshall. Subsequent chroniclers have leaned heavily on its accounts of the early years. Much there is of great, irreplaceable value, even if some contributions are less reliable than others – Jacques McCarthy's chapter on Ireland is a terrific piece of comic writing, but that is regrettably not the same thing as good history. It must also be remembered that the book was also intended to assist Marshall's other role as the scourge of professionalism in Yorkshire in the years leading up to the great schism of 1895 by its reminding readers of whose game it really was.

Yet the game has been well served in the last quarter-century. Dai

Smith and Gareth Williams's WRU centenary history *Fields of Praise* (1980) and Williams's collected essays *1905 and All That* (1991), set the bar extraordinarily high. Phil Dine's *French Rugby Football: A Cultural History* (2001), is original, perceptive and entertaining about the nearby country of which most British followers know too little. Greg Ryan's works on the 1888 New Zealand Native and 1905 All Black touring teams have revised our view of pivotal events thought already understood, with Tom Hickie performing a similar service for the Australian game. Tony Collins, writing about Britain, and Sean Fagan, in Australia, have produced definitive accounts of the schisms of 1895 and 1908, while reading Jean-Pierre Bodis's works on South Africa and Ireland, and most of all his *Histoire Mondiale du Rugby* (1987), prompted the thought that English-speaking rugby followers needed translations of his work rather than a new one by an Anglophone.

Frank Keating on fly-halfs and David Parry-Jones's trilogy on Welsh golden ages show that you do not need to be an academic to write informative and worthwhile history. Spiro Zavos has done similarly useful service for the southern hemisphere, supplementing history with polemic to make his books a Pacific (though anything but pacific) counterpoint to Stephen Jones's state-of-the-game trilogy *Endless Winter (1993), Midnight Rugby (2000)* and *On My Knees (2004)*, indispensable along with Donald McRae's *Winter Colours' (1998)* for future historians wanting to understand the turbulent years either side of 1995. Bob Howitt's *New Zealand Rugby Greats (1997)* has given the All Blacks an incomparable oral history. The museums at Palmerston North, New Zealand, and at Twickenham offer historical enlightenment to the curious fan and valuable archives and generous hospitality to the visiting researcher.

It is strange, then, that there has been no serious attempt at a general history of the game in English since Carwyn James and John Reason's *The World of Rugby*, written to accompany a BBC television series in 1979. It still reads extremely well, but inevitably lacks the 27 years of expansion and change that have come since.

This leaves space for an account which takes the story up to the present day – concentrated on the field of play but always mindful that those who play, watch, referee or administer have never existed in a vacuum but are the products of their time and place, acting within and upon a wider social context. At the same time, it should range widely in space as well as time, departing from the game's well-beaten tracks to acknowledge South African blacks as well as All Blacks, British Columbians alongside British Lions.

Should rugby players and fans care about the game's history? John Gwilliam, the only man to have led Wales to two victories at Twickenham, a history graduate who studied both Marshall's book and rugby's other great urtext, Dave Gallaher and Billy Stead's *The Complete Rugby Footballer in the New Zealand System* (1906), thought they should, advising the young player to gain:

> acquaintance with its history and keen interest in the ways of some of the great players of the past, their techniques and ideas. He must know of all the major battles in former internationals and the way in which the game has grown. This may seem of academic interest only, but an appreciation of the way the game has grown in the past is of great value in forecasting how the game will develop.

*You have been warned.*

# CHAPTER ONE
## *Fons et Origo*

'Our schools have been the *fons et origo* of modern football'
Revd Frank Marshall (1892)

'There is no real beginning. There is no date or fixture or person to be cited as the starting point'
*100 Years of Auckland Rugby* (1983)

The best-known account of rugby's origins cites both a date and a person. The story of William Webb Ellis, 'who with a fine disregard for the rules of football as played in his time first took the ball in his arms and ran with it, thus originating the distinctive feature of the Rugby game. AD 1823' is set literally in stone on the wall of the playing field at Rugby School. The legend was further sanctified in 1923 when combined Wales–England and Ireland–Scotland teams played a 'centenary' match on that field. It was to acquire a renewed status in 1986 when John Kendall-Carpenter, chairman of the World Cup organising committee and, perhaps uncoincidentally, an English public school headmaster, acquired a trophy and announced it would be called the 'Webb Ellis Cup'. So it remains, although Australians have, with characteristic matiness, rechristened it 'Bill'.

It is an attractively subversive story, impossible to disprove beyond doubt. Webb Ellis existed, was a Rugby pupil in 1823 and went on to Oxford University, where he achieved unquestionable sporting distinction, playing in the first cricket match against Cambridge. He became a clergyman, serving at St Clement Danes in the Strand, and died in 1872 in Menton, France, where his grave is a place of pilgrimage for passing rugby teams. Modern commentators sometimes assert that 'William Webb Ellis would be amazed if he could see this.' He probably would be, but not for the reasons implied.

No contemporary record was made of his alleged feat – none before an article in 1880 by Matthew Bloxam, who left Rugby in 1821. Thomas Hughes, author of *Tom Brown's Schooldays*, who started at Rugby in 1834, told the Old Rugbeian inquiry set up in 1895 to establish the game's origins that 'The Webb Ellis legend had not survived to my day.' Given reliance on oral tradition – in 1834, the rules had yet to be written down and were passed on by word of mouth – the implication is that it never existed.

Even though Victorian journalists might not have sought Webb Ellis out in the manner of their modern counterparts, it seems odd that, if he did play the pivotal role of legend, there is no record of his ever expressing an interest or claiming reflected glory, since he lived long enough to see his school's pastime become an adult sport with adherents across the British Isles, a ruling body and an embryonic international competition.

The Old Rugbeian inquiry sought testimony from the oldest surviving ex-pupils. Hughes implicitly rejected the legend, while Thomas Harris, Ellis's one surviving contemporary, recalled him as 'An admirable cricketer, but inclined to take unfair advantages at football. I should not quote him in any way as an authority.'

Suggestive as 'inclined to take unfair advantages' may be, it is scarcely enough to support the Committee's conclusion that the practice of handling 'in all probability' originated with Webb Ellis, let alone the bullish certainty enshrined on the playing field wall. The finest disregard on display was for the rules of evidence at any time.

There is a transatlantic parallel. Organised baseball too used a commission of inquiry and the testimony of ancients to fix its own preferred person, place and time of origin: Abner Doubleday in Cooperstown, upstate New York, in 1839. This story is demonstrably even flimsier. It is unlikely that Doubleday was in Cooperstown in 1839. Yet the legend has received a still more substantial setting in stone, with the location of baseball's official museum, the Hall of Fame, in Cooperstown.

The baseball group wished to show that their game was wholly American and not, as is now universally recognised, the direct descendant of the British game of rounders. In an era of US nationalism, this was essential to their claim that baseball was 'the national pastime', as opposed to the game's declining, unmistakeably English competitor, cricket, which was still strong enough in Philadelphia to field a team capable of matching English first-class counties.

The Rugby committee was convened when the growth of the game meant not only that former pupils had lost the near-monopoly of influence they had once enjoyed – the first five presidents of the Rugby Football Union (RFU) were all old Rugbeians – but the challenge of the working-class northern clubs was threatening to turn it into something very different. Like Marshall with his *'fons et origo'* remark, the committee was attempting to reassert a position as patent-holder.

Journalist Jim Manning called it 'the perfect hoax'. This is harsh. Rather than deliberate falsification, it is likelier both groups were guilty of the failing that underlies many unsafe criminal convictions and untrue newspaper articles: promoting a story because you believe, and desperately want, it to be true. A characteristically Victorian belief that great events must be the doing of great men may also have contributed.

Both groups were, in any case, missing the point. Nobody invents activities as elemental as kicking and running with a ball, or throwing it towards another wielding a stick. They doubtless date back to the first time somebody discovered that it is possible to inflate a pig's bladder, or that anything reasonably round and dense can be thrown accurately. The Romans played a game called *harpastum*, in which two teams competed to throw a large ball into the opposing goal. They fought for possession of the ball, then attempted to carry it to lines marked at each end of the field of play, driving in unison or passing to make progress. Medieval Irishmen played *cad*, attempting to carry an inflated bladder into goals created by bending trees into the shape of an arch. Welsh feast days might see inter-parish contests at *cnappan*, in which vast teams contended for possession of a wooden ball, which they would attempt to carry so far away that the opposition had no possibility of returning it, a process incorporating massed struggles for the ball in which, according to George Owen in *The Description of Pembrokeshire* (1603), 'you shall see a hundred or six score clustered together as bees when they swarm are knit together, the ball being in the midst of them, which the other party seek to open or undo by heaving or pulling' – a loose maul, albeit with stupefying numbers, in all but name. Frenchmen played *soule*, and Georgians (in eastern Europe) *lelo*.

Primitive forms of football caused so much official disquiet by being violently destructive of property and a distraction from more approved activities such as archery that 31 separate bans were proclaimed by state and local authorities in England, Wales and Scotland between 1314 and 1667. It remained, though, an essentially localised and informal activity with rules settled by custom, practice and negotiation.

Cricket was the first modern team game to evolve to the point at which rules are agreed and written down. It is this codification, not some mythic act of invention, that is the key moment in a game's history. It makes it portable – playable in different locations and between people from different places. Cricket's recorded rules date from 1727, devised for a challenge match between teams with well-bred sponsors – having money at stake was always a useful spur to codification. More general laws were agreed in 1744. By 1787, it had its ruling body in embryo, the Marylebone Cricket Club (MCC), and by 1814 a permanent purpose-built big-match arena, Lord's. Similar moves were afoot in individual sports – Jack Broughton drafted formal rules for the prize ring in 1743 and the Jockey Club was formed in 1752.

If anything, football appeared to be regressing in the early nineteenth century. Sir Walter Scott lamented the 'passing of football' in 1815. The growing pace of industrialisation and urbanisation meant lives – and the spaces in which they were lived and in which games might be played – were more regulated. The means to suppress unofficial football were increasingly available with the creation of police forces after 1829 and the passing of the 1835 Highways Act. Novelist Horatio Smith observed of London in 1831 that 'football and cricket grounds, bowling greens and the enclosures of green spaces set apart for archery and other pastimes have now been successfully parcelled out in squares, lanes and alleys'.

The folk game retained sufficient vigour for a French visitor to

Derbyshire in 1829 to remark that 'If this is what Englishmen think of as playing, it would be impossible to say what they might regard as a fight.' It survives to this day in the annual Shrove Tuesday match at Ashbourne, preserved in the manner in which Britain is wont to retain the last survivors of past times, like Blackpool's trams. Street football was still played in Dorking in 1888, while *cnappan* transformed Narberth into what Smith and Williams term a 'Welsh Pamplona' as late as 1884, but these were dying gasps of bygone custom.

While the forces of control and regulation made life more difficult for the ordinary citizen who wished to play football, they aided the cause of the public schoolboy – and of masters who wished to see the schools transformed from the brawlingly anarchic institutions some had become. Dunning and Sheard list 21 public school rebellions between 1768 and 1832. These were not the mildly festive uprisings, curable by detention and selective corporal punishment, portrayed by Frank Richards or by P.G. Wodehouse in *Mike at Wrykyn*, but serious outbreaks of public disorder. A riot at Rugby School in 1797 was put down only by a reading of the Riot Act and the attendance of soldiers with drawn swords. Rugby had a further eruption, followed by mass expulsions, in 1822.

Sport was a useful outlet for this surplus energy. Although football was organised by older boys rather than the masters, it was considerably more controllable – and more accessible to boys from the growing urban upper-middle classes who increasingly attended schools like Rugby – than hunting or shooting.

Most public schools had their own variety of football, whose rules, dictated by local preference and geographical idiosyncrasy, were passed down by word of mouth from year to year. This was not confined to England. Edinburgh's Royal High had its own game from 1810, while several American universities had their own versions – Harvard's still sufficiently violent and anarchic to be suppressed by the college authorities in 1860.

This, not Webb Ellis, is Rugby School's unanswerable claim on the game named after it – that its code emerged from a mass of competing possibilities. Rugby had its own playing field, a spacious patch adjoining the school buildings, from 1749. A memoir of old Rugbeian actor William Macready shows that football was well established by 1803. Rules developed gradually as players debated responses to contingencies. The adoption of 'running in', after the alleged style of Webb Ellis, is a case in point. Harris told the inquiry that 'picking up the ball and running with the ball in field was distinctly forbidden' in the 1820s. J.R. Lyon, who entered the school in 1830, remembered that it was allowed but the runner was subject to a barrage of hacking and 'collaring' – an account compatible with Hughes's recollection that in 1834 'Running with the ball to get a try by touching down in the goal was not absolutely forbidden, but a jury of Rugby boys of the day would certainly have found a verdict of "justifiable homicide" if a boy had been killed running in.'

Hughes said the practice grew through the 1830s and was particularly popularised by the skill in 1838–39 of Jem Mackie, 'the great runner-in'. Even so, 'The question remained debatable when I was captain of Bigside in 1841–42, when we settled it (as we believed) for all time.' There was an important qualification to legalisation: the ball must be caught rather than picked up from the floor.

Hughes's description of the game in *Tom Brown's Schooldays* shows that H-shaped posts and goalscoring were established by the 1830s:

> A set of gigantic gallows of two poles eighteen feet high, fixed upright in the ground some fourteen feet apart, with a crossbar running from one to the other at a height of ten feet or thereabouts ... it won't do ... just to kick the ball through these posts – it must go over the crossbar – any height will do, so long as it is between the posts.

The concept of taking the ball across the opposition's line earning one a try at goal – hence the term 'try' – was also accepted, as was the oval ball, a leather construction around an inflated pig's bladder. The first written set of rules, compiled in 1845, would define the vital concept of offside as 'A player is off his side if the ball has touched one of his own side behind him, until the other side touch it.' Those rules also permitted hacking – kicking below the knee – the opposing player nearest the ball, or anyone in a scrummage, and indicated that quick, decisive results and high scoring were not expected: 'All matches are drawn after five days, but after three if no goal has been kicked.'

The rules were drafted because the school had expanded to the point where word of mouth was no longer sufficient. The drafting committee included William Arnold, son of the former headmaster, and W.W. Shirley, later professor of ecclesiastical history at Oxford University. Their conclusions were reissued almost unchanged in 1846, described as 'a set of decisions on certain disputed points in Football, [rather] than containing all the laws of the Game which are too well known to render any explanation necessary to Rugbeians'.

Maybe so, but by this time others had become interested. In 1839, there were bemused eyewitness reports in Cambridge of 'a number of Rugby men, mostly freshmen, playing a new game' in which they 'made a circle around a ball and butted each other'. Debate over rules long established at Rugby entered a new phase at the universities as former pupils looked for ways of playing with and against those from other schools. Albert Pell, ringleader of the 1839 group, hoped to set up a football club in Cambridge, but no agreement could be reached on rules. That waited until 1848 when, after a seven-hour meeting in which 'Etonians howled at the Rugby men for handling the ball', the chairman's casting vote created rules based largely on Eton and Harrow's non-handling code. Goals were scored by kicking the ball under the crossbar, handling was limited to catching and immediately kicking the ball, and players were onside provided they had three opponents between themselves and the opposing goal.

The question is why Rugby's game should have emerged from a competing mass of school codes to become a national code rather than remaining a localised curiosity like Eton's Wall Game. It had several things on its side. One was a determined group of advocates. The *Football Annual* for 1868 would note that former Rugby pupils were 'more closely engrafted in the memories of the present century of football than the alumni of any of our other public schools'. It had written rules earlier than any other school – Eton was next in 1849. By 1839, Rugby's game was well-enough known for royalty – rarely on the cutting edge of popular culture – in the form of dowager Queen Adelaide to ask to see it played when visiting the school. Perhaps most valuable of all was the publication in 1857 of Hughes's *Tom Brown's Schooldays*, with its vivid description of the game. This was an instant bestseller with staying power, selling

11,000 copies within a few months, running through 50 editions in less than 40 years and staying in print to this day. As Tony Collins has said, 'Not only was it a good read, but it gave an ideology to middle-class leisure. It was about having a healthy mind in a healthy body.' Rugby's influence also spread across other schools. Marlborough, which in the 1850s adopted rugby with 'minor modifications' – chiefly the prohibition of hacking – had an ex-Rugby headmaster from 1852. The founding head of Clifton, another early adopter, was a Rugbeian.

Cambridge's vigorous debates in 1848 over handling and hacking drew the lines of eventual division. Their conclusion was important, since former students would be vital in introducing the game as an adult pastime. But their rules were as yet binding only on matches at the university. As football spread across the British Isles, each new grouping adopted a set of rules reflecting local influences and preferences.

University connections transmitted the game to Wales and Ireland. Students at Lampeter College played from 1850, when Rowland Williams, who had been a tutor at King's when Pell introduced the game to Cambridge, became vice-principal and professor of Hebrew. In Ireland, the pioneer was its Oxbridge equivalent, Trinity College, Dublin. A largely Protestant institution in a predominantly Catholic island – one-sixth of its students when the rugby club was formed in 1854 came from elsewhere in Britain – its distinctive sporting preferences, the Ascendancy made grass, are proclaimed to this day by the presence according to season of either rugby posts or a cricket square on the college playing field adjacent to its main buildings in central Dublin. The Trinity club, Dublin University, can claim to be the oldest continuously existing club in the world. Given the contribution of medical students to the game, Guy's Hospital in London would be a suitable title holder, but its claim to a foundation date of 1843 rests on little solid evidence beyond a fixture card from 1883 proclaiming '40th season'.

Neil Tranter's research has uncovered a 'football club' founded in Edinburgh in 1824 by John Hope, a graduate of the city's university, which had 85 members drawn from the local business and professional elite and lasted 10 years before succumbing to declining memberships and rising costs, notably the cost of hiring grounds in an expanding city. This is too early to assign to either rugby or soccer, but a distinctive Scottish rugby tradition began in the 1850s in the schools of Edinburgh and Glasgow.

Most accounts suggest that the game arrived at Edinburgh Academy in 1854 via the Crombie brothers, who had previously attended Durham School. Within three years, it had reached Merchiston Castle and Royal High. Differences in geography and culture meant that the Scottish school game developed more rapidly than the English. English schools did not play each other, as they were scattered across the country and each had their own version of the game to follow. Clifton and Marlborough essayed a contest in 1864, but 'so much bad blood was caused' that the fixture was not renewed until the 1890s. Rugby did not play another school until 1896. Scotland's leading schools, on the other hand, were closely concentrated in Edinburgh and Glasgow. As relatively recent foundations – Edinburgh Academy opened in 1824, Loretto in 1827 and Merchiston in 1833 – they lacked the ancient institutions' tendency to ancestor-worship, and their all-but-simultaneous adoption of the game gave limited scope for preciousness over their own version of the rules.

Merchiston played Royal High in the first inter-school match in 1858, and regular fixtures – aided by the happy coincidence that the sport-minded headmasters of Loretto, Merchiston and Edinburgh Academy had been together on the staff at Merchiston between 1858 and 1862 – rapidly ensued. Academy pupil John MacDonald recalled the matches of the period: 'We then played twenty a side and a scrum was a scrum indeed – fifteen pushing against fifteen in a tight maul, which often was immovable for several minutes. The steam rose from the pack like smoke from a charcoal-burner's pile!'

While comparatively few English public-school alumni stayed on in the towns where their schools were situated, Scottish former pupils more often than not continued both university study and professional careers in the same city. It was natural that they would also continue to play sport with friends from school, joining the former-pupil clubs pioneered by Edinburgh Academicals in 1858, with the older Crombie brother, Alexander, as the first captain. In time, this system would become an immense handicap for Scottish rugby, but in these early stages it was hugely advantageous.

In England, the game was moving on from its academic foundations with the creation of town clubs. Liverpool might seem an unlikely location for an early club, but a direct rail link with Rugby enabled a flow of the city's elite to the school. Liverpool's first match was played in 1857 with a 'Big Side' ball supplied by Richard Sykes, a sixth-form pupil from Manchester who three years later was among the founders of the club in his own city. The Sheffield club, founded in 1857, was from the start firmly in the non-handling camp.

It was in London that the schism between codes became formal. The sheer size of the city meant there was no difficulty finding the numbers of young men needed to create clubs, providing a choice of opposition that made it possible for them to move between different versions of football. Richmond, founded in 1861 to play Harrow rules, switched to Rugby a year later. Invited in 1863 to become a founder member of the Football Association (FA), Richmond declined. Secretary Edwin Ash explained that the club existed to provide recreation for young men who stayed in Richmond only as long as their preparation for army careers lasted, and that this shifting membership meant he could not guarantee it would last 'beyond this season'.

Blackheath, founded in 1858, did attend the FA's founding meeting, and was cast as chief spokesman for the Rugby tendency, which delegates made a genuine effort to accommodate in the agreed rules. The Rugby-like elements that were incorporated included an eight-metre-high goal, through which a shot at any height would count as a goal, the 'fair catch and mark' rule, throwing the ball into the field parallel to where it had gone out and any player nearer to the opposition line than the ball being offside. An initial draft also allowed players to run with the ball in their hands provided they had caught it or taken it on the first bounce, and to charge, hold, trip or hack – although not all at the same time. These two rules proved to be the splitting point. Edward Morley of Barnes proposed striking out both, arguing that tolerance of hacking would mean 'men of business, to whom it is of importance to take care of themselves, would be unwilling to play football'. The game would be 'entirely relinquished to schoolboys'.

Blackheath delegate F.W. Campbell responded with vigorous, socially condescending advocacy of a game for hooligans played by gentlemen, arguing that 'hacking is the true football game'. Opponents to this rule had begun 'late in life, and were too old for that spirit of the game . . . so fully entered into at the public schools and by the public school men in after life'. To abolish it would 'do away with all the courage and pluck of the game and I will be bound to bring over a lot of Frenchmen who would beat you with a week's practice'. Calling for a vote, he was defeated, and he walked out.

This was undoubtedly momentous, but both sides' predictions were wide of the mark (if less spectacularly so than Edwin Ash's estimate of Richmond's longevity). Frenchmen arriving in London and beating England's best would take nearer a century than a week. Blackheath did not, as Morley had jibed, fail to find 'any three London clubs to play them'.

Rules remained a matter of negotiation between teams. Edward Guillemard, who moved to London after leaving Rugby in 1864, remembered that:

Before the commencement of every match, it was absolutely necessary for the captains of the two teams to meet and exchange views on various points, it being usual to recognise the idiosyncrasies of the club upon whose ground the meeting was to take place.

Under one of these agreements, in 1866, Blackheath and Richmond, by now the leading clubs in London, abolished hacking in their meetings. F.W. Campbell's reaction is sadly not recorded. This did not presage rapprochement with the FA, which in the same year dropped their main remnant of handling: allowing a 'fair catch' and kick at goal from kicks by the other team. Even so, the divide was far from conclusive. The editors of the *Football Annual*, founded in 1868, evidently hankered after a common code. One London club, Clapham Rovers, formed in 1869, played the two codes on alternate weeks, with such success that they won the FA Cup in 1879.

Finding somewhere to play could be a problem, with matches being played in public parks. E.B. Turner, a medical student in the 1860s, remembered that 'The goals were not fixtures, and the posts and crossbars were in the custody of the park keepers who set them up on the reserved grounds and marked out the field of play with a few flags along the touch-line.' Spectators 'did not get in the way of the players more than they could help'. Guillemard found spectators on Blackheath and Richmond Green did not help, recalling that they:

Invariably declined to keep in touch, and the clear field of play was often not more than thirty yards broad. Then did the wily half-back see his opportunity and dive into the thick of the shouting throng so soon as the ball was in his hands.

Playing as one of the two full-backs in the formation of the time, he could often 'see nothing but the occasional flash of a coloured jersey nearing him at hundred yards speed'. Spectators entered the field at their own risk. Guillemard recalled that a fellow full-back once struck a spectator on the jaw 'and knocked him several yards in the direction of the touch-line'.

It must also be doubted how much entertainment value there was in these games. Turner recalled that forwards:

Stood straight up in the 'scrimmage' as it was then called and felt for the ball with their feet. As soon as it broke loose, they fell on it and when tackled waited until the scrum reformed and repeated the dose ad nauseam! Speed was at a discount and weight and strength only were of any value – 'hacking over' and 'tripping' were an integral part of the game.

Yet the game spread, and not only in the British Isles. Football took little time in reaching Germany. The German Rugby Union's centenary history includes a picture from 1850 of boys at Neuenheim College, Heidelberg (still one of Germany's main rugby centres), wearing suitably moody expressions and grouped around a ball which, if not precisely oval, is certainly not round. William Cail, later treasurer of the RFU, played a game resembling rugby as a student in Stuttgart in the 1860s.

The main transmission of the game, though, was inevitably through the British Empire, via both British settlers and the armed forces. Students and soldiers – that other concentration of young men with energy to burn – were the moving spirits in Canada. A match between officers from English regiments and civilians, mostly McGill University students, was recorded in Montreal in 1865, followed three years later by the foundation of the Montreal Football Club. Halifax, a military and naval base in Nova Scotia from its foundation in 1749, followed a similar pattern, with students from Dalhousie University playing the first match in 1867 and a town club formed in 1870 to play the resident garrison and visiting warships.

The baggage taken by British settlers and troops to the colonies was as much cultural as physical, sport being one of its basic components. Nowhere was this truer than in Australasia, which underwent a huge mid-century surge in arrivals as strong push-and-pull effects were exerted by the Irish famine and the gold strikes at Ballarat and Bathurst, Australia, in 1851. More than three quarters of a million people left the UK for Australia and New Zealand between 1848 and 1865, half of them in the six years from 1852 to 1857. Australia quadrupled in population – from 430,000 to 1.7 million – in 20 years from 1851, with Sydney tripling from 45,000 to 137,000.

Cricket, already defined and refined, was the first team sport to establish itself, with matches between New South Wales and Victoria starting in 1856 (the first USA–Canada match had been a dozen years earlier).

Football, still in flux, was more problematic. The challenge posed by the variegated population decanted into Melbourne has been vividly summarised by historian Gillian Hibbins:

> Each man played a lone hand or foot, according to his lights, some guided by a particular code of rules, others by none at all ... three or four Saturdays of this kind of play sufficed to show that something must be done to reconcile the different codes of rules.

Out of this chaos came Australia's own code, with the first recorded match of Australian Rules football (today Australian football, or 'footie' to aficionados) played between Melbourne Grammar School and Scotch College in 1858. A gifted and ultimately tragic old Rugbeian, Tom Wills, who had returned to his native Geelong – about 100 miles outside Melbourne – in 1856, was the leading spirit in developing the game and, in 1866, codifying its rules.

Wills, notably free of old-pupil piety, positively disliked rugby's overt violence, precisely echoing Edward Morley's argument on the other side of the world when he called it 'unsuitable for grown men engaged in making a living'. Australian Rules eschewed hacking and demanded that a ball-carrier bounce it every five or six yards – an action facilitated by switching from oval to round in 1867. It retained, and would ultimately develop as its great defining feature, the 'fair catch'. By the late 1860s, it was Melbourne's winter game.

Sydney proved more receptive to rugby, its interest in the sport, as elsewhere, incubated by a combination of elite schools, students and the armed forces. The first matches recorded were in 1865 – a game between members of the short-lived Sydney Football Club on 19 June, followed by two contests in July with the equally ephemeral Australian Cricket Club, all played at Hyde Park Racecourse. The key development was the debut a month later of Sydney University, which then played Sydney FC on 19 August. No score was recorded, but Australia's first match report recounted that 'the continual tussles, spills, kicks, cannoning of the ball off one and another's body seemed to cause as much amusement to the players as it did among the spectators' and opined that the game would be much better if players 'would dispense with their penchant for tripping'.

The University – still a tiny institution, with only 44 students in 1865 – would provide the continuity in the city's football. The team played the Military and Civil Cricket Club in 1866 and 1867 under rules described as 'a strange combination of Rugby and other rules'. In 1868, they played a new Sydney FC, before meeting the new Wallaroos club, whose influence on the early Australian game would match their own, in 1870. In between those last two dates, suggests Tom Hickie, the game had come close to dying out. It was rescued, in part, by the crew of the HMS *Rosario*, who provided the University with opposition for two matches in 1869.

The *Rosario* played a still more momentous role in international development a year later, as the opposition for the first recorded match in Auckland, New Zealand, in June 1870. Eighteen years after the event, an Auckland player recalled:

The game was played in the Albert barracks and it rained pitchforks and rivulets and as we Auckland players stood under the verandah I, for one,

37

almost hoped our opponents would not turn up, but shortly afterwards in marched the officers and sailors, bearing goalposts and a ball. The rules we played under were of the nondescript sort: no offside, no picking up and no holding, but shoving over was indulged in.

How much the Aucklanders knew about the game is unclear. After 90 minutes' activity, 'one gentleman who played the game informed me that Auckland won the match; but another informed me that Auckland received a good thrashing'. A club was formed, adopting 'the Westminster rules, somewhat modified'. Within a year, it switched formally to Rugby, but with no written copy of the rules available, 'the notion of Rugby rules was of course very vague'.

Various forms of football had been played in New Zealand for at least a decade. The South Island experienced its own gold-driven influx following the strikes in Otago in 1861 and Westland four years later, while renewed warfare with the Maoris brought fresh troops to North Island after 1861. Games were played under local rules at Christ's College, Christchurch, in 1862, the Christchurch club was formed a year later and a North Shore history suggests that a rugby ball was first seen in New Zealand on the Devonport naval base in the 1860s, fought over by soldiers from Irish regiments and sailors from ships including the *Rosario*.

Those pioneering sailors miss out on the distinction of participating in New Zealand's first-recorded rugby match on two counts. It is unclear whether the Auckland match in June 1870 can be classified as rugby, and the title had in any case already been claimed by a group of young men in Nelson, at the north of South Island.

Charles Monro, a 19-year-old Nelsonian recently returned from school in England at Christ's College, Finchley, was the moving spirit, proposing that Nelson Football Club, founded two years earlier, adopt the Rugby rules. The town also offered a ready-made opponent, Nelson College, a school intended as 'a miniature replica of Eton College', which had been playing football since 1860. The 18-a-side format admittedly stretched the resources of an enrolment of 61, but the requisite numbers – 10 forwards, 3 half-backs, 3 three-quarters and 2 full-backs – were duly assembled to play the town on the Botanic Reserve on 14 May 1870. Watched by a reported 200 spectators, town beat gown.

Monro lacked neither initiative nor connections. He spent much of his time in Wellington with his father, who was speaker of the New Zealand House of Representatives. Within a few months, he had rustled up a Wellington team, persuaded marine minister Julius Vogel to provide a Nelson team with passage across the Cook Strait and organised a match at Petone on 12 September 1870 in which 14 of Nelson faced 13 of Wellington. He 'played for his home side, was opposition selector and coach, and then referee'.

Rugby's game had come an immensely long way in the quarter-century since the first rules were written, establishing itself as one of the two main football codes in England and Scotland, with a firm foothold on the other side of the world. It had achieved all of this without a formal ruling body – indeed, had rejected the opportunity to participate in one in 1863. This was about to change.

39

# CHAPTER TWO

# Practising the Games of the Anglo-Saxon in their Youth

'I believe that rugby football is the best instrument we possess for the development of manly character'

Dr Hely Hutchinson Almond (1892)

'Two out of the four dates originally included were eliminated ... research ... having revealed that they are not memorable'

Walter Sellar and Robert Yeatman, *1066 and All That* (1930)

On the most stringent application of Sellar and Yeatman's test, 1871 was a memorable date, bringing both the first governing body and the first international rugby contest. Both events were triggered by letters to the press in a single week in December 1870. Wariness of years of match-by-match wrangling over interpretation is evident in the wording of the letter to *The Times* of 4 December 1870 suggesting a meeting so that 'some code of rules should be adopted by all clubs who profess to play the Rugby game'. The signatories were the secretaries of London's two leading clubs, Benjamin Burns of Blackheath and Edwin Ash of Richmond.

Delegates from 21 clubs, almost all from London, made it to the Pall Mall Restaurant on the corner of Pall Mall and Cockspur Street, close to Trafalgar Square, on 26 January 1871. Legend has it that there would have been 22, but the Wasps delegate had gone to the wrong place and liked it so much he decided to stay – which sounds like a rugby player. The RFU was duly constituted, with Richmond men as chief officers – Algernon Rutter as president; Ash as secretary. The task of composing the laws was deputed to a three-man committee, all lawyers and old Rugbeians. The bulk of the drafting fell on L.J. Maton, housebound by a timely broken leg.

His reward was a supply of tobacco from his fellow drafters and the presidency of the union in 1875–76.

By a fine irony, the committee's significant decision was the final elimination of hacking. It was mourned by some – Guillemard reminisced warmly about games where one might see 'a couple of players vigorously engaged in kicking each other's shins long after the scrummage had broken up' – but it had been done for by Blackheath and Richmond's renunciation and was finally buried by a *Times* letters-page controversy over the perils of rugby that raged intermittently through 1869 and 1870.

The RFU rapidly acquired imitators. The Scottish Rugby Union (called the Scottish Football Union until 1924) was formed in 1873. Ireland contrived to form two – the Irish Football Union was supplemented by the Northern Football Union only a few months after the former's formation in December 1874. There followed an extended courtship that produced an engagement by November 1878 but took until February 1880 for a full merger into the new Irish RFU (IRFU). The WRU (again called a Football Union until the 1920s) was formed in 1881, seven years after the establishment of the first overseas body: New South Wales's Southern Rugby Union (SRU).

The unions were the creation of established patent-holders. As noted earlier, the first five presidents of the RFU, who held office for eleven years, were old Rugbeians. Only one of Scotland's eight founding clubs was open: West of Scotland. Three were universities, the others for former pupils. The first president and secretary were members of Edinburgh Academicals, every executive member a graduate of Edinburgh University. The meeting to form the Irish union was called and hosted by George Stack, captain of Dublin University, which well into the 1860s had demanded that other clubs beat their second team before being allowed a fixture with the firsts. Stack was a medical student – almost one-third of the 389 Irishmen capped before 1914 were medics. He was also Ireland's first captain, leading 20 men clad in green-and-white-hooped jerseys against England at the Oval in 1875. He died little more than a year later in unexplained, possibly suicidal, circumstances, a miserable fate emulated two years further on by his fellow Trinity medic Richard Galbraith, half-back in that first Irish team.

Rapid exchanges of role were typical of the time. The union founders were young men, many still active players. England's first captain, Frederick Stokes, was president of the RFU three years later. Before he was 40, Arthur Guillemard had been a founder member of the RFU executive, England's first full-back, a referee in six internationals and president of the union for four seasons. Even he looked slothful alongside Ireland's George Scriven, yet another Trinity medic who, in twelve months from February 1883 onwards, played in two internationals, refereed another and was president of the IRFU, all before his 28th birthday.

Youthful officialdom had two consequences. One was long careers – several officials whose service began in the 1880s were still operating almost until, and in one case (WRU president Horace Lyne) beyond, the Second World War. The second was to give substance to rhetoric about the game being run for players. In time, this became tired and irksome – not least to the alleged beneficiaries – but in the early days it was based in reality.

The challenge which led to the first international match, Scotland v. England, was issued four days after Burns and Ash's letter to *The Times*. Two teams under those labels had played under Association rules at the Oval three weeks earlier. There were doubts about some of the 'Scottish' players – the qualifications of one alleged not to have extended beyond a fondness for whisky. On 8 December, a letter signed by the captains of five leading Scottish clubs appeared in the sporting weekly *Bell's Life*. It proclaimed 'a pretty general feeling among Scottish football players that the football power of the old country was not properly represented' at the Oval, argued that Scotland's strength lay in rugby and challenged 'any side selected from the whole of England' to a 20-a-side Rugby rules match in Edinburgh or Glasgow. Those responding were promised 'a hearty welcome and a first-rate match'.

An England team led by Frederick Stokes of Blackheath and including seven players from northern clubs – all from Manchester and Liverpool – travelled to Edinburgh to play Scotland on 27 March 1871. The abilities of Stokes, one of ten old Rugbeians in the team, are evident from a pen portrait in the *Football Annual* for 1871:

One of the very best and most brilliant of forwards, being always on the ball and always making excellent runs. Can also play in capital form half-back, is sure at tackling and a first-rate drop-kick and place-kick. An admirable captain and the numerous victories of his club are in great measure due to his efforts.

Not all of the portraits were so fulsome. A Harlequins half-back called Wilkinson was advised to 'practise his dropping'.

England travelled overnight by train to play two halves of fifty minutes at Raeburn Place, Edinburgh Academicals' ground, in front of a crowd variously estimated at between two and four thousand, whose shillings were collected by John MacDonald, enthusiasm undimmed by memories of interminable schoolboy scrummaging. Wearing all white with a red rose on their shirts, England confronted a Scottish team clad in blue jerseys and cricket flannels. It proved a spirited contest. Scottish forward Robert Irvine recalled, 'There were a good many hacks-over going on and as blood got up it began to be muttered, "Hang it, why not have hacking allowed? It cannot be prevented; far better have it."' Stokes and his Scottish counterpart Francis Moncrieff were unable to decide, but umpire Hely Hutchinson Almond, headmaster of Loretto College, warned he would not continue if hacking were allowed. It was not his last significant decision.

Guillemard, full-back for England and doubtless participating enthusiastically in that early outbreak of hacking, recalled, 'The match was very evenly contested until half-time, after which the combination of the Scotsmen, who knew each other's play thoroughly, and their superior training began to tell a tale.'

From a scrum five yards out, the Scots drove forward and grounded the ball. Amid vociferous English protests, Almond gave the try, and Malcolm Cross kicked the decisive goal. Scotland were to claim a further try, while Reginald Birkett of Clapham Rovers, who later took his club's hybridity to the logical conclusion of also playing soccer for England, crossed for the visitors. Neither, though, scored any points, as both conversions were missed – under the rules of the time, unconverted tries were worth nothing.

England's anger at a score which would not have been allowed under their rules contributed to their downfall. Scottish practice was that only the captain was allowed to appeal to the umpire.

Almond would write many years later that, had England followed this practice, 'I should have understood that the point raised was that the ball had never been fairly grounded in the scrummage but had got mixed up among Scottish feet or legs.' It was, he conceded, impossible to know where a ball was amid the scrums of the 20-a-side era. But amid multiple vociferations, he could not find out exactly what the problem was. In any case, he concluded magnificently, 'When an umpire is in doubt, I think he is justified in deciding against the side which makes most noise. They are probably in the wrong.'

Guillemard conceded that 'The Scottish forwards were definitely quicker on their feet and in better training than their opponents,' characteristics in keeping with the *Football Annual*'s observation that the Scottish game possessed:

> great liveliness and looseness. In England, a game very often is too much of a series of marks and scrummages, while in Scotland, by a strict attention to the rule respecting 'have it down', the game is altogether looser and the ball is kept in the air and over the field.

England's problem was that hacking had a purpose – breaking up scrummages. Without it, the admittedly partisan Guillemard complained, scrums became long-drawn-out shoving matches, with players joining on in twos, giving the appearance of 'a caterpillar whose last meal had stuck halfway down'. By 1875–76, the *Football Annual* reported, 'Matters seemed about as bad as they could be; forwards wasted their strength in protracted shoving matches, and backs neglected dropping almost entirely.'

Yet the 1876 Scotland v. England match in Edinburgh attracted 7,000 spectators, and Ireland was adding a fresh, if sometimes shambolic, dimension to international rugby. The 1870s also saw important new representative fixtures launched, starting with Yorkshire v. Lancashire in 1870. From 1872, the largest concentrations of young public-school-educated men in England clashed in the varsity match between Oxford and Cambridge universities. The North v. South fixture added a regional dimension two years after that. In Scotland, Glasgow played Edinburgh from 1872, while Ireland's international debut was underpinned by contests between its ancient provinces. The first inter-provincial club clash, between Belfast's North of Ireland Football Club (NIFC) – born to a cricketing parent in 1868 – and Dublin University in 1874 was followed by Ulster v. Leinster a year later and the debut of Munster in 1877.

The Scots had a solution to tedious matches: reducing teams from 20 to 15 players. Their initiative, accepted by the RFU, was implemented for the 1876–77 season. The same year saw the first recognition of the value of the running game, as it was agreed that games could be settled on tries if no goals were scored. Oxford had crossed the Cambridge line twice in the 1874 varsity match but only drew because they missed their conversions, a fate shared a year earlier by Edinburgh Academy when they scored seven tries to none against Fettes. Perhaps more important than either was the ruling in 1877 that the ball be put down after a tackle, rather than held until forwards arrived to set up yet another wrestle for possession. By 1878, the *Football Annual* could proclaim cheerfully that 'the old desultory style of forward play has been, as a rule, lost sight of, and a more vigorous system reigns in its stead'.

These changes were not universally welcomed. The acerbic Jacques McCarthy reckoned Ireland's novices were aided by the crowding and confusion of 20 a side. The team who played England in 1875 was composed of equal numbers from north and south who 'had not previously seen each other' but were united in being 'immaculately innocent of training'. Compliments on their tackling the following year were 'not an unmixed blessing, because they collared their own as often as the enemy, the jerseys being the same and the Irishmen were no better acquainted with each other than with the visitors'.

Ireland's first fifteen-a-side match, against Scotland in 1877, produced a fearful hammering, by six goals and two tries. This would be eclipsed by Wales's fate on debut four years later. The same forces of connection that took the game across England (Burton was the first Midlands club, in 1870, followed within two years by Coventry, while the foundation of Exeter, Clifton and Gloucester in the first half of the decade opened up the West Country) had inevitably brought it into Wales: individuals, notably teachers and former students who had played elsewhere, conveyed by an ever-expanding rail network, which made the movement of news, ideas and sports teams faster and more efficient. Neath, founded by a former Merchiston pupil in 1871, are the oldest of the great Welsh clubs. Within a decade, all of South Wales's major towns had clubs – several, such as Swansea and Cardiff, growing from and sharing space with cricket. The creation of the South Wales Cup in 1878 created immense enthusiasm, even if 1879 winner Newport's challenge to Blackheath, played in front of 5,000, produced defeat by the sobering margin of four goals and eight tries to nil.

It was a foretaste of Wales's first international, against England at Blackheath two years later. The Welsh Football Union was still a month from formation. Swansea playing Llanelli in a cup tie on the same day gave selection a pronounced eastward tilt, with six men from Newport and five from Cardiff. It was a well-educated team, with nine graduates, and God-fearing too, with three clergymen. The truly fearsome figure, though, was Lennard Stokes, younger brother of Frederick and captain of both Blackheath and England. First capped in 1875, he was remembered by Guillemard as:

> Six feet in height and of sinewy frame … champion sprinter at the sports of the United Hospitals. He was a faultless catch and field, and a very quick starter … with his speed of foot, wonderful dodging powers and clever 'shoving off' … he was also for several seasons the longest drop in the three kingdoms.

Many years later, Welsh three-quarter Richard Summers recalled 'a small crowd of Rugby enthusiasts, ranged perhaps three deep around the ground. There were no huge stands or terraced bank in those days. I am not sure that the playing pitch was even roped off.' Wales might have welcomed a barrier between themselves and Stokes: 'He had a most baffling, swerving run, and his left-footed kicking, which broke our players' hearts, astounded us all, for we had never seen a player who was able to kick with his left foot.' England won by seven goals, a drop goal and six tries to nil (82–0 in modern values). Yet Stokes said at the after-match dinner that 'I have seen enough to know that you Welshmen will be hard to beat in a few years' time.' Generosity to a foe beaten to the point of mutual embarrassment? Maybe. But perhaps Stokes remembered that crowd of 5,000 at Newport and recognised what such mass enthusiasm might presage.

46

For the moment, it was Scotland that provided England's serious competition. That it proposed the switch to 15 a side was no surprise. Scotland lacked England's sheer numbers but compensated by the concentration of its forces – its 1871 team was drawn from the five clubs whose captains had issued the challenge to England – and by thinking hard about the game. Far more than English schools, with which the ethic is generally associated, the Edinburgh schools epitomised Muscular Christianity. Almond, for 40 years headmaster of Loretto, proclaimed the aim of producing 'a race of robust men, with active habits, brisk circulation, manly sympathies and exuberant spirit'. Merchiston, famed for its combined forward play in spite of having only 130 pupils, developed these attributes through constant compulsory practice, spartanism – rising at seven for a walk or run followed by a cold bath – and elementary sports science. Each boy was weighed and measured twice a term. Almond believed that the Scottish schools had the advantages of pupils with hardier upbringings and an enthusiasm generated by regular matches against others, while the battle to win team places that gave boys 'a certain degree of school position' created an understanding of the self-denial and commitment needed.

Some advanced rather beyond 'school position'. Edinburgh Academy provided a player for either side when Scotland played England in 1881. While the Englishman Frank Wright was a late replacement playing his only international, the Scot Charles 'Hippo' Reid was anything but a stopgap. He was 6 ft 4 in. tall – the average Victorian male was the best part of a foot shorter – and 16 st., but as the Academicals' centenary history recalled he would have been formidable even without that physical presence: 'He usually had a hand in most of the scoring of his side, but his most striking and rare characteristic was his quickness to an opening, and the lightning-like rapidity with which he seized the opportunity.' He won 21 caps, a huge total at the time.

The intensity with which the Scots practised meant that they quickly grasped the greater opportunity for dribbling offered by the 1877 rule change requiring the ball to be released after a tackle. Reid was good at this too: 'No one could gain more ground with the ball at his feet . . . and it was no uncommon sight, even in international matches, to see him dribble through nearly all the opposing backs.'

The removal of five forwards created much more space for the fifteen players who remained, particularly if they passed the ball to each other rather than playing as individuals. Lennard Stokes's spectacularly successful late 1870s Blackheath teams may have been the first to do this and transmitted the idea to Oxford via forward Henry Vassall. There, Vassall found outside-half Alan Rotherham, who, as Arthur Budd percipiently noted, had gone to Uppingham, a non-rugby-playing school, and so had no preconceptions about how the game should be played. He decided his role was to link his forwards and backs, running with the ball then passing once his three-quarters were also on the move. In Scotland, Fettes and Loretto seized on this innovation. Almond was initially sceptical – charging into people or standing up runners was much more muscularly Christian than dodging or passing before a tackle – but concluded that passing made for unselfishness. Confronted by this tactic, Merchiston were reportedly unimpressed but baffled – a response shared by many over the next decade, as Fettes and Loretto had an immense impact. Their former pupils dominated varsity matches, providing 11 captains in as many seasons and one-third of the players in 1889. The combined Fettes–Lorettian Old Boys team assembled for a short annual fixture list was all but unbeatable, particularly when spearheaded by the half-back genius of Andrew Don-Wauchope, a fixture in the Scotland team from 1881. Don-Wauchope ran with a short, choppy stride that enabled rapid changes of direction, practised swerving by running around cricket stumps and was reckoned unstoppable once on the loose.

That such a small group had so large an impact was symptomatic of a game still in its infancy. As the game spread, others, not least in Scotland, were finding their own way of playing and demanding their say. The Border towns, who would add a very different dimension to the Edinburgh upper-middle classes, took to the game in the 1870s. Langholm (1872) were followed within five years by Hawick, Gala, Kelso and Melrose, who in 1877 seceded from a doomed-from-the-start two-year relationship with Gala and took with them goalposts, minute books, shirts and ball. By 1879, a Hawick v. Melrose match attracted such huge crowds that the gates were broken in. The 2,500 who paid were an impressive enough assemblage from towns with a combined population of 18,000 – and there may have been as many as 6,000 in the ground. It was a decade before Scotland chose a Border player, and Almond would claim that 'the best football in the world in recent years has been played at Merchiston' as late as 1892. Yet something different was clearly on its way. If anyone doubted it, the district's invention and enthusiastic adoption of seven-a-side rugby in the 1880s made the conclusion inescapable.

Challenges from further afield were also imminent. In New Zealand, Julius Vogel, the politician so helpful with inter-island transport for Monro's pioneering Nelson team, used similar techniques to populate his country – in 1871 introducing assisted passages that brought 100,000 British migrants within a decade. Gallaher and Stead, whose 1906 book begins by recounting the history of New Zealand rugby, record that 'When they came out to New Zealand, they constantly seemed to develop a new enthusiasm, and one greater than they had experienced at home.'

Distributed across a large country, New Zealanders rapidly showed impressive willingness to travel for matches – an Auckland team travelled 1,500 miles, much of it by sea, to play five games in 1875. It was also clear there was an audience for the game. In 1874, a provincial match in Dunedin pulled in 3,000 spectators. Rugby in New Zealand rapidly developed several distinguishing characteristics. Clubs were established in the main centres and quickly became highly organised. Greg Ryan has pointed out how strongly lists of senior clubs in 1870 resemble those of 2000. Representative teams were well established before the first provincial unions were formed in 1879. Even though provinces were abolished as political entities in 1876, these representative teams expressed a vigorous local patriotism. Contrary to legend, New Zealand rugby's strength has generally been concentrated in the main centres, and many small-town clubs were short lived, as key individuals or seasonal workers moved on. The New Zealand game was more socially inclusive than in England and Scotland – as Ryan points out, New Zealand's equivalent of the groups who dominated in those countries were too few to sustain rugby in New Zealand by themselves – but the educated and the professions were still strongly represented from the start.

But one wholly valid New Zealand stereotype is curiosity and innovation about tactics, particularly for forwards. Early play in

Wellington was, one chronicler recorded, 'very individual and not combined in its nature. Very heavy teams, bullocking . . . rough and tumble all-round play'. Visiting South Island teams, however, showed Wellington and others new ways of playing – Canterbury in 1876 providing 'an air of combination' and Otago's forwards ensuring 'a sound thrashing' a year later. Faced with the same teams, Auckland decided that, rather than confronting physical strength head-on, they should take two men out of their scrum and play them as wing-forwards, allowing a faster game.

Gallaher and Stead noted the emergence of local styles: Scottish-inflected Otago relying on heavy forwards; former public-school men in Canterbury 'more delicate and reminiscent of play on their native grounds'; Wellington producing fast forwards and Taranaki good half-backs. By 1885, S.E. Sleight, vice-president of the Dunedin Football Club, could claim:

> From Invercargill to Bay of Islands, clubs are everywhere springing up. Schools, colleges, trades, districts and industries send out teams to represent them. Whatever difficulties New Zealand may find in the way of continuous practice in cricket, the climate supports football as pre-eminently our national game, in which we ought to be first.

New Zealand nationality was as yet undefined. The country's settler population still defined themselves as British and would before very long be offered the option of joining a federation with Australia. While no longer a threat to settlers, Maoris still enjoyed de facto autonomy in parts of the country. There was no national rugby union at this point, but the pattern of provincial teams being active long before the formation of unions was followed at national level. New South Wales crossed the Tasman in 1882 and again in 1886, with a New Zealand team returning the visit in 1884. Results went New Zealand's way, while their haka in Sydney in 1884 led the New South Wales team to protest that it was hardly fair of the visitors to scare them out of their wits before the game began.

While Australian Rules had a presence, notably among South Island gold miners, New Zealand rugby faced less competition than its Australian counterpart. The Wellington club seriously considered switching codes in 1875, while Auckland clubs in 1877 only narrowly voted down a proposal to introduce Rules-style bouncing of the ball by ball-carriers. In Australia, rugby was forced to compete hard to survive in New South Wales and progress in Queensland.

Three Sydney clubs in 1870 became fourteen by 1874, when both the city's Premiership competition and the SRU – a founding vice-president, Edmund Barton, from the University club, would become Australia's first prime minister – were formed. In a city where space was a perennial problem, Moore Park had been secured in 1871, although it was still subject to the incursions of larrikins and parading artillerymen. The game expanded into the country. Seven clubs outside Sydney had joined the SRU by 1877. The social base, though, remained narrow. Hickie defines the SRU as 'an alliance between members of the Wallaroos, the University of Sydney and some of Sydney's private schools' – notably King's, Paramatta and Newington College.

A challenge from Victoria for a representative match in 1877 was rejected by the SRU, saying that rugby and Rules were 'diametrically different'. Yet the New South Wales Waratahs club played Carlton from Melbourne, Victoria, in June, and both they and the influential University club favoured rule changes, including the abolition of the scrum, to bring rugby closer to the Victorian game. It took the committed opposition of the Wallaroos – by self-definition the 'parent club' in Sydney – to defeat the rule changes. The Waratahs broke away to join the Rules fraternity.

Battle between the codes continued in 1882, with the footballers of Queensland, which was previously Rules territory, receiving simultaneous interstate invitations from New South Wales and Victoria. Preferring the SRU offer of fares plus accommodation to Victoria's promise of half the gate money, the Queenslanders set off for Sydney with a squad whose social composition resembled that of their heavily white-collar opponents but whose football experience was mostly in the other code. The subsequent battle for supremacy was fought not only on the pitch but in the *Brisbane Courier*, which declared itself for rugby because Rules was 'utterly unknown at home', meaning the UK – a compelling argument in a city with a high proportion of recent immigrants. Queensland's union – known as the Northern Rugby Union (NRU) – was formed in 1883. Having no affiliated rugby-only clubs, the union promptly set two up. In the longer term, the key to survival and prosperity was the schools. Brisbane Grammar School initially opted in 1886 to stay with Rules but changed a year later after two rugby-playing pupils were included in the state XV and became heroes after a victory over New South Wales, even then the direct route to a Queensland heart.

Had the proposal to drop the scrum been accepted, Australia would have headed off on its own trajectory – possibly in time merging with Rules but in any case ceasing to be rugby. This is what did happen in the United States, even though the initial story was one of great rugby success. Harvard accepted a challenge under rugby rules from McGill, Montreal, in 1875 and enjoyed it so much that in turn it persuaded Yale to give it a go. Their match on 13 December of that year attracted a crowd estimated at around 2,000, including 150 Harvard students: 'the largest crowd from Boston ever seen in New Haven'. Princeton and Columbia in turn adopted the new game. In 1876, the Intercollegiate Football Association (IFA) was formed, adopting rugby rules en bloc, except for deciding that four touchdowns would be equal to a goal. Parke Davis, a player of the time, however, remembered it as 'essentially a kicking game'.

Almost as soon as the rules were adopted, the Americans started changing them. As Stephen Reisman has pointed about, much about rugby was calculated to mystify and confuse, and American students had no tradition or older players to provide explanations. With few of the residual cultural ties to a British 'home' that limited change in Australia and New Zealand, the IFA amended what it did not like or understand at its annual rules meetings. The driving force was Walter Camp, who had played for Yale in 1876. Remembered to this day as the 'father of college football', he attended every rules meeting from 1879 to 1925, proposing changes that turned rugby into a different game. Exactly when it ceased to be rugby is a matter of definition. You can argue as early as 1880 – when teams were reduced to 11 and rugby's defining contest for possession was removed with the abolition of scrums – or as late as 1906, with the legalisation of the forward pass (which Canadian football resisted until 1931). Another evocative figure in the American game, John Heisman, pointed out that the intervening 26 years of amendment and innovation turned it progressively into a game planned in advance and controlled by coaches.

America's change had a knock-on effect in Canada. Rugby was reported to be a 'sport of the past' in Ontario and Quebec by 1882–83, as universities responded to change south of the border. There was, though, compensating development in British Columbia – the one part of Canada where the winter sports season is not truncated by brutal weather – with forces teams playing matches in 1876 and a Victoria town club formed in 1877 after playing against the British Navy, who became regular opponents.

There was growth elsewhere in the empire. The first recorded game in Fiji was in 1884, while the Ceylon (now Sri Lanka) Rugby Union claims a foundation date of 1878. That there was rugby in India in the 1870s is well known thanks to the defunct Calcutta club in 1876 using its assets to purchase the trophy contested annually by England and Scotland. Indian rugby was not confined to Calcutta. A letter to *The Field* in August 1872 from William Paterson, formerly of Blackheath and Manchester, reported that 'old Rugbeians and others' were playing once or twice a week according to rules 'more or less identical with those of the Rugby Union' in Bombay:

> It is perhaps rather hard and violent exercise for the climate; but now that the rains have cooled the earth and the fresh sea breeze is blowing over the esplanade, a very enjoyable game may be had. The spectators seem to enjoy seeing the fellows knocked about and, as these rules are a novelty here, the grounds on the evenings of play is a favourite lounge. The natives are greatly amused at it and turn out in large numbers. Unfortunately, already a dislocated shoulder and a sprained knee have not favourably impressed some people with the delights of the game.

What would not generally occur to Victorian Englishmen was that any of these numerous and greatly amused natives might be interested in playing. With the exception of New Zealand, where Maori participation was facilitated by Te Aute school, an elite institution in Hawke's Bay modelled on British public schools, and Fiji, where the British-trained Native Constabulary was involved from the start, native populations were not so much excluded as simply not thought of.

This was the early pattern in Uruguay and Argentina – neither part of the empire but both economically firmly in the British orbit, with railways and cattle ranching playing the role that lamb and dairy industries would fulfil for New Zealand. English cricket clubs were the incubator of rugby's development in these regions. Some reports put the first rugby match at the Montevideo Cricket Club as early as 1865, while a game which was 'neither one thing nor the other' was being played at the Buenos Aires club in 1873, the year before it formally adopted Rugby rules. Matches under titles such as England v. World and Bank v. City were the rule until 1886, when the first Buenos Aires v. Rosario (another cricket club) contest took place and a hispanic name, A. Calvo, appeared in the team lists. A match between Uruguayans and British members of Montevideo Cricket Club in 1880 evoked a vividly bemused account from one observer who found it 'at the same time sublime and ridiculous' and reported:

Young sons of distinguished families practising the games of the Anglo-Saxon in their youth and young Englishmen of blond Albion, face to face . . . on all sides [were] people strangely dressed who ran and shouted, pushed, fell, rose and finished by joining to form now a circle, now a pyramid, now a compact mass in which one could only distinguish heads without shoulders, legs without bodies and hands without arms.

South Africa would, of course, exclude its native population from far more activities than merely rugby. George Ogilvie, known as 'Gog' after the legible parts of his signature, had imported the rules of his old school, Winchester, when he became headmaster of Diocesan College in the Cape Town suburb of Rondesbosch in 1861. With a certain inevitability, these rules were christened 'Gog's game'.

The first clubs, Hamilton and Villagers, which were formed in 1876, played both Winchester and Rugby rules but by 1878 had, to Gog's profound displeasure, opted for Rugby. In an era of heavy immigration, with an average of 15,000 British settlers per year between 1875 and 1890, one particular arrival was influential. William Milton, twice capped for England in the mid-1870s, arrived in the Cape in 1878 – where he would rapidly rise to the position of secretary to premier Cecil Rhodes – and became a forceful, socially prestigious advocate of the game he had learned as a pupil at Marlborough. By 1883, the Western Province Rugby Union had been formed, funded with income from gate charges introduced from the late 1870s at Villagers v. Hamilton matches.

The first visitors from elsewhere in South Africa, from the mining centre of Kimberley, made the trek to Cape Town a year later. Contrary to what received South African orthodoxy would hold for more than a century, rugby was not confined to the English-speaking products of Diocesan College, the miners of Kimberley or the students of Stellenbosch, where the first Afrikaans-speaking club was formed in 1883. African house servants were seen playing football in Port Elizabeth in 1869. The first non-white club in Cape Town, Roslyns, was formed in District Six, close to the city centre, in 1882. By 1886, there were five clubs, four of which – Roslyns, Good Hopes, Violets and Arabian College – founded the Western Province Coloured RFU, a mere three years behind the white union.

In Europe, hopes of expansion still centred on Germany. The 1878 *Football Annual* reported that a headmaster in Brunswick with a taste for English pastimes had translated the rules into German and introduced the game to his pupils. With up to 100 at a time playing, the 'scrummages were really well fought out'. While alleging that Germans generally confined exercise to a stroll in order to drink beer or 'that sword exercise which results in the slashing of students' faces in duels', the account still pondered the possibility of 'England v. Germany, at Kennington Oval', which would naturally be accompanied by 'shouts of *mal* (goal), *abseits* (offside) and *wohl fallstosst* (well dropped)'.

Less remarked upon at this stage was development in France, where recuperation from the vigorous military exercise partaken by Germany in 1870 (to be fair to the *Annual*'s scribe, he had noted the 'stubborn steadiness and indomitable pluck of German infantry') was encouraging a serious interest in physical culture, with Anglophiles like Pierre de Coubertin seeing British sports as a possible aid to national renewal. The first French sports club, formed at Le Havre in 1872, was a British-dominated institution, with the insularity that that implied – even if one of the two founders was named Dreyfus. More authentically indigenous growth was, however, evident in Paris in the 1880s when the pupils of prestigious fee-paying *lycées* formed the Racing Club de France in 1882 and Stade Français in the following year.

The time was clearly fast coming when British teams might face overseas opposition. Cricket had been despatching teams to Australia since 1861 and started receiving them in return seven years later. The possibility of a rugby tour had been discussed in 1879 but fell through, according to Guillemard – who, as RFU president, presumably knew – when New Zealander and Australian hosts could not guarantee the British team's expenses. Guillemard felt this was no bad thing, as 'there is not enough Rugby Football in the colonies as yet to make the trip advisable', reckoning – on what evidence, we do not know – that the best 20 of New South Wales or New Zealand would do no more than give a British XV 'plenty of work'. Touring English cricket teams started playing Australians on equal terms in 1877, promptly losing what was later recognised as the first test match. For rugby football, though, greater challenges would first come from closer to home.

# CHAPTER THREE

# The Road to 1895

'I object to the idea that it is immoral to work for a living, and I cannot see why men should not, without objection, labour at football as at cricket'

Charles Alcock (1885)

'The history of all sports over which professionalism has gained sway is a catalogue of corruptibility and decay'

Arthur Budd (1893)

The challenges facing British rugby in the late 1800s came in the form of the north of England contesting the RFU's vision of the game, while other British unions challenged its view of the rules. In the north, rugby spread beyond the exclusivity of pioneer clubs like Liverpool and Manchester. Stuart Barlow's research on Rochdale shows the middle classes – which, like those of Wales and New Zealand, were smaller and more locally rooted than in London and its suburbs – encouraging working-class participation and rapidly being overtaken by it. Church-based clubs were succeeded by those:

> independent of middle-class partronage, based on street, district or public house. Players participated to represent their communities rather than to enshrine the ethics of 'Muscular Christianity'. The ethic of 'fair play' was subsumed by the desire to enhance local pride through securing victory against rivals.

The Rochdale club formed in 1867 was rapidly displaced by the 'open' Rochdale Hornets club. Before long, Hornets' derby matches with St Clements were attracting crowds of five or six thousand – more than internationals in London.

The northern game tapped into a growing population – in spite of emigration, the inhabitants of England and Wales more than doubled, from 15.9 million to 32.5 million, between 1841 and 1901. With textile mills ending Saturday working at 2 p.m. in 1850, and at 1 p.m. from 1874, and income up by one-third between 1850 and 1875, both a demand and the opportunity for increased leisure activities, either as player or spectator, were created. In the industrial north-east, rowers like Harry Clasper and James Renforth attracted colossal crowds to the Tyne. In Yorkshire and Lancashire, the football codes dominated, with soccer competing strongly in Lancashire. The Blackburn area, first the Darwen club in the late 1870s, then the Olympic and Rovers clubs from Blackburn itself, offered a challenge to the hegemony of southern aristocrats like Old Etonians and Clapham Rovers. Preston North End and Burnley FC were both rugby clubs before switching codes.

In Yorkshire, the forces described by Barlow were expressed almost exclusively in rugby. They were focused by the creation in 1877 of the Yorkshire Cup. The promise of its founder, James Hudson, that it would 'make Football the game for every boy in Yorkshire, and Yorkshire will be able to play the rest of England and beat it' was one of the better predictions of the era.

While their soccer counterparts created the FA Cup in 1871, the RFU in 1876 rejected the offer of the Royal Military Academy at Woolwich of a cup worth £150 for a club competition, concluding after a subcommittee had drafted rules that the idea 'did not commend itself'. The Hospitals Cup was launched in 1875, but a college competition at Oxford was rapidly abandoned when it was 'found to be making the college matches too bloodthirsty'. Historian Montague Shearman argued that 'in the excitement of a cup tie, the old Adam in the breast of the footballer will have its way and probably nothing but a neo-Platonist could play a cup tie without roughness'.

Neo-Platonists remaining in short supply, a fresh cup proposal was rejected in 1881. George Rowland Hill, archetype of that long-lived second generation of administrators as Hon. Secretary from 1881 of the RFU, wrote in the following year's *Annual* of the 'evil spirit' generated by cup ties, not only in Yorkshire but in a Hospitals Cup beset by 'exhibitions of rough and unscientific football'. Yet even Hill had to accept – tolerating a cup in his own county of Kent – that they were an unmatched means of generating interest in the game. In 1881, 15,000 watched a Yorkshire Cup quarter-final between Wakefield Trinity and Dewsbury.

There were benefits in this for the RFU. Larger crowds meant that internationals were increasingly played in the north. More than 15,000 attended the 1882 Scotland match at Manchester's Whalley Range ground. Only four of England's eleven home games in the 1880s – a number truncated by disputes with other unions – were played in London.

Playing standards rose. The Thornes team, whose 1882 Yorkshire Cup final defeat of Wakefield Trinity is claimed by the eminently sober Tony Collins as 'possibly the greatest upset in English rugby', were probably the first British team to assign forwards fixed positions in place of having them scrum down in the order in which they arrived. While Wakefield Trinity dominated the cup, playing in nine finals and winning four between 1879 and 1891, Bradford became, in Marshall's words, 'the premier club of England' in the early 1880s under the influence of centre Rawson Robertshaw, credited by Budd with extending the passing revolution by 'playing for his wings rather than himself'. Budd also reckoned the first pass from a half-back to a three-quarter was despatched by Payne of Broughton to Teddy Bartram in the North v. South match of 1881. Bartram promptly scored, his opponents doubtless shocked by this breach of propriety. His greater, still more shocking distinction was that he was widely believed to be paid for playing.

No sport sets out to be professional. It becomes, though, not only possible but likely when large numbers of people are prepared to pay to watch it and there are skilled players for whom extra income is important. Neither condition applied in London. Both did in Yorkshire, where social diversification was signalled in 1878 when Harry Hayley of Wakefield Trinity became the first working-class player to represent the county. Men on low incomes could not afford the cost of travelling to away games or the time lost from work. Clubs rarely objected to compensating them – why should they when they were charging people to watch? In 1874, Hull started paying half its players' train fares; by 1879, all of them. In 1883–84, their accounts included £18 for 'players' loss of time', payments which Wakefield

Trinity had been making openly for away matches since 1881. In 1886, following a public subscription, Bradford's England scrum-half Fred Bonsor was presented with a purse containing £80 and a watch worth £25 in front of a 10,000 match-day crowd. There were growing allegations of direct payment for playing, with Bartram the first and most obvious suspect – one reason why he did not play for England.

The movement of Scottish soccer players into Blackburn and Darwen in the late 1870s acquired a Yorkshire echo in the 1880s with the arrival of rugby players from Wales, which was just beginning to fulfil Stokes's predictions. Most, like the concentration of rugby-playing talent at Barker's Mill that enabled Thornes' success, were given jobs. None of this was illegal.

In 1879, the RFU started paying travelling expenses for representative matches. Rugby's founders had never considered the possibility of payment for playing, so there were no rules against it – except, revealingly, in Yorkshire, which in 1879 had borrowed cricket's prohibition on payments beyond 'expenses defrayed'.

The fears these developments created were summarised in the *Football Annual* for 1886 by Budd, fundamentalist amateurism's most articulate spokesman:

Gentlemen who play once a week as a pastime will find themselves no match for men who give up their whole time and abilities to it. How should they? One by one, as they find themselves outclassed, they will desert the game and leave the field to the professionals.

Rugby was not the only sport confronting this issue. Cricket had long allowed the parallel existence of professionals and amateurs – the latter defined more by social position than income. Huge public testimonials were raised for W.G. Grace and immense 'expenses' claimed by Walter Read – £1,137 (about 12 years' pay for a Lancashire millworker) for the Australia tour of 1887–88. In the USA, baseball accepted professionalism in 1868. Soccer was guided by pragmatic FA secretary Charles Alcock, who used his editorial in the *Football Annual* for 1884 to argue that professionalism was 'an event of the immediate future' that would 'remove many of the impurities which are presently seriously damaging the game' – a clear reference to concealed payments. He was proved right within a year, change being provoked by Preston North End, the former rugby club presided over by former forward Norman Sudell. Rowing went in a diametrically different direction in 1878, excluding not only those who competed for money but anyone who 'has ever been employed in or about boats, or in manual labour . . . [or] a mechanic, artisan or labourer', adding a year later, in case anyone had missed the point, 'or engaged in any menial activities'. It contained, John Lowerson has argued, 'assumptions that influenced every other sport's treatment of the amateur/professional divide'.

Rugby's response was never going to be as socially blatant. Tony Collins points to the game's ambiguous response to working-class players, tolerated as long as they played on the terms set by its rulers. Those terms were devised by a subcommittee including three Yorkshiremen and debated at the 1886 annual general meeting (AGM) of the RFU. The rules proposed were as follows:

Professionalism is illegal.

A professional is:

(a) Any player who shall receive from his club, or any member of it, any money consideration whatsoever, actual or prospective, for services rendered to the club of which he is a member . . .

(b) Any player who receives any compensation for loss of time from his club or any member of it.

(c) Any player trained at the club's expense or at the expense of any member of the club.

(d) Any player who transfers his activities from one club to another on consideration of any contract, engagement or promise on the part of any other club to find him employment.

(e) Any player who receives from his club, or any member of it, any sum in excess of the amount actually disbursed by him in account of hotel or travelling expenses incurred in connection with the club's affairs.

They were not received with universal enthusiasm. Horace Lyne of Newport, an RFU member by virtue of its location in ambiguously situated Monmouthshire, warned that Welsh as well as northern clubs would suffer if compensation for time off work were prohibited. The delegate from Dewsbury, where club president Mark Newsome's family firm provided jobs for players like Welsh international 'Buller' Stadden, spoke for clubs 'composed of working men, and they could not afford to lose them when engaged away from home'.

Budd's intention that 'no mercy but iron rigour shall be dealt out' was carried through. Harry Garnett of Bradford, voice of an always significant Yorkshire minority – they after all played weekly against clubs they felt were taking an unfair advantage – argued that 'If working men desired to play football, they should pay for it themselves, as they would have to do for any other pleasure.'

The RFU hoped that the issue had been settled. The first set of rules on amateurism were, however, merely the first shot in a longer conflict. Nor was it the only battle. Three surviving aspects of the original Rugby game – the almost complete primacy of the goal, control by captains rather than a referee and the absence of effective sanction against illegal play – were becoming untenable. Each national union had its own interpretation of the laws, and while differences were marginal, margins are where disputes occur.

Cup competitions, needing definite results, were a spur for points systems, used in both the Hospitals Cup and the South Wales Challenge Cup, although the latter's varied with 'confusing frequency'. New Zealand too showed its essential practicality by introducing points as early as 1875. The RFU, though, rejected a proposed system in 1882. Rowland Hill, the most influential voice, argued that points were 'prejudicial to scientific play. The fact that touchdowns score materially discourages dribbling.'

The belief that gentlemen would not deliberately misbehave coloured attitudes towards referees and their powers. The amendment to the RFU laws formally introducing umpires in 1874 also reaffirmed captains as the 'sole arbiters' of disputes. Yorkshire led the push for the introduction of penalty kicks as a punishment for offside. They lost in 1880, vehemently opposed by Budd and Edward Temple Gurdon, both former England players and RFU presidents-to-be. Yorkshire prevailed two years later, but it was not yet possible to score from the penalty.

The trouble was that gentlemen did not invariably conform to the ideal. By 1883, Hill was complaining that 'a crop of players has arisen that deliberately plays unfairly'. The lack of clear on-field authority left immense scope for dispute, particularly since, as one player recalled, 'The more plausible and argumentative a player was, the more likely he was to be chosen as captain.' In 1882, Richmond captain Frank Adams complained so vehemently about a knock-on ruling that the match with Oxford University was abandoned. The word 'deliberately' – the point of contention – was removed from the laws. Twice in the early 1880s the incontestably respectable Edinburgh Academicals abandoned matches after disagreements over interpretation.

Eventually, this wave of disputation swept into the international game, with far-reaching results. From 1881, neutral umpires were selected for international matches, but captains could still dispute decisions. In 1884, a complete international programme, all four teams playing each other, was completed for the first time. It would happen only once more during the 1880s, in 1887.

The 1884 match between England and Scotland was umpired by that busily versatile Irishman George Scriven, taking charge of his one international. England scored a try. The Scots said it was illegal. England pointed out that under their rules it was not, and that in any case the infringement was Scottish. There followed a half-hour hiatus during which Rowland Hill came onto the field with a copy of the rules. It was not until the after-match dinner that Scriven 'expressed himself in anything approaching decisive terms'. Scotland refused to accept the result, argued that the issue should be put to a neutral authority and, when England refused, cut the fixture off for 1885.

It was the Irish – themselves in dispute with Wales, whom they did not play in 1885 and 1886 – who proposed creating an international board to act as rule-maker and arbitrator. Instead of settling matters, this provoked further dissension over the proposal that each union should have three representatives. England, arguing that it had many more clubs, refused to participate on this basis, both its reasoning and its isolation anticipating disputes more than 100 years in the future. The Celts went ahead, formed the IRB and played each other – but not England – in 1888 and 1889. Realising that ultimately this would benefit none of them, both sides agreed to arbitration in 1890. The arbiters, Francis Marindin of the FA and Scotland's Lord Clerk of Justice Lord Kingsburgh – a title disguising former marathon scrummager and Raeburn Place gate-collector

John MacDonald – backed the RFU, giving it six seats, compared with two each for the other three members, and an effective veto by requiring a three-quarters majority for law changes.

The home unions had also fallen out in 1886 over the RFU's proposed points system – one point for a try and three for a goal – and its introduction of penalty goals, of which Hill would write two years later, 'experience has made converts of us all'. Points and penalty goals were now accepted by the IRB, along with the rest of the RFU rules, although scoring values remained in flux. Stability was finally reached in 1893, with three points – up from one in 1890 – for a try, two for a conversion, three for a penalty and four for a drop-goal. There was less contention over the introduction of referees in 1885 and the progressive conversion of umpires into touch-judges. In 1889, referees were given the right to send players off and three years later became 'sole judges of fact', although a right of appeal to the RFU over matters of law was retained.

England was not wholly starved of international rugby during its two years in solitary confinement, its players rescued by the invention of one of the game's defining institutions: the overseas tour, compelled by rugby's peculiar geography to be not so much international as intercontinental. Like London buses, two arrived almost at once. A British team went to Australia and New Zealand in 1888 and a New Zealand Natives team made the opposite journey later in the same year. In keeping with the age, both proved contentious. Both were commercial ventures, following cricket's pattern of tours as speculative enterprises. Rugby's first major tour indeed grew directly out of cricket, promoted by the Nottinghamshire duo of Arthur Shrewsbury and Alfred Shaw, respectively England's best professional batsman and best bowler, period. Much of the tour's popular appeal rested on centre Andrew Stoddart, already playing cricket with Shaw and Shrewsbury in Australia. The RFU refused official recognition for 'a money-making speculation', but decided not to interfere so long as amateur principles were maintained. This pious aspiration was not long in being breached. Shaw and Shrewsbury recruited via an agent whose 'very furtiveness made him an object of suspicion'. Three Dewsbury players refused their invitations and told their club what had been offered. James Clowes of Halifax accepted, and the Dewsbury club took revenge for an earlier incident by reporting him for professionalism. Clowes was duly banned.

The team assembled was hardly representative – predominantly northern, with four internationals and four who had played for North v. South among the 22 players. They were kept busy, with four months aboard ship and a programme of 53 matches, including 18 of Australian Rules football. While losing more than they won at Rules, they were unbeaten at rugby in Australia but found New Zealand more demanding, losing to Taranaki and Auckland. While they received this first warning of New Zealand standards – their victories were mostly close-fought – their combined back play was making an impact.

New Zealand interpretation held that heeling the ball from a scrum placed forwards offside. The inevitable consequence was remembered by Thomas Ellison: 'Back play was not generally the order of the day, and when it occurred it was not the result of systematic play.' In Britain, interpretation was still debated, but heeling-out, though deemed unmanly by those nostalgic for marathon heads-up brawls, was generally accepted. With local referees deferring to their visitors, the tourists were allowed to heel and demonstrate their skills. Stoddart's style was recalled vividly sixty years later by journalist Townsend Collins: 'he had a very close swerve, could break either way when he seemed to be almost in the arms of an opponent and had a quality of unexpectedness which was very disconcerting to opponents', although 1871 veteran Robert Irvine said that the Scots always rated the unselfish Robertshaw more highly for his 'wide, accurate passing' and reckoned they had little to fear from Stoddart. Still, his impact on New Zealanders was considerable. Stoddart also excelled at Australian Rules and took the captaincy when the original leader, Robert Seddon of Swinton, drowned in the Maitland River in New South Wales. He was away for 14 months on the two tours.

Shrewsbury was delighted with rugby's stance on professionalism: 'If the Rugby Union can get players to come out without paying them anything, so much the better for us.' But there is little doubt money had changed hands. Stoddart was offered a £50 down payment to 'bind' him for the rugby tour, for which two lesser-known players were offered £200 each and the sole Welshman, W.H. Thomas of Cambridge University, received £90.

On their return, the RFU, usually keen to root out offenders against amateurism – six clubs were suspended between 1888 and 1890 – proved strangely uninterested in checking out widespread rumours of illicit payment. Clowes' suspension was lifted and other team members asked to sign a declaration that they had not been paid – foreshadowing the treatment a century later of players who went to apartheid-era South Africa. The most plausible explanation is offered by Tony Collins: that any investigation would have exposed Stoddart, a southern gentleman regarded very differently to the working men of the north. Even under cricket's more liberal regime, his expenses claims occasioned controversy in 1896.

In consequence, Stoddart and his tour-mates were available to face the visiting New Zealand Natives – a further cricketing echo, as the first Australian cricket team to visit Britain were the Aborigines of 1868. The Natives' programme made Shaw and Shrewsbury's team look like slackers on the job. They were away for just over a year and played one hundred and seven rugby matches, plus at least eight of Australian Rules while passing through Melbourne. Seventy-four were played in less than six months in the UK, including such improbable feats as playing Llanelli, Wales, Swansea, Newport and Cardiff in ten days (one of which was Christmas Day). The wonder is that a twenty-six-man party, led by Joe Warbrick and containing four of his brothers, won any matches in Britain, let alone forty-nine, including the international against Ireland. It was not a wholly happy experience – years later, Pat Keogh alleged that its relentlessness contributed to ten of the team dying before they were forty-one. Part of an obituary for one of the last survivors, 'Tabby' Wynyard, read:

> Severe hardship and a continual shortage of clothing and luxuries, even food, owing to the fact that 'gates' in Britain were generally very poor, a few coppers only being charged ... they were often compelled to reside ... at third-rate boarding houses and hotels, and on several occasions arrived at snow-clad railway stations at midnight with nobody to welcome them and had no option but to sleep on the benches there.

The tour's modern chronicler Greg Ryan describes this as an extreme account but leaves little doubt of attendant controversy.

Warmly received in northern England and Wales, they were less fondly regarded in the south. These feelings were reciprocated by the formidably articulate Ellison, who felt Yorkshire, who inflicted their heaviest defeat, 16–4, were a better team than England. Anticipating many of his countrymen, he was unimpressed with British play, which was:

> one style and description, from start to finish, hooking, heeling-out and passing all day, whether successful at it or not. I never played against a team that made any radical change of tactics during the course of a game. They all seemed to have tumbled into a groove, and stuck there.

Any British fans expecting to see spear-wielding primitives were as shocked as their military counterparts had been two decades earlier by Maori warriors who proved to be militarily sophisticated, tactically innovative and were only ultimately contained by sheer weight of British numbers. Ryan notes that before the 1920s, Maori participation was 'comparatively limited and confined to an acculturated elite'. Six of the squad had attended Te Aute school, and a minority of *pakeha* (white New Zealander) players were added after poor preliminary matches in the team's home country.

The visitors were subjected to allegations of veiled professionalism, drunkenness and bad sportsmanship. The latter were rooted in extraordinary incidents during their match against England. Once again, Ellison recalled, Stoddart was at the centre of events:

> I lured him into my arms by applying the feign dodge. By a quick wriggle, however, he escaped but left a portion of his knickers in my possession. He dashed along and the crowd roared; then suddenly discovering what was the matter he stopped, threw down the ball, and, in an instant, we had the vulgar gaze shut off by forming a ring around him.

While the Natives were protecting Stoddart's modesty, England forward Frank Evershed seized the discarded ball and ran over for a try, which the referee – none other than Rowland Hill – awarded. Three of the native team walked off in protest, only returning when Hill restarted in their absence. England scored again for a 7–0 win. The RFU then demanded an apology for the walk-off, Marshall in a notably po-faced passage saying 'this step was, as may very well be imagined, most distasteful to the Union, but the principles of the game have always been of the first importance to the minds of the Union Committee'. The apology was duly given, then repeated when the RFU deemed it insufficient for the tour to be completed. It still had five weeks to go in the UK. There was no official welcome for the tourists when they returned to London a month later. For his part, Ellison not unreasonably wanted to know why Hill, the RFU's senior official, was allowed to referee an England match.

On their way home, the Natives confirmed a developing pattern of cross-Tasman superiority by winning 15 of 16 matches in Australia and drawing the other. Ryan asks why so remarkable a team was allowed to drop into retrospective obscurity. One reason, he argues, is that they predated the creation of a national union and so the team does not fit into All Black iconology. They had, however, played in black, and it was Ellison who both proposed the adoption of their black shirt with fern leaf when the newly formed union discussed the issue in 1892 and led the team to Australia a year later.

The creation of the New Zealand Rugby Football Union (NZRFU) was not a smooth process. Both Canterbury and Otago, via the Dunedin club, were already affiliated to the RFU and reluctant to accept what Otago's delegate to the first meeting of the NZRFU in 1892 termed 'government . . . by Wellington'. Canterbury's delegate explained that his province 'had thrown out of office those who favoured the union'. Neither province joined. In 1893, they seriously contemplated forming a South Island union together with fellow refuseniks Southland. Their resistance was broken by an NZRFU resolution preventing affiliates from playing non-affiliated unions. Canterbury signed up in 1894. Otago, angered by losing their oldest and most lucrative fixture, followed, along with Southland, in 1895.

Ellison's contribution to New Zealand life – he was also the first Maori admitted to the legal profession – did not stop with the invention and leadership of the All Blacks. He wrote the first New Zealand coaching manual, *The Art of Rugby Football* (1902), describing inter alia how his Poneke club perfected what became the distinctive New Zealand pattern of play with seven forwards, each with a specialised role, supported by wing-forwards (initially there were two), whose duty was to put the ball into the scrum and protect the half-back. He argued: 'the protected half-back of the wing game can send all, or nearly all, of his passes out to the backs, whereas the pestered and utterly unprotected half-back of the other systems is lucky when he gets half of his out'.

In 1892, it had taken two months of intensive pre-season training to prepare Poneke for the system, which brought them and the Wellington province team immense success. *The Art of Rugby Football*'s pioneering is not confined to being first in a fruitful New Zealand literary field. Ellison's disregard for the rugby of the other hemisphere and conviction that things were not what they had been – labelling the wing-forwards of 1902 'nothing more than aimless off-side jokers' – anticipated much rugby discourse to this day, while his suggestion that it should be possible to score from a punt would be echoed, surely unconsciously, in Michael Green's comic classic *The Art of Coarse Rugby* (1960).

For Australia, repelling troublesome trans-Tasman invaders was a perennial problem – although with the compensation of crowds of 10,000 to see the conquering Natives at Brisbane – but its game was progressing in other respects. Within a decade of the formation of the NRU, Brisbane had 72 clubs, while Sydney by the end of the century would boast 79. The formation of the Greater Public Schools Association in 1892 and the adherence of new recruit St Joseph's, which has since supplied more than 50 Wallabies, consolidated rugby's hold in the elite schools, and there was also growth from the late 1880s in the state sector. While the discarding of the 'North' and 'South' labels and their replacement by state names in 1892 did not presage the creation of an Australian Rugby Union – Queensland and New South Wales were still separate colonies and Australian federation was eight years away – they avoided potential confusion with the new NZRFU and reflected an emerging sense of local identity independent of Britain.

South Africa, its identity considerably more conflicted, was next to enjoy the empire-reinforcing ritual of a tour from Britain. It too developed institutionally, creating a rash of anniversaries that would be a thoroughly mixed blessing a century later. The South African Rugby Football Board (SARFB) was formed in 1889 at a four-team tournament in Kimberley, and this pattern of provincial teams being brought together in a single location for tournaments would continue for many years. The same year saw the foundation of the Transvaal Rugby Union, representing a region transformed from backwater to boom by the discovery of gold three years earlier.

The 1891 tour was recognised by the RFU, once Cecil Rhodes had personally promised to guarantee the costs. Edwin Ash went as manager of a 24-man party led by William MacLagan of London Scottish and Scotland. It included eight internationals – four each from England and Scotland – and no fewer than fourteen Oxbridge Blues, twelve from Cambridge. They were introduced to Transvaal premier Paul Kruger in Pretoria and found South African conditions demanding. Paul Clauss, one of the Scots, recalled the Kimberley ground as:

> Absolutely desolate of grass, hard and covered with reddish dust; so that, with the bright sun overhead there was a considerable glare. Frequently, too, one lost sight of the ball in the pillars of dust that rose up in the wake of the players as they ran.

Unsurprisingly, 'it was no joke being tackled'. Tackling, along with kicking and fielding the ball, was reported to be a South African strength. Team play, though, had not developed, with Marshall's correspondent reporting 'Forward and back alike were very loth to part with the ball when once they had possession of it.' MacLagan, veteran of 26 international matches dating back to 1878, a wing noted for tackling that 'was sound but destructively ferocious', was well equipped for this type of rugby. Irvine bluntly noted that 'roughness has often been imputed to him', and an unnamed teammate reckoned him 'an ill-natured devil'.

His team won all of its 19 matches, conceding only a single point while travelling more than 4,000 miles, mostly by train. It left a permanent memorial in South Africa: the Currie Cup, presented to Griqualand West (the scorers of the single point) for the best performance against the tourists and in turn donated as the prize for South Africa's inter-provincial championship.

In Canada, the loss of Ontario and Quebec was being steadily compensated for by growth in British Columbia. The construction of Brockton Oval in Stanley Park, Vancouver, gave the British

Columbian Rugby Union, founded in 1889, a permanent, visually spectacular ground shared with baseball, cricket and lacrosse, which regularly accommodated crowds of several thousand by the early 1890s. Cross-border contact was established with the US, a team who visited San Francisco in 1894 finding to their evident satisfaction that 'Individually, California was superior for weight and speed but lacked the cohesion displayed by the winners.' Rugby in the Canadian province of Manitoba was more flamboyant but with less staying power. From 1896, it was replaced by Canadian Football. This, however, was not before members of the Assiniboia team, based around Cannington Manor – a settlement formed in 1882 to 'bring gracious living to the empty frontier' and graced from 1889 by three old Rugbeian Beckton brothers 'who had somehow failed to mature beyond adolescence . . . and followed up every victory or defeat with a carnival of alcohol-inspired high jinks' – had left a lasting impression upon Winnipeg. The East Assiniboia team kicked up a 'rumpus' in the Walker Theatre after they had 'defeated Winnipeg and had been handsomely wined and dined by them . . . two of them spent the night in the cooler'.

In Argentina, a similar fate awaited the first Buenos Aires team to travel to play Rosario, in 1890. They arrived 'shouting and uproarious'. Local police, unfamiliar with rugby teams but well aware of political tension in the capital, took them for the advance guard of a revolutionary army and detained them.

France too was not long removed from revolutionary moments – a military coup expected in 1886 only failed when its leader lost his nerve. It too acquired a governing body, although the Union des Sociétés Françaises de Sports Athlétiques (USFSA), founded by Pierre de Coubertin, was an umbrella body for all amateur sports. By 1892, it had a national championship, admittedly a flattering title for a contest between the only two entrants, Racing Club – whose first rugby XV in 1888 included a future cardinal, Petit de Tulleville – beating Stade Français. Not everyone yet recognised it as a legitimately French activity. When Cyril Rutherford, later a significant administrator, played his first game in France in the Parc de Vincennes in 1895, a curious spectator ridiculed 'a gang of idiots chasing on the grass after a ball'. An early Nantes team lost six players on military service when they were imprisoned for 'exhibiting themselves in an indecent dress' by playing in football kit rather than military dress. That there were clubs in Nantes, Toulouse and Bordeaux was a pointer to an increasingly provincial future.

Across the Channel, the return of uninterrupted international action was rapidly followed by a never-to-be-repeated sequence of consecutive Triple Crowns – beating the other three teams in a season – by each of the four competitors. For Scotland in 1891, Wales in 1893 and Ireland a year later, it was a first crown. England, who were the 1892 claimants, had previously won the Triple Crown in 1883 and 1884.

Scotland at last recognised that the Borders might provide Edinburgh students and advocates with international teammates as well as club opposition, capping Adam Dalgleish of Hawick in 1890. Other nations were seduced by the attacking potentialities of the new formation pioneered by Wales from the mid-1880s, sacrificing a forward for a fourth three-quarter, but the Scots remained loyal to the nine-man pack and a rugged, dribbling-based style practised by a vigorous, durable pack including players like John Boswell of West of Scotland, a noted drop-kicker who won 15 caps, and Robert MacMillan of London Scottish, who played 21 times between 1887 and 1897.

Ireland, too, remained loyal to a forward-based style. New Zealand Natives captain Joe Warbrick retained a warm regard for the way they 'used to career down the field with the ball at their feet and were next to irresistible. They never attempted to pick up unless in our 25'. Here too there was diversification, with Catholic schools like Blackrock and Rockwell broadening the religious mix, and the foundation of clubs like the Limerick duo of Garryowen and Shannon in 1884 (Young Munster followed in 1895) broadening the geographical mix. Even so, there was little warning of the country's 1894 triumph. Ireland had won only four of thirty-two matches before 1890, and one out of twelve between then and the 1894 competition. A team whose success had the air of fiction fielded a three-quarter named H.G. Wells. Another, Lucius Gwynn, was selected two years later to play cricket for England, declined because of examinations and died of tuberculosis before he was 30. Forward Tom Crean was destined to win the Victoria

72

Cross, while Ireland's strong fraternal tradition was represented by the Lytle brothers from NIFC. John Lytle sealed the decisive win over England with the only score, a penalty, on a Belfast day designed for forwards: 'mud was over our ankles, and it was almost impossible to keep a foothold' recalled one player. Ireland tackled ferociously and relied on those storming foot-rushes.

Wales's triumph a year earlier was a little more predictable in one sense, although they came to the tournament with a poor record against England and Scotland. Wales had previously won only two matches out of nineteen against the two sides, and the Scots thought Wales were serious opposition only for half an hour before blowing up, producing results like the 1887 debacle when Scotland won by four goals and eight tries to nil. Welsh passion, though, was reflected in vastly growing crowds. Cardiff's annual gates rose from £364 in 1885–86 to £1,233 in 1890–91 – not quite a match for Bradford's £2,000-plus but vastly more than a Midlands club such as Coventry, who pulled in £113. More than 20,000 people watched Cardiff play Newport and Swansea in 1893–94.

These colossal assemblies reflected Wales's spectacular population growth – the country gained a million more inhabitants between 1871 and 1911, much through migration from the depressed agricultural areas of the west of England. Cardiff's population quadrupled between 1871 and 1901.

Local loyalties were fierce – a newspaper in Llanelli, always an exemplar, telling players that their task was:

> not one merely of beating 15 picked men from each of the other teams in the Western District of South Wales. It means much more. It means vindicating the honour of Llanelli against her many detractors . . . It means raising her name and her fame amongst the towns. It tends to bring more trade, a more vigorous public spirit and a healthier social life.

So vehement were those rivalries that Wales downgraded its cup to a competition for junior clubs in 1887 after entries tailed off due to endemic disputes. It was not, though, parochial in the sense of rejecting outside contact – 12 of Cardiff's 31 fixtures in 1888–89 were against English clubs.

Wales also had its own style of play. Warbrick recalled opponents in 1888 operating through 'a succession of short passes, with very little danger of their being intercepted'. While Cardiff's adoption of a fourth three-quarter in 1884 was a short-term expedient – bringing Frank Hancock into the team without losing another strong three-quarter – it was rapidly recognised as offering much greater attacking options and adopted within two years by most Welsh clubs. Newport resisted longest, because of the opposition of Arthur Gould, arguably worth two three-quarters by himself. First capped in 1885, he was to Marshall, writing the year before Wales's breakthrough, 'the central figure in the football world, the greatest centre three-quarter that has ever played'. Gould had the speed of the track champion he was when not playing rugby, an ability to swerve and sidestep that made stopping him, according to Gwyn Nicholls, his eventual successor as Wales's midfield general, 'like trying to catch a butterfly with a hatpin', an all-round kicking game and was, in the words of his devoted but clear-eyed admirer Townsend Collins, a 'supremely great individualist with judgement super-added', an instinctive genius who nevertheless honed his skills with more practice than anyone else.

Around him grouped younger players of the impish quality that delights Welsh crowds but whose sleight of hand fulfilled the practical need to compensate for the superior size and power of the Englishmen and Scots. The James brothers of Swansea – small, curly-haired, half-Jewish half-backs, labourers in the White Rock copper works which stood where the Neath-Swansea Ospreys' Liberty Stadium now stands, practised interpassing so deft and deceptive that an Irish captain advised his teammates to 'go for the one who hasn't got the ball – because he'll be the one that has'. They evoked, as John Morgan and Geoffrey Nicholson have pointed out, the same bafflement outside Wales as their political compatriot and contemporary David Lloyd George: a sense of the exotic, unworldly and inexplicable. Gould had a clearer view of them as 'not conjurors, but an exceptionally clever pair of halves who have brought half-back play to a state of perfection'. The James brothers ruled themselves out of selection for Wales by joining Broughton Rangers in 1892, but their spirit lived on in their Swansea teammate Billy Bancroft, a daringly tantalising sidestepper at full-back who foiled a Scottish rush during the Triple Crown year by volleying the ball back over the charging forwards' heads. Townsend Collins recounted a Merchistonian's plaintive 'That's not rugby' meeting the prompt Welsh reply, 'No, that's Banky.'

The Triple Crown was a triumph made in Newport, unbeaten that season and with eight players in the teams that played Ireland and England, and nine against the Scots. Club captain Tom Graham, an incomer from Newcastle who won three of his twelve Welsh caps that season, was as important as Gould. Collins remembered:

> He asked for thorough training and assiduous practice; he called for the study of theory and the understanding of tactics; the dressing-room became a school for footballers – on the lines of a Workers Educational Association class where, in the give-and-take of discussion, tutor and students make education a cooperative effort.

The decisive match, against England, was in doubt due to a frozen pitch. Five hundred coal-filled buckets were brought in, creating what a London journalist compared to 'a scene from Dante's inferno . . . five hundred fires blazing far up into the dark night', as snow continued to fall and 'dark ghoul-like figures' fed the fires. Walking the pitch at midnight, Collins thought it playable. So it proved the next day, as Gould scored two tries then Bancroft secured a single-point victory with a drop-goal landed with sure-footed assurance – and, in some accounts, against Gould's orders – from frozen ground near the touch-line.

Less anticipated than either Ireland or Wales's first Triple Crowns was that England's of 1892, which was won without conceding a point, would be their last for nearly 20 years. Nine of the players who beat Scotland that year were from Yorkshire or Lancashire (there had been ten against the Maoris). By 1894, England were led by Dickie Lockwood, a 5 ft 4 in. centre from profoundly unfashionable Heckmondwike who had first been capped at 19, within a year earning Ellison's admiration. In maturity, Marshall saw him 'combining in one person to the highest degree all the essential qualities of a centre-three-quarter . . . of almost infallible judgement, always turning up at the right time and invariably being in the right spot, he always does the right thing'.

The County Championship was introduced in 1889. Yorkshire

won it then, and every year until 1896, except 1891, when they lost to Lancashire. Yorkshire Cup entrants doubled from sixty-four to one hundred and twenty-nine in three years from 1887, while 27,654 people (more than for that year's FA Cup final) attended a third-round tie between Leeds and Halifax in 1892–93. That match was played on the Headingley ground, the construction of which in 1889 had been enabled by Leeds becoming, as Leeds Cricket, Football and Athletic Co. Ltd, the first football club to become a limited company, raising £25,000 in share capital to purchase the 22-acre site.

Yorkshire used the power of its growing number of affiliated clubs to push for RFU annual meetings, always held in London, to take place in alternate years in the north. They got a majority in 1891 but fell short of the two-thirds needed. Hill, who was happily citing superior numbers in the IRB dispute, wrote that London was 'more convenient for representatives from all parts', with meetings there 'not affected specially by the views of workers in any particular district'. Changing would create unrepresentative meetings controlled by sectional interests and 'reprisals will inevitably arise'.

The feeling in the north was that they already had. With Marshall, Yorkshire treasurer from 1888, providing leadership, the weaponry of the 1886 regulations was deployed against offenders. The RFU went after clubs – six were suspended for periods of up to fourteen weeks between October 1888 and January 1890 – and players. Lockwood's mastery extended to stonewalling enquiries about the precise sources of his income, surviving one three-day inquisition.

External factors exacerbated tension. A downturn in the textile trades, reflected in Yorkshire Cup final crowds levelling off in the 15–17,000 range in the early 1890s, while previously comparable FA Cup finals were doubling in attendance, made extra income more important for working-class players – almost the entire team at Bradford. Labour unrest, with major disputes in Bradford, Leeds, Hull and Wakefield between 1890 and 1893, plus the formation in Bradford in 1893 of the Independent Labour Party, reflected class and political tension, compared to the relative tranquillity of the mid 1880s, when soccer had resolved its issues.

Ultimately, conflict centred on a single issue: whether or not to allow 'broken time' compensation for time off work. The leading

Yorkshire and Lancashire clubs wished to restore the tolerant pre-1886 status quo. The case against was put, with characteristic clarity, by Budd:

> If A.B. of the Stock Exchange were to ask for compensation for loss of time for a two-days football tour, such compensation to be fixed on a scale commensurate with his earnings, the football community would denounce it as a scandal. A.B. the stockbroker has therefore to stop at his desk because he cannot afford to play, but C.D. the working man is to be allowed his outing and compensation for leaving his work, which under any other circumstances he could not afford to abandon. If a man who gives his whole time to a game is bound to best the amateur, who devotes only his leisure to it, the inevitable law of survival of the fittest must intervene, and it simply becomes a question of how the amateur can survive.

Budd had enjoyed great success advising Oxford University in the early 1880s. H.H. Vassall recalled that he had demanded 'constant practice . . . crowds of men [were] ready to play six days a week if given a chance, the difficulty was to stop them getting too much practice'. A columnist from the left-wing weekly *Clarion* asked why losing was so unacceptable if the game was supposed to be enjoyed for its own sake.

Budd and his allies were to win on this occasion. At the 1893 AGM, James Miller of the Yorkshire Rugby Union (YRU) proposed that players be compensated for 'bona fide loss of earnings'. Miller argued:

> These men were constantly called upon to lose their wages in order to play for their county or their club and at the same time they were debarred from recompense for the loss of time involved. Why should not the working man be able to play the game on level terms with the gentleman?

Hobson of the Midland Counties retorted that his club was formed largely of working men who did not want payment, while J.W.H. Thorp of Cheshire asserted that 'The pseudo-working man and the bastard amateur do not represent the working man of this country.' Marshall, heckled violently by Yorkshire club delegates, said the resolution would allow them to go on breaking the rules. When the vote was taken, the resolution was lost by 282 votes to 136. Hobson and Thorp's contributions underline the point made by Tony Collins, that the Yorkshire clubs lost because they failed to convince those they needed on their side rather than because the establishment wielded 120 proxies – for which Collins can find no evidence – or counted Oxbridge colleges as individual clubs.

Hill's counter-resolution that 'only clubs composed entirely of amateurs shall be eligible for membership' was adopted. The RFU followed through with fresh regulations, although a clause placing the 'burden of proof' on accused clubs and players because of the 'methods of concealment hitherto adopted by leading clubs' was rapidly dropped following protests from not only Lancashire and Yorkshire but Durham, Gloucestershire and the Midlands. In the next year, Huddersfield, Salford, Wigan and Leigh were suspended. At the 1894 AGM, a resolution offering a £20 reward for information leading to suspensions, proposed by 'Tottie' Carpmael of the Barbarians club – nobody seems to have asked if it would professionalise the recipient – received 163 votes.

The inevitable breach came in 1895. The strongest Yorkshire and Lancashire clubs, who had organised themselves into county leagues, known as Senior Competitions, since 1892, had further fallings-out with their county unions over payments and, in a foretaste of the early twenty-first century, promotion to and relegation from their self-selected competition. In late 1894, Yorkshire clubs declared the RFU view on professionalism 'not a reasonable and just interpretation and cannot be accepted by us'. In January 1895, eighteen of them (with four apologising for absence) proposed forming a 'mutual protection society, called the "Northern Union"'. The RFU predictably vetoed this, then backed the YRU in July when it rescinded the Senior Competition's powers. The leading Yorkshire clubs resigned from their county union. Some inevitably hesitated over taking the final step of secession – Bradford were effectively pushed into it by their players, while on 12 August the RFU chose this sensitive moment to reissue its code on professionalism. The Yorkshire clubs met on 27 August and, duly resolved, came together with their Lancashire counterparts at the George Hotel, Huddersfield, two days later to form the Northern Rugby Union on the basis of 'payment for bona fide broken time only'.

# CHAPTER FOUR

# Between Schism and War

'Nothing in the world pays a team as well as the accurate performance of sound and sensible tactics. Individual brilliance is a beautiful thing to see, but it never wins a match on its own account'

Dave Gallaher and Billy Stead, *The Complete Rugby Footballer in the New Zealand System* (1906)

'A pre-eminent expression of Welsh consciousness, a signifier of Welsh nationhood'

Gareth Williams, *1905 and All That* (1991)

That 1895 is the most important date in the history of rugby league is patently obvious. It is the point of foundation for an entire sport. It is, though, almost as significant for rugby union. It turned an element in its regulations into a ruling ideology, the test against which every new idea, development and aspiring nation would be measured. What Marxist-Leninism was to the Soviet Union and papal infallibility to the Roman Catholic Church, amateurism would be to rugby union for the next century.

The schism had a profound effect in Britain. It made the Home (later Five, still later Six) Nations championship the centrepiece of British and European rugby. Without the loss of the Northern Rugby Union clubs, England's overwhelming advantage in numbers and wealth would surely have made it, even allowing for eccentric organisation, the dominant nation. The schism amputated England's most fertile region and also hampered Wales, the next best-equipped nation. In an undivided code, the championship might not have been as unbalanced as its soccer equivalent – an Anglo-Scottish near-monopoly – but it could not have been the unpredictable, highly competitive tournament that became the British season's central ritual. Wales, for example, was the top team of the twentieth century but had a success rate of below 60 per cent in Home Nations matches, while back-marker Ireland topped 40 per cent.

Rugby league (the Northern Rugby Union until 1922) played an ambiguous role. It was The Other, so identified with professionalism that the slightest contact was fatal. It was a seceding province with no legitimate existence – Taiwan to Mao's China. In Wales, the league scout became a pantomime villain, albeit one likelier to be ducked in the sea at Penarth than erupt through the stage trapdoor at the Swansea Empire. Yet it was also a safety valve, a place of refuge for those who needed to turn rugby talent into legitimate income. If league had not existed, rugby union would have had to invent it.

Northern Union was not so much proscribed as attaindered at the RFU AGM on 19 September 1895. While amnestying players and clubs who returned to the fold by 1 November, the RFU ruled that 'The members of the Northern Union clubs are, under our rules, declared to be professionals.' Contact with league's grounds, players, referees and officials was banned. As Tony Collins has pointed out, it is instructive that the resolution 'makes no mention of payments to players, but simply goes after anyone connected with the Northern Union'.

The Northern Union did not regard itself as professional, indeed saw broken-time payments, capped at six shillings each week, as a defence against all-out professionalism. That particular battle was to be lost within three years, with the Northern Union legalising straightforward payment in 1898. For several more years, it required players to have outside jobs, banning those unemployed or in unacceptable work. It evolved rapidly into a different game in the search for a more attractive spectacle – abolishing the lineout and reducing all goals to two points in 1897 then embracing radical change in 1906 by reducing teams to thirteen men and replacing the battle for possession after a tackle with a play-the-ball. Some clubs, including Bradford and the first Northern Union champions, Manningham (who became Bradford City), changed codes to soccer. The great Lockwood was declared bankrupt in 1897, with debts of £300. A breakaway by 14 clubs to form their own competition in

1901–02 doubtless had the YRU chuckling at the irony.

The YRU needed all the cheer they could get. It had looked initially as if the damage might not be that bad. Yorkshire won the County Championship, possibly out of habit, in 1896. England picked five northern forwards against Scotland. The trouble was that the 22 clubs who met at The George in 1895 were only the beginning. Those who stayed found they had lost their most attractive and demanding fixtures, impacting on crowds and income. The first two post-schism Yorkshire Cup champions, Leeds Parish Church and Hull Kingston Rovers, went over at the end of their cup-winning seasons. In Lancashire, Swinton and Salford went over in 1896, followed in 1897 by Barrow, which cast the gentlemanly officials of Liverpool, Manchester and Liverpool Old Boys in an unattractive light by revealing that fixtures promised for not going had failed to materialise. By 1897, there were only 13 clubs left in the Lancashire Rugby Union. Four years later, only eleven, down from a pre-schism peak of one hundred and thirty-two, entered the Yorkshire Cup. Total RFU membership as a whole nearly halved, from 481 clubs in 1893 to 244 a decade later. In fifteen seasons up to the schism, England had won twenty-three matches and lost nine against the other three nations, winning three Triple Crowns. In the next fifteen, it won twelve and lost twenty-nine, with no Triple Crown or championship until the fifteenth year, 1910.

The 1890s are the sole decade in which Scotland had the best won–lost record in the championship. This could have happened whatever occurred in England – Scotland won four out of their five meetings immediately before the schism – but it removed the likeliest obstacle. Their success continued into the next decade, with Triple Crowns in 1901, 1903 and 1907. Almond's reference to 'the peculiar Scottish genius for football' appeared to make perfect sense, particularly if one cares (as Almond probably did not) that Scottish players had refined soccer beyond recognition in the 1870s and 1880s with their subtle combined passing tactics, consistently beating England. The social homogeneity of its teams – the whole XV that beat Wales in 1901 had been to public school – remained an advantage, not least because it made them immune to Northern Union temptation. Their style made a deep impression on Wales's Gwyn Nicholls, who wrote: 'I want to see any fifteen in the world

81

who can stand up against a real, big, rough-edged, dashing Scottish eight, with the pipes skirling them on.' Nicholls's description of 'The avalanche, the six, seven or eight component parts of which are all wielded into one rushing, crushing whole, the course of which a miracle alone can arrest' offers a foretaste of later evocations of All Black packs. Among these well-brought-up chaps were some with the testing-the-limits-of-the-acceptable ruthlessness associated in more recent times with Colin Meads and Martin Johnson.

MacLagan had a successor in kind in 'Darkie' Bedell-Sivright of Cambridge and Edinburgh Universities, who won 22 caps and copious lineout ball between 1900 and 1908. Townsend Collins's perception that 'he seemed to me to lack completely the chivalry which sets a crown on a great footballer' came from another country. It was, though, the Scotsman R.J. Phillips who felt forcefulness 'a rather obvious component of his play'. Phillips recalled with evident relish the view of a Border spectator that Bedell-Sivright had long had it coming when he finally met his physical match, laid out 'going high' on Ireland's Basil Maclear.

Scotland, led by James Aikman Smith, whose administrative career lasted from 1887 to 1931, was also acquiring its reputation for reflexive conservatism. Yet it operated a highly elastic definition of 'Scottish', fielding a three-quarter line of a New Zealander, two Australians and a South African against England in 1903 and was enterprising in ensuring that it had the best ground as well as the best team. In 1899, the Scottish Rugby Union became the first union to own a purpose-built ground, funding Inverleith with debentures after falling out with Edinburgh Academicals over Raeburn Place. Other unions were still nomadic. Wales's matches were increasingly confined to Swansea and Cardiff but had been shared more widely, the proposal in 1885 to give Llanelli its first match provoking a typically Welsh row when one delegate called it 'an out of the way place'. Ireland used Lansdowne Road from 1876 but did not secure a lease until 1906. In 1905, much local ingenuity attended a first international in Cork, with grandstands improvised out of empty barrels supplied by local brewers and bound together with wire securely enough to satisfy the safety inspectors.

Ireland had claimed a second Triple Crown in 1899, the unorthodox half-back brilliance of Louis Magee complementing traditional forward strength. This was the first full season after yet another dispute, this one arising from Wales's predictable difficulties with the post-1895 settlement. With the northerners gone, Wales was the only country where working men likely to attract Northern Union attention were still a significant factor. Llanelli were distinctly unamused when six players departed together for Rochdale Hornets in 1896, while Cardiff's William Jones earned unflattering publicity in the *Yorkshire Post* when he took a £10 signing fee from Hull, then continued playing for Cardiff and won selection as a Wales reserve.

The crisis was provoked not by the Northern Union, but by a Welsh desire to mark the colossal achievements of Arthur Gould. A national testimonial was launched in January 1896. The WRU not only did not disapprove but subscribed £50. The RFU predictably did disapprove and had little difficulty persuading Scottish and Irish IRB delegates to agree. Wales, pointing to a presentation worth £100 to Richmond's W.E. Bromet, refused to blink and instead left the IRB. Ireland and Scotland refused to play Wales in 1897, during which time Gould was presented with the deeds to a detached house and – with a Welsh-accented raspberry – voted onto the WRU committee.

At this point, the RFU reconsidered the 'exceptional circumstances' of the case. After vigorous debate, Gould was reinstated. Wales rejoined the IRB in February 1898, promising to observe the rules on amateurism and that Gould, now a selector, would not be chosen for internationals. Scotland signalled continuing displeasure by refusing to play Wales again in 1898. Recounting the story in the 1920s update of *Football: The Rugby Union Game*, RFU man George Bernays rationalised that 'The striking distinction worthy of emphasis between this and the ordinary case of professionalism is that A.J. Gould was in type, heart and in fact an amateur.' By this reasoning, an amateur was whoever the RFU said, irrespective of material evidence. Gould's reinstatement was proposed by the usually unbending Hill, who described his role as an 'unpleasant duty'. No longer threatened from the north, the RFU could accede to the mounting concerns of clubs fearful of losing lucrative Welsh fixtures, while avoiding the risk of driving Wales towards the Northern Union. In return, Wales was permitted a degree of local flexibility over 'blindside remuneration', crackdowns coming only if, as when payment was compounded by allegations of match-fixing at Aberdare in 1907, the breach was outrageous. Rugby celebrity had other rewards – Wales wing Willie Llewellyn's chemist's shop remained untouched when stores around it were looted during the Tonypandy riot of 1910.

Duly restored, Wales's rise continued. Gould was succeeded at centre by the powerful, cool-headed Gwyn Nicholls of Cardiff, one of many Welsh players who were, in Gareth Williams's memorable phrase, 'West Country men by birth, but Welsh by location, adoption and inclination'. Townsend Collins reckoned him not quite Gould's equal as an individual player but his superior as a team player, with an outlook expressed when he wrote 'In an ideal Welsh game, you really see 15 great chess masters working in partnership and without consultation, each man knowing instinctively not only the best thing to be done but that all the other fellows know it also.'

A good proportion of the masters came from Swansea, who were the unofficial Welsh champions from 1899 to 1902 and then unbeaten between December 1903 and October 1905. Scrum-half Dickie Owen would win 35 caps (half-backs were becoming steadily more specialised and differentiated). He was described as 'prematurely old, shrivelled and puny' by Townsend Collins, who added that these looks were as deceptive as the feints, missed move and reverse passes devised by one of the sharpest tactical brains the game had yet seen. Versatile midfield-back Billy Trew won 29 caps, with 'unobtrusive skill and unfailing judgment' and the capacity to rise to the occasion: 'great in club football, he was even greater in international games'. Both were publicans, as with Lockwood the reward for fame – Trew had begun as a boiler-maker.

The late 1890s saw the rise of the 'Rhondda forward'. This, as Townsend Collins noted, was a physical, not a geographic type, a tough competitor as likely to hail from Llanelli or Newport as the valleys, who deployed the strength and physicality of the manual worker. It was a reminder of what England had lost in the 'Yorkshire forward', whose comparable attributes were much respected by Scottish connoisseurs.

Not that all other nations appreciated this new type of player. In 1903, the Irish allotted more than £50 for dinner after their Scotland match and only £30 for Wales. The IRFU treasurer explained that the Scots had been given champagne and the Welsh beer (but plenty of it). The Scots 'were gentlemen and appreciated a dinner when it was given to them. Not so the Welshmen.' Scottish referee Crawford Findlay told Welsh centre Rhys Gabe (a teacher) that he was surprised Wales selected miners, steelworkers and policemen and felt they should join the Northern Union. Findlay may have taken his social distaste onto the field. More than 40 years later, Townsend Collins was still splenetic about the referee's performances in 1904, disallowing a match-winning Welsh try against England, then against Ireland ruling out another match-winner, giving Ireland a 'mysterious penalty' and showing 'blindness to Irish faults . . . harshness to Wales'. Ireland won 9–6, and Findlay complained that Welsh forward Alfred Brice had accused him of selling the match. The WRU apologised, but Brice would not: 'I cannot apologise for a thing I never said.' A policeman for once on the wrong end of 'his word against mine', he was suspended for six months and never played for Wales again.

Pre-eminently the product of a new Wales – industrial, urban and largely English-speaking – Welsh rugby withstood the last blast of an older order: Evan Roberts's religious revival of 1904–05. There were setbacks, with half a dozen clubs closing and Jenkin Thomas's famous implication of diabolism at Kenfig Hill, but the devil proved to have the more compelling tunes. The Findlay-refereed setback at Belfast in 1904 was Wales's only defeat against anyone other than Scotland between 1900 and 1905, and the only season in this spell when the winner of the Wales v. Scotland match did not also take a Triple Crown. Wales took revenge in 1905 with their most powerful performances yet, beating hapless England 25–0 on the way to another Triple Crown before the end of the year brought opposition as diabolically formidable as any known to Jenkin Thomas.

There had been no further invitation to a New Zealand team since 1888, even though it had had a national union since 1892. Aside from indulging in a decade of internal punch-ups, British rugby – and in particular the RFU – still remembered the allegations of professionalism, now upgraded from infraction to capital heresy, against the Native team. In New Zealand, Thomas Eyton, who spoke with authority as promoter of the 1888 tour, wrote eight years later of insuperable obstacles to a repetition, notably that 'there is hardly a first-class footballer in this Colony who can afford to go for a six- or nine-month tour with only bare travelling expenses. Yet such is the Rugby Union's dictation.'

The next tour of any consequence came in 1902 – a distinctly motley crew of Canadians, most with little or no rugby experience and only five players from the strongest province, British Columbia. Privately sponsored by two Montreal entrepreneurs, it started promisingly with an 11–8 win over Ulster in December 1902. The Canadians beat Bristol and held a Gloucester team including nine current or future internationals to 11–3 but lost thirteen of their twenty-three matches, including a 34–4 hammering by Devon Albion in front of eight thousand spectators and a 29–3 defeat by Cardiff. Their visit remains an intriguing curio, with limited impact and consequences.

South Africa, a much quicker, easier journey than New Zealand, got three visits by representative British sides and Australia one – rather pointedly not crossing the Tasman – before Bedell-Sivright's team played five matches in New Zealand as an afterthought to its Australia trip in 1904. After winning all 14 in Australia, they lost the test 9–3 at Wellington and also fell to Auckland. Bedell-Sivright was singularly graceless in defeat, and Wales wing Teddy Morgan returned home predicting the 1905 tourists would lose to Wales, England and Scotland.

Some misgivings were shared in New Zealand. Otago had voted against the tour, although southern contrarianism also had its uses. Otago had also protested violently and successfully against the NZRFU's initial acceptance of a combined Australasian test against Bedell-Sivright's team. Joint Australasian teams were common, surviving in the Olympics into the 1920s. Otagoan obduracy averted a serious threat to the as-yet-unborn All Black tradition.

Selection had been convoluted and haphazard. The journey to Britain – a bonding opportunity with the parallel risk of falling out – was so contentious that skipper Dave Gallaher and deputy Billy Stead resigned and sought a vote of confidence, which was passed less than resoundingly. Jimmy Duncan, the coach (although in deference to British sensibilities he was not called that), was completely marginalised. He found other ways of passing the time, later recalling fondly 'the numbers of young ladies and old widows who were desirous of taking me into partnership as a sleeping partner only'.

This unpromising band hit Britain with an unanticipated impact rarely matched between the invasions of the Vikings in the tenth century and the Australian rugby league team of 1982. Their first match was against Devon, that season's county champions. Within three minutes, five-eighth Jimmy Hunter scored the first of his forty-two tries on tour. The tourists ran in 11 more to win 55–4. All 23 matches in England were won by a cumulative score of 721 points to 15. England, not for the last time handicapped by eccentric selection, were beaten 15–0. Half-back Dai Gent, dual-qualified and a recent Wales trialist, reckoned it could have been double that but for heavy rain. Ireland fell by the same margin, although Gallaher and Stead's evocation of their forwards still echoes, allowing for changes in technique, in Munster packs a century later: 'there is none finer, none more exhilarating than that of a pack of Irish forwards sweeping down the field in one combined rush with the ball at their feet and under the most perfect control'. Scotland had done much better, leading until the last few minutes when New Zealand scored two tries for a 12–7 win. Legend alleges that the Scottish Rugby Union, fearing the All Blacks would not attract a decent crowd, had refused to offer a guarantee and were furious when the tourists left with the profit from a 21,000 gate. As Ryan points out, their refusal, repeated when South Africa visited in 1906, was simple prudence for an organisation still paying off the costs of building Inverleith – although there was a marked absence of hospitality for the visitors. Scotland were furious that wing Nelson Fell, named after his New Zealand birthplace and key component of that multinational 1903 three-quarter line, refused to play against his compatriots. Deciding that 'I do not love thee, Dr Fell', Scotland did not pick him again.

When the All Blacks reached Wales in December 1905, they had won 27 straight matches, scoring 801 points to 22. Players like the prolific Hunter, with his 'zigzag, eel-like bursts for the line', Billy Wallace, first of a remarkable succession of All Black full-backs who would see the position's attacking possibilities while British counterparts were chained to their defensive posts, and forward Charlie 'Bronco' Seeling, of whom Sewell wrote 'this splendid specimen of manhood had everything necessary to the composition of a forward', were recognised as individually brilliant amid a team whose combination and teamwork were everything, and more, that Nicholls had dreamed of.

None of this happened by accident. New Zealand was a dynamic and innovative nation. Its population grew proportionately faster than anywhere in the world between 1881 and 1921, and it was first to introduce votes for women (1893), state labour arbitration (1894) and old-age pensions (1898). Rugby, the main sporting expression of this national vigour, was taken with intense seriousness. Regular club training, at least twice a week in the training halls provided in each district, often before 'a critical assembly . . . present to make suggestions and give hints', was an essential part of the process ('the man who does not train shall not play') that turned those halls into 'a busy centre of eager and ambitious athletic manhood every evening from seven o'clock until half-past ten'.

The national team had devised its own way of playing. The seven-man scrum could match a British eight because each of its members was a specialist, chosen for and practising constantly his specific position. Packing in a 2–3–2 formation, they drove inwards to create pressure on the opposing hooker, rather than pushing straight ahead as British teams did. Everything was geared to quick ball – the put-in by the wing-forward, scrummagers aligned to aid rapid channeling and the scrum-half ready to unleash a back division in which the five-eighth offered variations unknown to British defences. They had thought through more efficient ways of passing 'at the moment of being tackled' and of attacking from the lineout: 'we believe in our forwards being as quick as the back division in taking the ball'. They kept records of why and how tries were scored. All of this, and much more, was explained in detail in Gallaher and Stead's book, *The Complete Rugby Footballer in the New Zealand System*, which, as Gareth Williams has written, 'brought a startlingly new technical dimension to rugby literature, raising it to a level of sophistication previously unheard of and rarely exceeded since'. Reading it years later, England centre Jeff Butterfield, a great creative player and early proponent of coaching, said, 'No wonder it took us 70 years to catch up with New Zealand.'

It was written post-tour in response to British debate over their success. The English critic E.H.D. Sewell and the Wales-based Townsend Collins had attributed it to the quality of their individuals rather than their system. The *Daily Mail*, even then keen to locate decadence and undeterred by the reality that two-thirds of the team came from the four main towns and most had blue-collar or clerical jobs, had emphasised superior fitness created by the outdoor colonial lifestyle. New Zealand's prime minister Richard Seddon, first in a line of populist premiers large in both personality and build, and his British representative William Pember Reeves did nothing to discourage this impression, using the team to publicise their still new nation – it had rejected joining the Australian Federation only six years earlier – and encourage potential immigrants.

So far, so positive. But there had also been ferocious criticism of the wing-forward. The coolly analytical Gabe explained why:

When the opposition heeled the ball, he performed the function of the scrum-half, but when New Zealand obtained possession he remained still and was legally offside, being in front of the ball and not in a scrummage. Moreover he was guilty of passive obstruction, for the opposing scrum-half was obliged to run around him.

The *Manchester Guardian* called Gallaher – who played the position – 'a professed obstructionist', while the *Daily Chronicle* characterised the wing-forward as 'an irritating person . . . who plays such a decidedly unlawful game'. If the word 'cheat' was not used, it could hardly have been more strongly implied.

Bloodied by hostile press and crowds, the All Blacks came to Wales and at last encountered opponents who had both the talent and the low cunning required to cope with them. Wales had known the date of the match for more than a year and had sent representatives to look at the All Blacks a month earlier. Their players, unprecedentedly, had two pre-match practice sessions.

A crowd of 43,000 attended the first match with serious claims to be for the championship of the world. In more than 60 years' rugby-watching, Townsend Collins reckoned it one of the three toughest matches he saw. It turned on two moments. Wales shared the general dislike of the wing-forward. Manager George Dixon recalled Gallaher being received with 'a degree of bitterness'. They were not, though, too proud to try to slay New Zealand with their own weapon, selecting seven orthodox forwards plus Cliff Pritchard of Pontypool in direct opposition to Gallaher.

For 25 minutes, Owen gave the impression that he had forgotten Pritchard's existence. Then, from a midfield scrum between halfway and the New Zealand 25, he broke to the right, the New Zealand defence moving with him to cover the three men outside. Owen reversed direction and passed to Pritchard, running hard to the left of the scrum. Owen would recall that 'barring accidents, a try was certain'. There was no accident. Like the chess masters described by their captain, Pritchard and Gabe combined to send Morgan careering over on the left. It was the only score. However, it is not its progenitor, Owen, who devised it at the second practice session, nor the scorer, Morgan, who is linked forever more with this match.

In the final few minutes, centre Bob Deans – at 6 ft 1 in. and 13 st. 4 lb described as 'the Goliath' of the New Zealand backs – was brought down at the Welsh line. The Scottish referee, John Dallas, ruled that he had not scored. End of the matter in one sense; only the beginning in another.

This incident is rugby's equivalent of Geoff Hurst's second goal in the 1966 World Cup, debated ever since but becoming, as Gabe would say nearly 50 years later, more nebulous by the year. New Zealanders have emphasised Deans's deathbed claim, only three years later, that he did score and Teddy Morgan's 'confession' to a later All Black party that, as the Welsh tackler, he believed Deans had scored. Welsh opinion is more impressed by Gabe's counter-statement that he was the tackler and felt Deans try to struggle forward rather than, as he would have done if he was over the line, grounding the ball. When Deans claimed after the match that he had scored and Gabe asked why he had struggled, 'there was no answer'.

There is an element of invented tradition about this. Gallaher and Stead make no mention of the incident in their account of the match. Like most good debates, it is inherently insoluble. Its consequence, though, was that both countries took something from the game. Wales had its victory, while the All Blacks acquired a legend that Sir Keith Sinclair described as 'New Zealand sport's equivalent of Gallipoli'. It made this a unique moment. Whereas most nations' great moments are somebody else's misery, Wales v. New Zealand in 1905 is shared, a defining moment for New Zealand, a new nation, and for Wales, an old one that had undergone a profound transformation over the previous half-century and for whom rugby, in the absence of more conventional institutions, was becoming the main means of collective national self-expression.

In spite of attracting huge crowds and playing brilliantly, the All Blacks waited 19 years for another invitation. The First World War had something to do with this, yet South Africa's Springboks, next in the remarkable succession of touring debuts that illuminated Edwardian Britain, received a second invitation before the war, only six years after their first. The Springboks – who chose their name to stop the British press labelling them – could not have the same impact. Notions of certain British superiority had been irrevocably broken a year earlier, and the South Africans were better known to British players than the All Blacks had been, after British tours to South Africa in 1896 and 1903.

The 1896 team had enjoyed themselves hugely – Irish forward Tom Crean, a 210 lb man who could run 100 yards in less than 11 seconds, suggested they limit themselves to four tumblers of champagne on match days – and encountered better opposition than their predecessors of 1891. It was no longer 'a matter of chance when the ball found its way to the three-quarters', and South Africa won the last test of four, aided by a referee who penalised the tourists' wheeling of their scrum. In 1903, South Africa were stronger still. The first two tests were drawn, then the Springboks won the decider – the first match in which the South Africans played in green jerseys, an Old Diocesan set donated by skipper Barry Heatlie.

In Cape Town, tourist Alf Tedford, one of Ireland's finest forwards, noticed 'the keenness of the Malay and coloured populations'. Non-white rugby had also moved on. The South African Coloured Rugby Football Board (SACRFB) was founded in 1896, its affiliates including the Griqualand West Colonial RFU, the first explicitly non-racial sporting body in South Africa. The GWCRFU secretary was Isaiah 'Bud' Mbelle, the first African to pass the Western Province civil-service examination, later brother-in-law of the journalist and activist Sol Plaatje, who was one of the key figures in the development of the African National Congress. There were strong echoes of the SARFB's start-up seven years earlier – the same four provinces meeting in the same place, Kimberley. When the SACRFB started a provincial competition, the Rhodes Cup, in 1898, it was won by Western Province.

Well connected as it was, though, the SACRFB could not escape the structural inequalities of South African society. Historian Jeff Peires has described the early days:

> The game itself was played in appalling conditions. Most fields were without grass, and many more were riven by ditches, located on slopes or acting as private thoroughfares. Boots were considered a luxury, and each team had at most a single set of jerseys. Such circumstances bred dedication and selflessness; sacrificing one's wages to buy the team colours, walking all night to be at a match the following day.

The invaders who did most to benefit white South African rugby were possibly neither those of 1896 or 1903, but the 450,000 British troops who conducted the Second Boer War from 1899 to 1902. Such benefits were well concealed, as 27,000 Afrikaners were confined to prisoner of war camps in Ceylon and St Helena, but, as one observer noted, 'Rugby football in particular claimed a remarkable enthusiasm and it was noticeable how very keenly the Boer fell to the purely British game.' In 1902, a camp newspaper appealed for fewer games to be played, because 'the men cannot last at that rate', while on St Helena there were frequent matches between two prisoner camps two hours' walk apart. Jean-Pierre Bodis lists 66 international players who served with the British forces – Crean and another Irishman, Robert Johnston, winning Victoria Crosses, while two died – and a remarkable incident in which a Boer officer challenged his local British counterpart to a match two weeks before peace was concluded. Afrikaners came out of the war determined to reassert their identity – beginning to develop their own language as a written medium in place of the Dutch that Captain Maritz had used to issue his challenge – and found rugby an effective vehicle. Paul Roos, Springbok captain in 1906, recalled his father saying, 'In the war, we were swamped by numbers. In this, you are man for man.'

The novelist John Buchan dismissed Afrikaners as 'not a sporting race', but the astute Gallaher, one of the 66, knew considerably better, warning that 'there is something about the climate and the country that makes one feel instinctively that here is a place where Rugby Football would thrive if it would anywhere in the world'.

Within months of those words being published in 1906, he was proved right. A Springbok team divided evenly on linguistic lines, led by the bearded, patriarchal Roos – one of six Afrikaner graduates of Stellenbosch and much later the town's National Party MP – fell little short of the All Blacks' achievements. They lost only to Scotland and Cardiff, and inflicted Wales's only home defeat – by an incontrovertible 11–0 – between 1900 and 1911.

The Springboks showed an unfortunate capacity for shipping memorable tries, within seven days conceding two scores remembered as long as anyone lived who had seen them. Kenneth Macleod, a Scottish prodigy who would have been capped at 15 if his headmaster had permitted it, had 'most members of the Press Box forgetting their first duty' as they cheered home his swerving run. A sporting polymath who gave up rugby at 20 when his elder brother died, then played cricket for Lancashire and soccer for Manchester City, he would end up in South Africa as Natal Amateur Golf Champion.

Ireland's Basil Maclear, who picked up a loose ball and ran 75 metres, breaking through tackles, changing direction and three times handing off Springbok winger Stephanus Joubert, one of the Stellenbosch six, had already been to South Africa, winning the Queen's Medal during the Boer War. An army officer who played in white kid gloves, he was English, but Rowland Hill rejected him after a brilliant club performance, deeming the opposition inadequate. Ireland, where he was stationed, were less fussy, more perceptive and had their reward with victories in all three of his matches against England.

Roos, a theologian, impressed in the pulpit as well as on the field. Against Wales at Swansea, centre Japie Krige gave the great Nicholls a miserable last afternoon in test rugby, dummying brilliantly to create a try for Joubert, and full-back Arthur Marburg's defence ensured Wales were kept scoreless. Collins was suitably impressed:

93

The All Blacks were professors convinced of the correctness of their theories, satisfied with themselves, confident of their mission and ability to teach. The Springboks were students anxious to learn, and at the end they were a very great team. The Springboks' conception of combination was better than the All Blacks; their passing was better.

Other comparisons were pointed. Without mentioning the All Blacks, Leonard Tosswill left no doubt what he meant in recalling the 1906 Springboks:

Perhaps what appealed to us most was the fact that they played the game in the same way as ourselves, with the same formation, but they did it with a difference. Their straight running, tackling and kicking was a joy to behold; there was nothing in their method that was in any way questionable.

The South Africans were invited back out of turn in 1912, when they beat all four home nations. Ireland were demolished 38–0, and full-back Gerhard Morkel – one of ten Morkels to play for South Africa between 1906 and 1928, self-confessedly slow but with exceptional anticipation and positional sense – entered folklore with two colossal penalties against England. The Springboks also received a British team in 1910. New Zealand had to contend with persistent attempts by the Scottish Rugby Union to have their players professionalised for receiving the agreed subsistence rate of three shillings per day in 1905 and settle for the visit of an Anglo-Welsh touring team in 1908.

Intended to reaffirm the benefits of the amateur game for an errant dominion, this became a magnificently counterproductive exercise in mutual incomprehension. A 29-strong party, 20 public-school educated – as Geoff Vincent notes, closer to the usual profile of an England team than a Lions or Wales squad – made a point of not training on the way out, were slaughtered 29–0 and 32–3 in two of the three tests, drawing the other 3–3 in a mudbath. They rather undermined their missionary purpose when Leicester prop Frederick Jackson was found to have played Northern Union and was sent home, cheered all the way up the gangplank. He later returned to New Zealand and sired an All Black prop.

New Zealand were offered convincing evidence of the worth of their system of training and forward specialisation. Taranaki took revenge for the Natives of 1888 by scoring a try as players gathered round an injured man. The tour manager George Harnett returned home saying wing-forward play was worse than ever and Britain 'should keep touch with the South African players who, besides being amateur to the core, are genuine sportsmen, who play clean and honestly'.

The extraordinary Edwardian succession of visiting touring teams was completed in 1908 by Australia's Wallabies, end product of the federation created – with unresounding majorities in Queensland and New South Wales – eight years earlier. The first match as a united nation had been played only four days after the vote, against the British team captained by the Revd Martin Mullineaux. Four years later, the Wallabies began the rivalry with New Zealand that has produced more test matches (finally overtaking England v. Scotland during the 2006 Tri Nations) than any other. Australia had struggled consistently against New Zealand since federation and lost all three tests to the 1904 British team that went on to lose in Wellington.

The Wallabies became Olympic rugby champions in 1908 – Australia's only gold of those games – and were immortalised in song, but it was not an entirely happy experience. Their captain, Herbert Moran, a tough, wry doctor, reckoned their finest achievement was getting through five months without anyone catching venereal disease. Rugby was a sideshow to the Olympics – which was still in its infancy – and the only opposition were county champions Cornwall, representing England. New Zealand and South Africa had declined invitations, while Wales, Scotland and Ireland ignored theirs and France were late withdrawals. Australia won 32–3 on a wet, heavy pitch with a swimming pool running alongside it – mattresses were placed around the edge of the pool to prevent injury and poles were used to fish the ball out. Beyond the Olympics, the touring team lost not only to Wales but to Cardiff, Swansea and Llanelli – originating the *Who Beat the Wallabies* verse in terrace anthem *Sospan Fach* – and did not play Ireland or Scotland. Moran recalled that his team felt hostility from the RFU, spectators and the press and speculated that disillusionment with Britain contributed to only seven of his thirty-one-strong squad serving during the First World

War. There were other distractions. Australia had just undergone its equivalent of England's 1895 schism, and there was a second Australian team, many of them teammates a year before, touring the Northern Union. There was copious speculation about further defections. Moran recalled, 'The subject was constantly before our minds.'

With the 'Barassi Line' dividing Rules and rugby country firmly established by the end of the nineteenth century, rugby boomed in newly federated Australia. The representative-match income of Sydney's Metropolitan Rugby Union (MRU) tripled between 1902 and 1907. Fifty-two thousand people, a world record, watched the All Blacks in Sydney in 1907. Simultaneously, there was discontent among players. As the *Bulletin* reported: 'the players are realising that the Union gets all the loot, while they have a monopoly of the bruises and kicks'. The received version of Australian league's foundation is that the revolt followed anger when an injured player, Alex Burdon, was left without income after a serious injury. The injury to Burdon, a wharfie and barber, in 1907 undoubtedly had a 'last straw' quality about it – the MRU had cancelled its player insurance scheme that season while spending £12,500 to buy the Epping racecourse as a permanent ground. Sean Fagan's research shows, though, that plans for a breakaway were well under way before that, fuelled by the anger of players at the inadequacy of three shillings per day as expenses and at their offhand treatment by officials. In 1905, New South Wales hooker Harry Hamill refused a tour of New Zealand, insisting that he needed at least ten shillings per day – still 5s less than he was earning – to make it possible.

The trio who set up the New South Wales Rugby League (NSWRL) in 1907 – politician Harry Hoyle, entrepreneur James Giltinan and cricketer Victor Trumper – also had the advice of those organising the 1908 'All Gold' professional tour of Britain from New Zealand, which included several members of the 1905 All Blacks. They recruited Australia's outstanding union player, Dally Messenger, days after he had played for the Wallabies against the All Blacks.

While the NSWRL claimed the allegiance of 138 first-grade players when it was launched in the summer of 1907, its success was no foregone conclusion. There was little to choose between crowds when competitions ran in parallel in 1908, and the Wallabies returned from their tour in first-class transport while the Kangaroos had to appeal to the Northern Union for their fares. League, though, steadily established an ascendancy, striking the vital blow on the return of the two touring teams when James Joynton-Smith, former owner of Epsom racecourse, promoted charity matches between the two teams. The Wallabies who took part, for fees of £50–£200, were professionalised and forced into league. By 1910, a league international against Great Britain outdid an All Blacks test on the same day by 28,000 spectators to 8,000. In the following year, league's share of rugby's gates in Sydney was 88 per cent. Still more damaging was the decision of Marist schools in 1913 to switch to league, followed by the Christian Brothers in 1915, taking the Catholic working class firmly into the other code. Bodis argues that although 21 of the 135 men who played for New Zealand between 1901 and 1914 signed for rugby league clubs at home, in England or Australia, the All Black of 1914 resembled his counterpart of 1905 'like a brother'. Australian union, though, retreated into an upper-middle-class ghetto.

Among the countermeasures tried by Australian union was inviting a touring student team from California in 1910. This proved a hopeless loss-maker, deepening already acute financial problems, but was far from the lunacy it might appear to be. Reacting to the growing savagery of American Football, which prompted something close to a moral panic in 1905, with President Theodore Roosevelt leading the protests, the universities of California and Stanford abandoned football 'until such a time as an acceptable game should be developed in the east' and took up rugby. They were encouraged by the British Columbian Union, which was delighted to find potential opposition on the doorstep. From 1906 to 1914, the two universities' major annual fixture – the 'Big Match' – was a rugby match. Rugby was also played in the schools of California. Martin Mullineaux, captain of the 1899 British touring team to Australia, lived in San Francisco, coached at Palo Alto High School and refereed important matches. California and British Columbia's best clubs played for the Cooper-Stokes Cup between 1907 and 1911.

This was welcome not only for North Americans but for Australia and New Zealand. With no immediate prospect of further invitations to Britain, they were pleased to find alternative opponents closer (if hardly close) to home. The student team of 1910 returned home as disappointed as their hosts, but for different reasons, with only three wins from fourteen matches, plus a highly impressive draw with Ranfurly Shield holders Auckland. Australia sent a full team in 1912, which lost to both universities and only just beat All-California 12–8, a match now recognised as a full test v. the USA. The Wallabies left behind Daniel Carroll, who enrolled at Stanford and later coached the 1920 and 1924 US Olympic squads. He also played another retrospectively-recognised test, lining up with his adopted country in 1913 when the All Blacks despatched a full team to California. Intended to boost American rugby, it had precisely the opposite effect. They won all 16 matches, including a 53–3 test victory, scoring 610 points to 6. Even a nation less committed to winning than the USA might be discouraged by such results. Disappointment undoubtedly contributed to the drift back to the American game, starting with the University of California (which was struggling in the 'Big Match') in 1915. Deprived of its defining rivalry, Stanford resumed American Football four years later.

New Zealand missionary work had happier results in Fiji. Press reports show rugby being played regularly, mostly by expatriates, from around 1900 and the formation of a club competition in 1904, with Civil Service and Constabulary among the pioneer clubs. In 1907, a Wairarapa provincial player predicted that Fijian rugby would make its mark on the world, and essential progress was made towards that aim six years later when former Otago captain Paddy Sheehan, who was working on the plumbing for the Grand Pacific Hotel, organised the setting up of the Fiji RFU.

South America showed greater staying power than the north. Argentina – where the River Plate Rugby Union was formed in 1899 – moved gradually away from its exclusively British origins, a progress measured by the steady transformation of the Argentina team in the annual Argentina v. Extranjeros (foreigners) match started in 1905 from Argentine-born sons of British families to local Spanish-speakers. The first local club, Facultad de Ingeniería, was formed in 1904. A second, Facultad de Medicina, was short-lived but produced Che Guevara's main rival as the most memorable rugby-playing Argentinian medic. Bernardo Houssay would be notable for inspiring the translation of the rules of rugby and the union constitution into Spanish in 1908, even if he had not gone on to win the Nobel Prize for medicine in 1947. A more durable club, Gimnasia y Esgrima, was founded in 1910. The same year saw an RFU team led by England player John Raphael visit Argentina, winning all six matches, including a 28–3 defeat of a local union XV. Another famous name, Racing Club, entered that year but was expelled within six weeks for 'the bad conduct of players and public'.

In Japan, too, the game had taken root and been adopted by the indigenous population. The British had played in the treaty ports for years – a famous picture shows a match from 1874 – but had shown no interest in involving the locals. That changed in 1899, when Edward Clarke, a Cambridge graduate from the British community in Yokohama, and Tanaka Ginnosuke, also a Cambridge graduate, introduced the game into Keio University. Clarke recalled that his students 'seemed to have nothing to occupy them out of doors in the after-summer and after-winter days. Winter baseball had not yet come in, and the young fellows loitered around wasting the hours and the lovely outdoor weather.' By 1901, they were crossing racial barriers to play the Yokohama foreigners, losing 35–5, Clarke converting the try scored by a student named Shiyoda.

Clarke believed that 'the great success of English-speaking people is largely because of the love of games'. It was not only his and Argentina's experience that showed it could translate into other languages. On New Year's Day 1906, after the All Blacks's defeat by Wales, the New Zealanders provided the opposition for France's international debut, winning 38–8 at the Parc des Princes – as yet little more than 'a footer pitch in a park', with Wallace claiming a hat-trick. France first played England in the same year, following this with Wales in 1908, Ireland in 1909 and Scotland in 1910, completing the transformation of the Home Nations championship into the Five Nations.

French rugby took on its familiar shape in the 20 years before the First World War, with the majority of its leading clubs formed as power shifted progressively from Paris to the provinces and in particular the south-west. Stade Bordelais broke Paris's championship monopoly in 1899 then established one of their own, winning four consecutive titles from 1904 to 1907. Two years later, they beat Stade Toulousain in the first all-provincial final, marked by a regional sports paper with the words 'Bordeaux and Toulouse will avenge . . . all the provinces for the great injustices they too have endured and for the unjustified humiliations that Paris believes it can inflict'. The finals of 1913 and 1914 saw success reach France's south-western extremes, the Basque Country and Catalonia, with the victories of Aviron Bayonnais and A.S. Perpignan. The first French team, in 1906, contained 11 Paris-based players. By 1914, nineteen of the twenty-four players capped during the season were from the provinces – six from Bayonne and four from Tarbes.

British influence mattered. Bodis cites the Bordeaux wine trade in general and British shipping-company manager J.J. Shearer in particular as playing a vital role in the game's vigorous growth in that city, while Aviron Bayonnais's champions were coached by a Welshman, Owen Roe, who in Bodis's words 'came to learn French and never really did in 40 years'. They were outweighed, though, by the proselytisation engendered by the Ligue Girondin de l'Education Physique, founded by Philippe Tissié in Bordeaux in 1888, which brought sport to thousands of schoolboys in the region and was directly involved in the formation of clubs like Stade Bordelais (1893) and Pau's Section Paloise (1902). The Ligue promoted *barette*, a rugby-like game where tackles were made by touching the ball-carrier and shouting *touché*, equally suitable for and, in time, adopted by girls. Rugby was introduced into Bayonne's schools in 1897 and adopted nine years later by Aviron, a rowing club formed in 1904. Rugby's local resonance was recorded in 1913:

On Sunday evenings after a match, large crowds would assemble in the Place du Theatre, where the latest results would be chalked up as they came in and jeered or applauded as local prejudice required. The large café in the square was owned by a former player, Louis Saubian, who would give public demonstrations of how to heel a ball with the aid of a pile of chairs.

Nor was Aviron's impact confined to Bayonne – or to rugby. The *beret basque* worn by their supporters became a national fashion and, in time, a French stereotype.

Crowds too were growing. There were 28,000 spectators at the

Paris University v. Stade Bordelais final in 1911, with reports of touts selling five-franc tickets for up to sixty francs. No more than 5,000 people saw France play England in 1908, but there were 20,000 for the visit of Wales in 1910 and 25,000 to see Scotland in 1913. This was not because the French team was successful. It won only one of 26 championship matches before 1914: against Scotland in 1911. Thierry Terret suggests that French aesthetic preferences, and perhaps the emphasis on evasion rather than contact in *barette*, did not help: 'Strength was a value that was neither admired nor sought after. The rugby player was a fast-moving athlete who knew how to fake and spin around, to trip and break away – a playing style that pleased French reporters, who showered praise on the athletes.'

The French were remarkably gracious adversaries. A 1906 Springbok recalled a large, bearded Frenchman leaving the field when a Bok went down with a cut knee, returning with 'a small black bag rather resembling a maternity bag', which the South Africans viewed with concern, until he 'solemnly produced bandages and salve from his bag and proceeded to render first aid'. Later, a Springbok suggested to a French player, '*Essayez-vous* a drop-goal, *Monsieur*.' The Frenchman duly 'bowed and solemnly attempted the drop amid shouts of bravo!'.

These were not isolated incidents. Wallace recalled that before France's debut test 'the French captain would not hear of tossing. We were the honoured visitors and therefore it was their pleasure to allow us to choose which way we would play and also have the right to kick off.' Tom Richards, of the 1908 Wallabies, reckoned the French 'the best spectators of all, friendly and impartial', while England's Edgar Mobbs complimented the 'great impartiality of the public' in 1910.

This was not, however, the experience of his compatriot James Baxter, referee of France's match at home against Scotland in 1913. Penalties he awarded to Scotland while wearing what one spectator called 'a superior smile' so enraged the crowd that he had to be smuggled out disguised as a policeman in a car driven by French wing Pierre Faillot, who was immune from public ire, if not attention, having scored two tries in France's victory in 1911. The IRB warned that fixtures would be suspended unless measures were taken against a repetition, and Scotland refused to play France in 1914. It was not the happiest moment for France to present the first of many applications to join the IRB. It was rejected with the explanation that this was not permitted under its constitution.

Nor was this the only aspect of French rugby occasioning concern across the Channel, with growing suggestions that they had their own distinctive interpretation of holy writ concerning amateurism. Stade Bordelais confirmed this in unsubtle fashion by advertising in the Scottish press – roughly akin to seeking a marriage annulment via *L'Osservatore Romano* – for 'a good stand-off half', offering 'a good business situation' for the right man and then, just to ensure that the Scottish Rugby Union took an interest, writing to Glasgow Academicals and Glasgow University seeking information about a player they wanted to sign. Since this happened in 1912, the wonder is that Scotland were still playing them in 1913.

France's leadership of Continental European rugby had not been in doubt since they had claimed gold at the 1900 Olympics, the first of Olympic rugby's succession of loosely organised events with minimal participation (a fair description of the entire games in 1900), by beating Germany, whose rugby federation was founded that year. Rugby in Spain was originated by an Englishman named Stuart Nicholson in Bilbao, who turned to Racing Club when he wanted eye-catching opposition for a three-team tournament, also involving British and French exiles, in Barcelona in 1901.

That development went no further, but much greater success was enjoyed by Romanians returning from studies in France. The journalist Chris Thau has recorded that every player in Romania's first rugby match in 1913, also the year when the national federation was founded, was a native Romanian. A championship was won by Romania Tennis Club in 1914 and continued annually.

Students returning from France are credited with starting the game in Italy as well – Piero Manani returned in 1909 to Milan, others to Turin. Clubs were formed in both cities and played exhibition matches against visiting French teams, but both Italian clubs had gone by 1912. Like Spain, the country would have to wait until after the war.

France played in the final pre-war international match, losing 39–14 to England on 13 April 1914 at the Stade Colombes. The truly memorable match that season was an Ireland v. Wales brawl in Belfast a month earlier, with both teams apparently channelling their domestic tensions into the game. These tensions were industrial in Wales, political in Ireland, where the NIFC had suspended their season to release their players and their ground to Sir Edward Carson's Ulster Volunteers. Collins reckoned it the roughest match he ever saw, the Welsh pack immortalised as 'The Terrible Eight' led by the Revd Alban Davies, Church Militant made flesh. England's victory meant that they had won all four matches and the championship for the second year running (the term Grand Slam was four decades away, and Triple Crowns were what mattered, the assumption being that France would always be beaten). It was England's third title since moving to their new purpose-built home at Twickenham in south-west London in 1910. Which came first, ground or revival, is a chicken and egg question, but the decision to build a ground costing £25,000 with a capacity of 37,000 was testimony to a confidence fully justified when the costs were paid off by 1913. The north was still rebuilding, but compensating work had happened elsewhere. The Bristol Schools Rugby Union was formed in 1898, followed by the city's Combination for second-class clubs in 1901. Leicester had arrived as a powerful club, winning the Midlands Cup from 1898 to 1904 and developing their Welford Road ground under the guidance of Tom Crumbie, a remarkable club secretary.

There were still periodic purges under the rules on amateurism, although the RFU created an exception for itself by employing a paid secretary from 1904. Coventry were suspended in 1909 and two years later lost their ground to a short-lived Northern Union club. In 1912, Torquay, Plymouth and Newton Abbott were investigated and the following year a speaker at a Plymouth rugby dinner said, 'Broken-time payments have been made in these parts for 30 years . . . personally, I find the Northern Union the purer body.' Ten players and officials were banned. One player felt compelled to write to the press: 'If it is the desire of the RFU committee practically to limit the game to players who learn it at the public schools and in the services and universities, such a finding is reasonable . . . Rugby is too good a game to be confined to a particular class.' This shameless subversive was Ronald Poulton, England captain, perhaps the most vivid personality of one of its greatest eras.

England were well served for quality and character. Adrian Stoop, a sharp-witted, sometimes abrasive Dutch-descended Harlequin, had reorganised English back play, standardising specialisation at half-back, analysing angles of running and passing, and attacking from wherever the opportunity presented itself rather than waiting for forwards to earn favourable field positions. Those principles were never better demonstrated than in Twickenham's first few seconds as an international ground in 1910, when Stoop fielded the Welsh kick-off and instead of returning the kick, as orthodoxy demanded, switched direction, broke upfield and put in a short punt. England won the contest for possession and wing Frederick Chapman crossed in the corner. England beat Wales for the first time in 12 years.

It was not quite the end of Wales's golden era. In 1911, they would add a further Grand Slam to those of 1908 and 1909 – the first sealed only when the IRB rejected a protest from Scotland after a kick ahead in their 6–5 defeat at Cardiff struck the chief constable of Glamorgan, who was walking in the in-goal area. For years, however, Wales were wary of England's new ground.

Slightly before Stoop had come James Peters, a Devonport naval yard supervisor who in 1906 was England's first black player. A debutant for England in the first international at Twickenham was the formidably quick and unorthodox flanker Charles Pillman, who, the 1912 Springboks remembered, 'never put his head in a scrum but stood behind his half-backs and trailed across the field at speed when our backs launched an attack'. By 1914, regulars included Cambridge University's John 'Jenny' Greenwood, who shocked teammates on the trip to Scotland in 1913 by reading a book relevant to his studies – reportedly unprecedented behaviour for a student player.

Poulton (who added the name Palmer in 1914 after a large bequest from his biscuit magnate uncle) was capped for England before he won his Oxford Blue, his student contemporaries baffled by a dashing individualism that had one later teammate confessing 'damned if I ever knew where he was going'. What Townsend Collins termed 'a quality of unexpectedness' played even greater havoc with opposing defences. When Oxford finally picked him, he scored five tries in a single varsity match. One opponent asked, 'How can one stop him when his head goes one way, his arms another and his legs keep straight on?' He was charismatic, serious-minded – close friends from Rugby school and Oxford included William Temple, later Archbishop of Canterbury – and by 1914 England's captain. He scored four tries in that final demolition of the French. Four months later (Wales having declined a singularly ill-timed invitation to play Germany), war was declared.

# CHAPTER FIVE

# Answering the Whistle

'Good old Rugby Football, all over the British Isles its exponents were in the van of those who went'

W.J. Carey, Bishop of Bloemfontein (1921)

Indeed they were. As Leonard Tosswill put it: 'Men who had learned to "play the game" on football grounds might be trusted to do no less in the greater game of war . . . [he] answered the call of his country as he would to the whistle – without questions.'

The response from rugby's institutions was also rapid. Within a week, the Scottish Rugby Union subscribed £500 to the National Relief Fund and offered Inverleith to the military authorities (in New Zealand, a similar offer led to Lancaster Park, Christchurch, becoming a potato patch). A few days later, the RFU suspended matches for the duration, and Wales soon followed suit.

Former England captain Edgar Mobbs mailed home postcards showing him knocking down Kaiser Wilhelm with a hand-off, while John King of Headingley, Yorkshire's only recent England regular, with 11 caps between 1911 and 1913, left harvesting to his sisters and joined the Yorkshire Hussars as a private.

Rugby's response was used against sports which carried on, such as soccer. A letter from the historian and former rowing Blue A.F. Pollard in *The Times* of 7 November bemoaning 'the persistence of Association Football Clubs in doing their best for the enemy', followed by a leader-column assault, caused the FA to protest that its clubs had already supplied 100,000 recruits. Sheffield United's win in the following spring's FA Cup final, the last match before fixtures were suspended in England (Scotland continued throughout the war), was branded 'a disgrace to the city' by a local paper.

There were parallel disputes in Australia. Rugby union, whose players and followers were more middle class and likelier to think themselves British, cancelled its 1915 premierships. League did not, but the NSWRL's annual report for 1915 urged players to join up, and matches were used for both recruitment and fundraising. In Australian Rules, middle-class clubs pulled out in 1916 – University went a year earlier, never to return – but those from the inner suburbs continued.

Organisational skills honed in rugby were put to military use. Leicester secretary Tom Crumbie was reckoned to have brought in 4,500 recruits, while WRU secretary Walter Rees was awarded the rank of captain for his efforts as a registration and tribunal officer.

The toll taken on those recruited was hideous. Young middle-class men – the archetypal rugby players – became junior officers, first in the sights of machine-gunners as they led charges out of the trenches. More than 33 per cent of British junior officers were killed, against 15 per cent of more senior officers and just under 13 per cent of other ranks. Flu in 1918–9 was comparably devastating but less discriminating. One hundred and thirty international rugby players are known to have died on active service. Among the twenty-eight Englishmen was James Watson of Blackheath, who died at sea aged twenty-four within six months of playing centre alongside Poulton-Palmer in that final match against France. Watson had followed his club's resolution that 'it is the duty of every able-bodied man of enlistable age to offer personal service to his king and country'. He was followed by King, by now a lance-corporal, and Mobbs, whom legend depicts punting a ball towards the doubtless nonplussed German trenches. Poulton-Palmer died in May 1915, as much a symbol of the 'lost generation' of war dead as his fellow old Rugbeian Rupert Brooke, consigned to his corner of a foreign field less than a fortnight earlier.

Eleven players from the 1913 England v. Scotland match did not survive the war. Bedell-Sivright, one of 30 Scottish caps who died, fell at Gallipoli, while Ypres claimed Basil Maclear, one of the nine Irishmen. The dozen New Zealand deaths included the incomparable Gallaher. There were nine Australians, five South Africans and thirteen Welshmen. The twenty-three Frenchmen, more than one-fifth of the men capped before 1914, included Jo Anduran, capped in 1910 because France were one short for the marathon trip to Swansea, where they lost 49–14, and his Paris art gallery was within walking distance of the station.

International players were only a small proportion of the whole. E.H.D. Sewell, who compiled a study of rugby's war dead, mourned the death in 1917 of B.H.M. Jones as 'the severest loss the Rugby game has suffered. Players of his ability arrive on the scene about once every ten years.' King was one of 47 Headingley players, nearly a quarter of the membership, who died. Waterloo lost 51. Forty-five of the sixty men who played in London Scottish's top four teams on the last Saturday of the 1913–14 season did not return, while Bristol's Memorial Ground commemorates, with sadness only deepened by the loss of the previous name, Buffalo Bill's Fields, more than 300 players and members. In New Zealand, Auckland's College Rifles club supplied 330 men to the colours, of whom 54 died and 80 were wounded. The New South Wales Rugby Union's (NSWRU's) annual report for 1916 listed 115 dead. French writer Paul Voivenel's nostalgic and evocative recall of an incomparable 'King of Matches', the championship quarter-final in 1914 between Aviron Bayonnais and A.S. Perpignan, was shot through with the memory that 15 of the 30 players did not survive the war.

Aside from Captain Mobbs's idiosyncratic contribution to infantry tactics, some rugby was played at the front. French soldier Henri Amand recalled changing in a trench before playing alongside international player Geo Andre in a match rapidly truncated by a German shell. A Welsh prisoner of war wrote to his local paper in 1915 that his regiment had defeated both Yorkshire and Rest of Camp, while the New Zealand Division was among the teams competing in 1917 for the 'Somme Cup'.

The game gradually resumed on the home front as it was realised that not only would the war not be over by Christmas, it would take much longer than that. Rugby league players who had joined the forces began to turn up in representative charity and fund-raising matches. It was here that the doomed Jones impressed Sewell, scoring from halfway at Old Deer Park and performing brilliantly against a team of New Zealanders in the year after he left Birkenhead School. In April 1916, a North of England team fielded against Australian forces at Headingley included four Northern Union players, including Welshman Ben Gronow – who as a union player had supplied the kick-off caught by Stoop at Twickenham in 1910 – and 'prince of centres' Harold Wagstaff, who had 'never seen a rugby union match, much less played in one'. Wagstaff's brilliant individual try contributed to 14 points scored by the Northern Union contingent.

In October 1916, the RFU regularised the situation, allowing Northern Union players to participate for and against bona fide naval and military teams but adding 'these rules only obtain during the war'. Major R.V. Stanley showed the entrepreneurial team-raising talents deployed at the service of Oxford University for a star-bedecked annual match by putting together a formidably strong Army Service Corps (Motor Transport) team based at Grove Park depot in south London, recruiting seven league players, including Wagstaff. In the 1916–17 season, they won 25 matches out of 26, scoring 1,110 points to 41, and lost only to a United Services team including eight full union internationals. Some military protocol was preserved. Wagstaff played inside Harlequins wing L.L. Nixon, whom he addressed as 'sir', while being called 'Wagstaff' in return. When the war ended, Horace Lyne, since 1906 president of the WRU, reprised his conciliatory role of 1886 by suggesting that league players who had served in the forces should be offered reinstatement. He found no support from the RFU committee, which reimposed the status quo at its first post-war meeting.

While the war ended in 1918, there were sufficient men still in uniform the following year for the renewal of peace to be celebrated by the playing of an international, inter-services King's Cup. This involved teams from the Royal Air Force, South African Forces, Australian Expeditionary Force, Canadian Expeditionary Force, New Zealand Army and the British Army (playing as Mother Country). The New Zealanders won this proto-world cup, beating Mother Country at Twickenham in the final, and in all played 38 matches across Britain and France, including a 6–3 win over Wales at Swansea. This was followed, on the way home, by a 15-match tour of South Africa. The touring team paid their own way but were aided by racing tips supplied by a New Zealand jockey.

This visit marks the real beginning of rugby's most intense international rivalry. Among the New Zealand Army stars in Britain was 'Ranji' Wilson, a loose forward of partly West Indian descent who won ten caps before the war. He was not taken to South Africa. There is no knowing what would have happened if the New Zealanders had challenged South African susceptibilities on race. Perhaps the tour would have been banned or public disorder created. But rugby's purported value system emphasises the fellowship of teams – when someone rejects a teammate, they reject you. At the first time of asking, New Zealand failed that test, simultaneously giving up the right to choose their own team. A precedent had been set.

# CHAPTER SIX

# Gathering Storms

'It is said rugby is a game for players. I am often tempted to think that it is a game for the legislators who lay down the rules under which rugby must be played'

Rowe Harding (1929)

'The south-west [of France] in its historic rebellion against the abusive power of the north seized upon the game of rugby football as its main means of expression and its space for joy'

Daniel Herrero (1990)

Historic southern hemisphere dominance is shown in the IRB's retrospective world rankings. They are indicative rather than definitive, but so are contemporary rankings. Players were unaware that their performances might later be analysed for rankings – but does position in the IRB list matter in the slightest compared with the imperatives of winning the match or competition at hand?

The historic series shows that the southern trio shared top place all the way from 1912 to the rise of Clive Woodward's England in 2002, excepting one day's leadership by France in 1987 and two weeks' by England in 1995. South Africa or New Zealand were top for 77 of the 79 years between 1912 and 1991.

On-field dominance was not reflected in off-field influence. In 1919, New Zealand and the two Australian unions called for the creation of an 'International Board of Control' representing every country where the game was played – essentially an extension of the IRB. As NZRFU London representative C.J. Wray argued in 1921, if dominions were consulted over imperial defence and premiers invited to London for conferences, why not in rugby union? With due deference, they appealed to the RFU for 'some voice in the deliberations of those who govern the game'.

The RFU offered the minor concession of a place on its committee from 1921. In the same year, France's latest application was rejected by an IRB whose capacity for institutional change had been exhausted a decade earlier when the RFU – facing a Scottish campaign for equal representation – accepted the reduction of its own delegation to a less overwhelming (but still veto-wielding) four places. The IRB would spend most of the 1920s wrestling with the intractable problems of the scrummage, ameliorative intent endemically unequal to the disruptive ingenuity of front-row forwards.

New Zealand continued to press. The IRB's best offer, made in 1924, fell just short of insulting: a conference on the laws held every five years in London, with each union responsible for its own expenses and the IRB free to ignore its conclusions. The southern unions failed to take the hint. In 1929, the majestic Paul Roos travelled to London to present their case, and the IRB agreed to the creation of a consultative body, provided the dominions accepted the IRB's rules of the game. The dominions did accept this, but the four home unions stalled and the issue lapsed after 1932. In his history of the IRB, English administrator Eric Watts-Moses speculates that the home unions were preoccupied with relations in France – expelled from international competition in 1931 – and also unhappy that New Zealand and New South Wales continued to be allowed 'dispensation' from parts of the rules.

The most significant of these were the 'Auckland Rules', a series of dispensations adopted during one of the periodic panics over league competition in New Zealand's largest city. These included referees putting the ball into the scrum, defenders not being allowed to cross the middle line of the scrum until the ball was out and in the scrum-half's hands, and a ban on direct kicking to touch between the two twenty-five-yard lines. There were threats of secession – or expulsion – from the NZRFU when they were first proposed, but they were accepted in 1920 and limited touch-kicking was sanctioned by the RFU a year later. Years later, Aucklanders remembered men like five-eighth Karl Ifwersen, a reinstated former league international and, according to journalist Terry McLean, 'a tactical genius', making the game more fluidly attractive than ever before or since. Fifty years on, Laurie Knight remembered 'fast, good-handling forwards whose support of clever back lines has never been equalled'.

With worries of its own, New Zealand was nevertheless firmly committed to helping rugby union survive in Australia. Queensland was lost entirely to league by 1919. Historian Tom Hickie suggests that New South Wales would have risked that fate if Herb Evatt, later leader of the Labor Party and president of the United Nations General Assembly, had succeeded in taking Sydney University across codes in the same year. Evatt lost at an AGM which Hickie describes as crowded with 'hitherto inactive supporters of the union'. A further boost came when Randwick, destined to supply both great players and attacking philosophy, joined the Sydney premiership first grade in 1923.

New Zealand support sustained morale and income. The All Blacks paid five visits in six years from 1920, while New South Wales's Waratahs took four return trips between 1921 and 1928. The process of debt clearance was completed by the 25,000 crowd, largest for a union match in Australia since 1907, who watched Cliff Porter's team en route for Britain in 1924. Australia in 1986 retrospectively recognised thirty-eight matches as full internationals – twenty-four against New Zealand (who won eighteen), three defeats by the 1921 South Africans, seven matches against the New Zealand Maoris (W4, L3) and the four tests on the 1927–28 tour of Europe (with wins over Wales, Ireland and France) – recognising that even if the team was called New South Wales it was a de facto Australia XV.

Matches fully recognised as tests, and domestic action, gave New Zealanders much to remember in the 1920s. Tests against South Africa finally started in 1921 with the visit of the Springboks, who called 120 players to trials and chose 29, of whom 23 had seen war service – highly conducive to popularity when New Zealand had 17,000 war dead and 41,000 wounded from a population of little over a million. New Zealanders also appreciated watching worthy opponents, although 114 lineouts in the first test at Dunedin tried spectator patience and the third was a 0–0 draw in weather foul even by Wellington standards. The Springboks matched the haka with a 'Zulu war cry' of their own and shared the three-match series.

A ferocious game against the Maoris also left a warning of the wrath which the South African connection was to inflict on New Zealand. A South African journalist's cabled report – 'Most unfortunate match ever played . . . Bad enough having to play officially designated New Zealand natives; but spectacle thousands Europeans frantically cheering on coloured men to defeat members of own race was too much for Springboks, who frankly disgusted' – was leaked, to a furore, in New Zealand.

The match was played at Napier, the centre of both New Zealand and Maori rugby during this period thanks to a remarkable Hawke's Bay team which won the Ranfurly Shield in 1922 and held it through five years and an unprecedented twenty-four challenges. Coach–selector Norm McKenzie made efficient use of Maori talent – none greater than George Nepia, chosen for the 1924 tour of Great Britain as a 19 year old. New Zealand rugby was sufficiently culturally important for deputy premier Gordon Coates to attempt a late intervention in team selection and confident enough to rebuff him: 'We do not presume to interfere in politics and would prefer that politics does not interfere with us.'

Coates was reflecting informed opinion. George Tyler, a veteran of 1905, proclaimed it 'the weakest team ever to leave New Zealand'. It returned as precisely the opposite, after 30 straight wins. This included a 17–11 defeat of one of England's strongest ever teams, in which New Zealand played for more than an hour with 14 men after giant forward Cyril Brownlie, next to offend after three general warnings by referee Albert Freethy, had become the first man sent off in an international match. They did it on limited possession. British forward play had advanced since 1905 and controlled the bulk of possession against the tourists, even though Maurice Brownlie, Cyril's brother, was universally recognised as a magnificent forward, prototype for a succession of abrasive, mobile, ball-handling Kiwi giants.

Britain had no answer though to the speed, combination and skill of the All Blacks, who worked around the five-eighths axis of Bert Cooke – a darting genius in the Welsh mould (his parents had left Llanelli in the 1890s) – and the less obvious but still deadlier eye for angle and opening of Mark Nicholls. Welsh winger Rowe Harding recalled:

One great player single-handed can effectively be stopped; but two, playing together in a side where the other players are sound, honest footballers, can accomplish miracles. Nicholls and Cooke were an extraordinary combination. Each was the antithesis of the other and yet each completed the other.

The man behind them was arguably even greater. Nepia, previously a five-eighth, played full-back in all 30 matches. Described by the Australian writer Denzil Batchelor as possessing 'a face fit for the prow of a Viking longship', his judgement and anticipation in attack and defence, tackling in which his 'embrace of man and ball was like an octopus' and massive kicks ensured him rugby immortality before he was 20.

The sole asterisk against the 'Invincibles' is that they did not play Scotland, that year's champions. It was not their fault – the Scots declined on the procedural grounds that the RFU rather than the IRB had invited New Zealand – although some suspected grievances from 1905 were still simmering.

The All Blacks' next major tour took them, minus their Maoris, to South Africa in 1928. The Maoris, although not Nepia – who was left behind after a hoax telegram said he was not available – received the consolation of a 16-match tour of Britain in 1927. By passing through shortly before the New South Wales Waratahs, the Maoris allowed Pontypool – not usually on tourist tracks – the rare distinction of beating two touring teams in one year, one of Wales's few bright moments in a miserable decade.

Miserable was also the word for the 1928 All Blacks. Skipper Maurice Brownlie, 'a cold, hard man' according to forward Jim Burrows, fell out with abrasive deputy Nicholls, who played only the fourth and last test. Like many teams visiting South Africa, they were tired by endless long-distance rail travel. Without Nepia, Nicholls argued, and with kicking skills downgraded by the different requirements of the Auckland dispensation, they were outkicked by cannon-like South African outside-half Bennie Osler. Worse still was the scrum. New Zealand stuck with its seven-man scrum and two-man front-row, even after a 1921 IRB ruling handicapped it seriously by requiring the ball to pass beyond the first man before being touched.

The Springboks' only international opponents since 1921 had

been the unrepresentative 1924 British team who met for the first time on boarding at Southampton and in Harding's words suffered from 'a lack of good reserves and never got properly together as a team'. By contrast, the 1928 Springboks prepared intensively, calling 60 men for a week of trials in Durban with the message that, work commitments or not, not attending meant not playing. At their disposal was the latest in scrummaging weaponry, the 3–4–1 formation which combined the 2–3–2's ability to focus pressure with the weight of the extra man. Western Province and Transvaal's scrums massacred the All Blacks before the first test at Durban. There, the Springboks won 36 of the 51 scrums and, Nicholls remembered, 'they heeled from fully 95 per cent of loose rucks'. He went on: 'They pushed our pack all over the field, they got possession from the set scrums at will and, during one period of the second half, they heeled from 16 scrums in succession.' South Africa won 17–0. Osler, a perfectionist with a chaotic personal life who trained five times a week for two pre-season months and four times a week in season, and had been known in matches to throw passes he considered sub-standard back at his scrum-half, scored fourteen points from two penalties and two drops.

It says much for the All Blacks that they rallied to draw the series – Springbok captain Phil Mostert paying tribute to their 'intensive backing up' and 'bewildering passing' – but Nicholls, whose ten points won the final test at Cape Town, reckoned that Durban 'shattered the aura of invincibility which had sheltered and sustained the morale of the All Blacks'.

The following year supported that view. Queensland rugby was resurrected in 1928 with a schools festival hosted by Brisbane Grammar School and a visit from Sydney University. Five clubs were in action in 1929, which also saw discussions of a merger with the Brisbane Rugby League when the BRL fell out with the Queensland body. Resuming fixtures with New South Wales allowed the return of an unambiguous national XV. Australia included veteran five-eighth Tom Lawton, a Queenslander who, as a Rhodes scholar in the early 1920s, was close to both England selection and suspension for having played league (he eventually persuaded the RFU that with no union at home it was league or nothing), and the astonishing 'Wild Bill' Cerutti, who played top-class rugby for 20 years in what

Spiro Zavos has called 'a confrontational manner that suggested he either did not understand or, perhaps more accurately, did not agree with some of the laws of the game'. They were unhampered by gratitude towards New Zealand for assistance in the dark days, inflicting a 3–0 defeat in a four-test series.

All that went wrong for Australian rugby in 1929 was the jailing of Rob McCowen, Queensland's first Wallabies captain, for 14 years for defrauding his law clients. Fraud appears rugby's crime of choice. Rex Grossman, a founder of the Otago University club, and England flanker Tony Neary are among others to have been convicted, although if one Jack the Ripper theory is right, rugby's most famous criminal was Montague Druitt, secretary of Blackheath in the late 1870s.

New Zealand v. South Africa was not the only series launched in the 1920s. In 1924, a Fiji team drawn entirely from its Native Union, founded in 1915, went on tour. It started in Western Samoa, where New Zealanders had introduced rugby after taking over from German colonisers in 1920. The tourists played the home team on a pitch in Apia featuring a tree on halfway, kicking off at 7 a.m. to allow the Samoans to get to work and the Fijians to catch their boat to Tonga. Both teams played in bare feet – a practice Fiji maintained until 1938. Fiji, including loose forward Atunaisa Laqeretabua, who would still be there in 1938, won 6–0. They were less successful in Tonga, losing their first match 9–6 but recovering to share a three-match series 1–1. Samoa's first taste of international rugby was also its last for many years, but Fiji and Tonga played again in 1926, 1928, 1932 and 1934 – Tonga winning the two 1920s series and Fiji those in the 1930s.

Boots remained de rigueur in Europe, but other attributes were missing when international action resumed with France v. Scotland on New Year's Day 1920. This went into French folklore as *'le match des borgnes'*, with five players – two Frenchman and three Scots – missing an eye following war service. One of them, French forward Marcel Lubin-Lebrere, nearly lost more than an eye later that season in Dublin. Out for an evening stroll, he heard the Marseillaise being sung 'not very well' and located the singers, a Sinn Fein cell, at the same time as the British Army, who took him into custody and took some persuading that the monoglot Lubin-

Lebrere was not something new in the way of subversives. Ireland's matches continued uninterruptedly during the violence before and after the creation of the Irish Free State in 1922. In 1921, when Wales visited Ireland, two men were killed outside the team hotel. Two years later, the WRU insured their players for £1,000 a man. Rowe Harding remembered:

the armoured cars hurrying through the town, the search parties holding up pedestrians to search for firearms and the rifle shots which broke the silence of the night. Our captain refused to accept a small square package from a representative of a firm of chewing-gum manufacturers because he suspected it might be an infernal machine, and a card party was abruptly terminated by the staccato notes of rifle-firing outside the hotel.

Ireland lost a union president in 1916 when Frederick Browning fell victim to the Easter Rising and gained a Republican martyr with the death – famously commemorated in song – in 1920 of Kevin Barry, who had played for Belvedere College and University College Dublin. The post-war years were tough. Ireland won only five matches between 1920 and 1924 – Lubin-Lebrere's near-thing preceded France's first win over them – but Irish rugby survived and stayed united, while football was breaking into North and Free State in 1922. Financial confidence, and commitment to the North, was demonstrated by the opening in 1924 of the 30,000-capacity Ravenhill Road ground in Belfast, costing £18,000. Irish teams retained some traditional qualities – 11 doctors and medical students played against Wales in 1920 – but the game was spreading and diversifying, with rapid growth in Munster after a sticky period in the early 1920s. On-field fortunes also improved, with nine wins out of twelve and two consecutive shared championships between 1926 and 1928. Centre George Stephenson – an elegant straight runner and watertight defender – rose from Queen's University Belfast thirds to Ireland inside a year and stayed a decade, setting a record of 42 caps that endured into the 1950s. Tough forward James 'Jammie' Clinch won 30 caps while, as befitted a doctor and son of an international, epitomising traditional Irish attributes. These were particularly appreciated in Wales, where he promised to 'make an orange' of tough Neath forward Arthur Lemon and, greeted with shouts of 'send him off' at Swansea, said he was 'touched that they remembered me'. Still more evocative of the forces that kept Irish rugby in one piece was Ernie Crawford, an Ulsterman and doctor who practised in Dublin and played for the once heavily Protestant, but now increasingly Catholic, Lansdowne club. He won 30 caps, the first aged 28, and was seen by England's Wavell Wakefield as 'a kind of brooding intelligence directing the play and waiting like a spider for the unfortunate man who has to try to pass him'. Given to directing streams of abuse and encouragement at teammates, he was cool enough in 1922 to lean calmly against a goalpost with arms folded as a Frenchman touched down, confident that the touch-judge would spot a foot in touch 30 yards back. His confidence was justified.

If anywhere, though, exuded confidence in the 1920s, it was England. The social force of middle-class prosperity was behind the English game. Rugby was being taken up by both private and grammar schools, which were expanding after the Hadow report in 1918 recommended all 11 year olds should go to secondary school and the creation of state scholarships in 1920. Ground was regained in the north. Yorkshire clubs increased from 29 in 1914 to 39 in 1920 to 54 in 1923. Two hundred and thirty-one new clubs were formed during the 1920s, taking RFU affiliations back to pre-1895 levels while many older clubs were expanding – Wasps had three teams in 1907, six by 1924 and nine in 1935. Twickenham expanded to meet an ever-rising demand for tickets – by 1925, it could accommodate 53,000, more than a third seated. New technological forces were felt, with the first radio broadcast from the ground in the 1927–28 season.

While the German Rudolf Kirchner in 1928 saw rugby as a means by which the 'cultured Englishman can carry off a national defeat without any resentment' and a game in which he has 'become accustomed to share his honours with other nations', not much of this was actually happening, particularly at Twickenham. The invincible 1924 All Blacks were the first visitors to beat England since the 1912 Springboks. Scotland finally broke the home nations duck against England in 1926, while Ireland had to wait until 1929 and Wales 1933. The first half of the '20s was England's, with Grand Slams in 1921, then in 1923 and 1924 – the only time anyone won consecutive outright titles between the wars – and again in 1928.

The immediate post-war period was identified with a classic complementary half-back pairing, both naval men. Scrum-half Cecil Kershaw was a submarine commander, while W.J.A. 'Dave' Davies was Welsh-born, in Pembroke Dock, and had started as a dockyard apprentice. Kershaw was thickset, powerful, broke fast from the base of the scrum and mixed it with forwards. Davies, in whom radio commentator Teddy Wakelam saw 'an air of divinity student mildness', had acute tactical sense. Wakefield wrote with gratitude that he 'instinctively seemed to know when his forwards must have relief'. In addition, he was 'at his best when things went none too well' and 'defeat never worried him'. After a losing debut against the 1912 Springboks, he was undefeated in 22 further England appearances.

The decade, though, belonged to Wakefield. He would have been memorable if he had done nothing but play – a force of nature 6 ft tall, 14 st. and, as the distinctly pacy Rowe Harding confirmed from personal experience, faster than most wingers. He was, in Howard Marshall's words, 'the complete footballer', who could 'run and handle the ball as well as any three-quarter or control in a dribble like Stanley Matthews'. His impact went beyond that, true to a credo of rugby as 'the game for the tactician, for the man who is mentally alert' – in the 1923 varsity match, he let Oxford have the ball for 20 minutes to tire them with heavy tackling, then initiated an all-out attack.

In 1925, Leonard Tosswill wrote that the contemporary forward was:

> expected to be almost as fast as a three-quarter, to break up the scrummages and join in all attacking or defensive movements on equal terms with the backs, to be an adept in passing and, at the same time, to be no less proficient in his own peculiar department, out-of-touch play, wheeling and dribbling, than the older type of forward.

This owed much to Wakefield's example; still more to his thinking. Captaining his country from 1924 to 1926, he did for English forwards what Stoop had done for backs, introducing and refining New Zealand-style specialisation, developing cover defence and 'corner flagging' by back rowers and using what became known as 'second-phase possession' – drawing opponents into contact then heeling quickly – as an attacking weapon. Wakefield's 31 caps remained an English record for more than 40 years, most of which he spent as a Conservative MP before elevation to the Lords.

His great ally for England was Gloucester's rumbustiously combative Tom Voyce – great-uncle of the current England player – who had survived gassing at Passchendaele and other war injuries. Essayist H.J. Henley wrote: 'No one could play more politely than Voyce when the game was allowed to pursue a tranquil course; but heaven help the other fellow who took a liberty and forgot the rules.'

Wakefield pictured Voyce as 'the happy warrior':

with the ball in a lineout, struggling to make a few yards with three or four opponents round his neck or knees. It may be that he is wasting his energies and not really furthering the attack, but he is thoroughly enjoying himself and the very fact of this fighting spirit of his puts heart into the forwards with him.

Wakefield's England probably reached their peak at Swansea in 1924 when, Dai Gent wrote, Wales were 'completely bewildered by the nature of their passing and the numbers of men concerned with it'.

There might have been a third consecutive title in 1925 but for a Scottish team whose best decade of the century reached a remarkable peak. Textile-trade recession was reflected in the presence of only a single Borderer, Douglas Davies of Hawick, but the big city hothouses were still producing a decent crop. Dan Drysdale, first of a remarkable line of Heriots full-backs, secured the defence with an unhurried competence born of innate positional sense. The Glasgow Academical duo of Jimmy Nelson and Herbert Waddell formed a stable and accomplished half-back pairing, and there was both fire and durability in a pack featuring 'Jock' Bannerman, who played 37 consecutive tests between 1921 and 1929 and wound up facing Wakefield from the Liberal bench in the House of Lords.

For Scotland, the triumphs of 1925 are closely identified with their Oxford University three-quarter line. This was another colonial construction. Wing Johnny Wallace had already played (and would play again) for Australia. Centre George Aitken had captained New Zealand in 1921. Wing Ian Smith was Australian born, while the one native Scot, centre Phil Macpherson, was scarcely less exotic in coming from Gaelic hotbed Newtownmore. They never played as a unit for Oxford and only five times for Scotland, coming together slightly by accident after Eric Liddell, destined for posthumous screen fame in *Chariots of Fire*, concentrated on training for the 1924 Olympics and Leslie Gracie, chaired off Cardiff Arms Park after a match-winning display in 1923, gave up international rugby.

There were doubts, expressed vigorously after Scotland's 1925 opener against France, about their defence. Little matter when the creativity of Macpherson, a subtle sidestepper, sent Smith on one of the greatest scoring sequences in rugby history.

Smith combined extreme pace with balance and power. Rowe Harding said he was fast enough to cover both wings and unstoppable by anything less than a wholehearted tackle, and 'even that was often unsuccessful'. He had a high knee action and a homing instinct for the corner.

He had given notice the previous season with four tries in a 35–12 massacre of Wales – his marker, Harold Davies, asked to meet him after the game, having failed to get near him while on the field. Smith prepared for the 1925 championship with five tries in Scotland's final trial, then claimed four in the opener against France, including a second-half hat-trick. Three more in the first half against Wales in Swansea completed six consecutive tries in less than eighty minutes, with a fourth after the break to complete Welsh déjà vu. At this point, partly because the opposition improved and Macpherson missed the Ireland match due to injury, but mostly because of the force of gravity, Smith reverted to human form. Wallace, whose two tries in each of the first two matches would normally have occasioned much more notice, crossed again in a hard-won 14–8 victory in Dublin.

By a happy accident of timing, the season climaxed with the opening of the Scottish Rugby Union's new Murrayfield stadium, built on land purchased in 1922 from the Edinburgh Polo Club. Inverleith's 30,000 capacity had never been tested. The new ground, which held 70,000 and featured a giant grandstand hailed by *The Times* as 'second to none in the world of sporting spectacles', even if their reporter was unimpressed by the location of the press-box, was packed. England had lost only one of their last twenty-one championship matches, and not to Scotland since 1912, although hopes of a third consecutive Triple Crown fell with a draw against Ireland at Twickenham. In a contest of exhausting tension and physical commitment – Wakefield took several days to recover – England led 8–5 at half-time and went further ahead when Wakefield scored from one of his patented moves, driving over after a cross-kick from centre Len Corbett. Scotland struck back with a try from Wallace, making him the second of only five men (and the last until 1983) to score in all four games, then took the lead 14–11 with a Waddell drop-goal (still worth four points). In an excruciatingly tense finale, England full-back Tom Holliday narrowly missed a drop-goal, and Corbett, 'through sheer exhaustion', was held a yard short. An understandably exultant *Glasgow Herald* warned that 'It will be the duty of Scottish sides in the coming years to confirm the Murrayfield precedent.' That duty would take some confirming, although Scotland shared championships with Ireland in the next two seasons, then won outright in 1929. Smith continued until 1933, his final total of 24 tries a championship record which still stands and a mark for all international rugby that lasted until David Campese overtook it in 1988. Too bad they never, with the exception of Wallace, who returned to Australia in 1926, played the All Blacks.

The decade's unhappy exception was Wales, its very different social base savaged by industrial decline. The trends of previous decades were reversed, as 430,000 people, half of them in rugby's key 15–29 age group, left Wales between the wars – 'a Black Death on wheels', in the words of serious humourist Gwyn Thomas. They were escaping an economy in which mining employment dropped by almost half, shedding 127,000 jobs and lowering the wage bill from £65 million to £14 million between 1920 and 1933. England was a beneficiary of this migration of youth and talent. More than one-fifth of new arrivals in Coventry, which experienced a population growth from 128,000 to 220,000 between 1922 and 1939, were Welsh. This influx bolstered the strength of local rugby and, in particular, of games teaching in schools, both of which would contribute to the city club's post-war prowess.

Many of the most gifted Welsh players took their skills north. Tony Collins calculates 25 Welsh players a year went to northern England between 1919 and 1926, and a total of 392 between the wars. This included 70 internationals. Still greater losses were teenagers like Cardiffians Jim Sullivan in 1921 and Gus Risman a decade later, who became historic figures in their adopted game. In 1920, Ebbw Vale secretary Thomas Rees asked the Northern Union if his club could switch code. The Northern Union, displaying the genius for missing chances that survived its change of name in 1922 to the Rugby Football League, said it could not guarantee confidentiality because other clubs had to be consulted, and the idea lapsed. League's single inter-war venture into Wales at Pontypridd, gateway to the Rhondda, during a long coal dispute was a snowball cast into hell.

Rugby union was not immune to political disturbance. Gareth Williams records a referee with a revolver strapped to his waist at Glyncorrwg amid 'a sort of guerrilla warfare' in the Afan Valley in 1926. A year earlier, striking miners put unwanted leisure to use by constructing a new ground for Penygraig, replacing a fearsome hilltop pitch. The *Western Mail*, voice of the coal owners and the Cardiff ascendancy, attributed crowd incursions at the 1921 match against Scotland in Swansea to 'irresponsible hooligans, posing as followers of Lenin and Trotsky'. Simple overcrowding, with 60,000 packed into St Helen's, was the likelier explanation. Referee James Baxter, familiar with public disorder from Paris eight years earlier, stopped the match for ten minutes and contemplated abandonment. The delay meant the visitors had to rush unshowered but happy to their train station, 14–8 winners thanks to a try touched down among spectators sitting in the goal area by Allen Sloan of Edinburgh Wanderers.

No political agitation was needed to create chaos. Wales's selectors did that by themselves, picking eight different half-backs for four matches in 1921. They picked 35 players in 1924, making 13 changes after an England match marked by Swansea spectators singing 'Yes, we have no three-quarters' and Sewell's comment that 'the only Welsh combination seen was the way in which the pack lost its temper as one man'. The following season, the 13-member 'match committee' was replaced by a 'Big Five', who retained a capacity for the bizarre and inscrutable. Nothing sums up Welsh selection better than that Albert Jenkins – a centre of genius, even if Llanelli's famously partisan press said so – won only fourteen caps across nine seasons. The quintessential local hero, a fitter's mate and dock labourer known universally in Llanelli as simply 'Albert', he turned down an offer of £500 to join Hull in 1919. An immaculate figure with swept-back brilliantined hair, he was a devastating runner, a fine passer – Harding recalled receiving three scoring passes early in a match and dropping the lot, so hard and direct was the pass – a defender who could disrupt an entire opposing three-quarter line before collaring the wing and a dropper of massive goals. Llanelli legend credited him with the ability to play unaffected (save a moment's absence with a simulated injury) after six pints of bitter. Harding recalled his display in the invasion-disrupted match against Scotland in 1921:

> He made opening after opening only to see his efforts nullified by the ineptitude of his colleagues. Finding that victory by orthodox methods was hopeless, he took the game into his own hands and in ten minutes he had dropped two goals and narrowly missed dropping two more.

That the crowd then broke in and Welsh momentum was lost typifies Jenkins's international career.

Harding was a quick wing who earned the ire – once gained, never forgotten – of Llanelli by leaving for Swansea and wrote his own piece of rugby history with the first British player memoir – previous books were essentially coaching manuals, even if leavened with a little autobiography. He provoked a rumpus – less of an authorial aspiration then than it is now – by trenchant chapters in which he described his Cambridge teams as 'professional gladiators, devoting all our time and energies to winning the varsity match', argued for broken-time payments on tour and for British employers to follow French examples and find jobs for players.

He also recalled with mortification Wales's chosen pack failing in practice to outscrummage six Cardiff policemen. Technique remained primitive, with little New Zealand-style specialisation, never mind the refinements introduced by Wakefield in England. However, the policemen probably knew what they were doing.

Harding also commended Glamorgan's veteran chief-constable Lionel Lindsay as one employer who did find work for rugby players. Cardiff teams from 1923 to 1939 fielded an average of ten policemen, while there were six in the Wales pack in 1926. Miners like Arthur Bowdler of Ebbw Vale, wont to rush home from internationals to fulfil his night shift underground, were increasingly the exception.

But whatever the composition of the team, the force was not with Wales. A misleadingly promising post-war start, with good seasons in 1920 and 1922 highlighted by massive defeats of England bizarrely out of context with the era – England's only losses in thirty championship matches between 1913 and 1925 – was followed by only seven wins in the next six seasons. Five of them were the 'annual consolation' against France, and even that was denied in 1928.

France too started well but faded. In 1920, they beat Ireland and, reckoned Ernest Ward of the *Morning Post*, 'with luck might have won all four of their matches'. Former England full-back Herbert Gamlin thought the better team lost when his compatriots squeezed home 10–6 in Paris. Two matches, with a first win in Scotland, were won in 1921, when French rugby also won institutional independence. By far the most popular of the amateur sports which pooled income under the USFSA's rule, rugby voted through its clubs to break away in 1919. Fearful of losing rugby altogether, the USFSA offered the clubs – led by former Stade Français player Frantz Reichel – a reformed structure, with every sport allowed its own autonomous federation. This was agreed, and the Fédération Française de Rugby (FFR) came into being on 1 January 1921.

The number of French clubs tripled to 800 between 1920 and 1923, most newcomers located in the south-west, where Toulouse established itself as the capital of French rugby, nodal point for a rapidly expanding network of small town and village clubs, five times national champions between 1922 and 1927 and home of the weekly rugby journal *Midi-Olympique*, established in 1929.

Yet those two wins in 1921 were more ceiling than springboard. There were only four more, including landmark defeats of England in 1927 and Wales the year after, in the remaining eight seasons of the decade, plus bitter disappointment in the 1924 Olympics. It was bad enough to have lost the 1920 Antwerp games gold medal to an

American team dominated by players from Stanford, which had only just reverted to American Football. The 1924 games were in Paris. As in 1920, the RFU refused to participate, leaving three entrants. The USA, essentially a Stanford team with three holdovers from 1920 and a sizeable contingent of American Footballers wont to try to 'knock the ball carrier into the next country' rather than simply tackle him, had beaten Devonport Services but lost to Blackheath and Harlequins on the way over. Neither they nor France had any problems with a Romania team with greater experience of rail travel – four days in third class getting to Paris – than international rugby. France expected to win, but its players accepted a 17–3 defeat gracefully. Not so the crowd. They booed the US national anthem and both the winning team and referee Albert Freethy needed police protection. There has not been an official Olympic rugby tournament since.

One possible explanation for France's international failure was the intense emphasis on the club championship. The first radio broadcast, in 1923, was not an international but the championship final between Stade Toulousain and Aviron Bayonnais. France's Republican uniformity conceals an extraordinary range of strongly felt regional and local identities – Charles de Gaulle would bemoan the impossibility of governing a country with 300 varieties of cheese. Rugby became an apt means of expression, for good and ill, of the south-west's identity, its festivity, patriarchy and what ethnologist Sebastian Darbon termed 'a certain conception' of the group and 'a taste for violence'. The Federation's decision in 1921 to organise the championship on a regional basis ensured a plentiful supply of local derbies to channel ancient grievances. Phil Dine suggests that the style of play which emerged in the 1920s, brutally violent in its defence of the locality, must in part have reflected the trauma of invasion and trench warfare in the previous decade. Harding thought that by 1929 French club rugby was stronger than anything in Britain, but playing improvements were accompanied by growing concern over violence and ill-concealed professionalism. In 1925, former international Geo Andre condemned the Carcassonne v. Perpignan final as:

a match of brutes . . . on the terrace, there were battles, and on the pitch, there was a battle royal . . . the game was played in the most vicious possible spirit ... played in this way, rugby is more like the ancient games of the Roman circuses.

Carcassonne were coached by former international Jean Sebedio, 'The Sultan' from wartime service in Syria and, between 1913 and 1923, France's first working-class international. Sebedio moved to Lezignan where, in Dine's words, 'He cultivated his persona by sitting in the middle of the pitch with a long whip and a wide sombrero, making his players run round him like circus horses' while he equipped the referee's room with a skeleton complete with cigar clamped between its jaws, introducing it as 'the last referee to give a penalty against Lezignan'.

Not far from Lezignan was Quillan, whose population of 3,000 might have expected to support, at best, a reasonable junior club. In 1928, 1929 and 1930, its team reached the final of the national championship. In 1929, Quillan beat Lezignan, population 6,000, in a notably savage final. The local magnate, hat manufacturer Jean Bourrel, recruited quality players – particularly from Perpignan, who supplied six of the 1929 champions. Quillan may have been no guiltier than other clubs, but the sheer improbability of their rise symbolised the *amateurisme marron* (shamateurism) of the time. Wing Jean Bonnet, their last survivor many years later, recalled, 'Financially, I never received a cent. M. Bourrel paid for a worker to take my place when I was away, while others had jobs at the factory.' Players also advertised Bourrel's products – Bonnet remembered the team going to Paris in yellow hats.

Quillan's mass recruitment from Perpignan made their matches charged even by the standards of the time. In 1927, Quillan hooker Gaston Rivière died from his injuries after a match against Perpignan, giving literal truth to writer Paul Voivenel's characterisation of the era as '*Rugby de muerte*'. Three years later, Agen's 18-year-old hooker Jean Pradié, still a schoolboy, died following a late tackle by his Pau counterpart, French international Jean Taillantou. The dashing, tragic Yves du Manoir, an aristocratic outside-half killed in a flying accident on 2 January 1928, the day of a Scotland match from which he was unexpectedly dropped after seven caps, is France's official rugby martyr of this era. Pradié should perhaps stand alongside him. Questions were asked in the

National Assembly, and it was evident that French rugby could not go on like this.

France played a more benign role elsewhere in Continental Europe. Members of its military mission started the first club in Poland in 1921, while one Jean Nau has been credited with introducing rugby into Russia in 1927. Czech rugby was pioneered by children's writer Ondrej Sekora, who brought a ball and the rules, which he translated, from France in 1926. In Spain, rugby was relaunched by Baudilio Aleu Torres, who returned to Barcelona from veterinary studies in Toulouse in 1921 and launched the Santboiana club, playing on a pitch the players had cleared themselves – a tree was tolerated and used as a coat hanger until it was uprooted after a few games. Three other Barcelona sports clubs were persuaded to try the game before the end of the year. Madrid's first match two years later, an exhibition between Biarritz and Tarbes, was watched by 12,000 spectators, a proportion of whom took exception to a Biarritz score and rained cushions on the pitch. Early matches were handicapped by the absence of rules translated into either Spanish or Catalan, while organisation was hampered by conflicts reflecting Spain's wider political and regional tensions, with schisms between Madrid and Catalonia and among the Catalans. France sent a team including du Manoir to Madrid in 1927, but the Spanish XV was organised by a breakaway governing body and the game is not officially recognised. When Spain finally played a recognised international, at Barcelona's Montjuic Stadium in 1929, as part of that year's Expo and with the Spanish royal family in attendance, it was an all-Catalan team playing in Catalonia's colours. Their opponents were Italy, a year on from the relaunching of their game, setting up the Federazione Italiana de Rugby (FIR) and recruiting several foreign coaches, mostly French. Italy's Fascist leaders initially favoured rugby, but Volata, a mixture of handball and soccer played by eight-man teams, favoured by party secretary Augusto Turati, emerged as a rival, and the FIR was suppressed in 1929. Spain beat Italy 9–0 and then, playing in Spanish red, went down to Germany, which had also been the beneficiary of French encouragement, including regular fixtures from 1927. France had won the first meeting in Paris, but the team which had beaten England only six weeks earlier had gone down 17–16 in the return in Frankfurt, watched by 12,000 people. France would soon be rewarded for having done such missionary work.

Canadian rugby, its main centres a continent apart in British Columbia and Nova Scotia, revived rapidly after the war. Contact with California continued, and the *Daily World* newspaper in 1921 donated the imposingly named World Trophy for an annual match between the University of British Columbia and either Stanford or California. More than 9,000 people watched the invincible All Blacks in 1925, and revival in the east saw McGill and Toronto universities playing each other from 1923 and the resurrection in 1929, after more than 50 years, of the Ontario v. Quebec provincial match. Even so, it was in Winnipeg, where the Mounties had sustained the game, that the Canadian Rugby Union was formed, with an admirable absence of superstition, on Friday, 13 September 1929.

In Japan, too, universities were vital to the game. Doshisha and Waseda played the first inter-university game in 1923. Prince Chichibu, younger son of then Crown Prince Hirohito, became a fan after watching Keio play Waseda. Although forced to return to Japan after only a single term at Oxford when the emperor died in December 1926, his enthusiasm had been stoked by attending matches in London, and he became patron of the Japan Rugby Union, which was formed in 1926.

In Argentina, the game remained a matter of clubs rather than universities. It offers a candidate for the team of the '20s in San Isidro, champions from 1917 to 1930. They had powerful forwards – Hugo Mackern, doyen of Argentinian rugby journalism, remembered them as 'slow but very effective' – including the worst possible player to confront in a punch-up, 1928 Olympic heavyweight champion Arturo Rodriguez Jurado. In 1927, San Isidro held a visiting British team captained by Scotland's D.J. MacMyn to 14–0, even though reduced by injury to 14 men for most of the match. MacMyn reported that the Argentinians had:

> all the qualities that are required for international football. They were big and strong and fast. They were tremendously keen – some, by virtue of their Latin temperament, over-keen. What they lacked was experience of first-class football and a knowledge of the finer points of the game.

Another British observer thought them characterised by 'exceptional physical condition and individualism, the latter being of an exceedingly difficult nature to eradicate'.

British rugby's next significant tour was the first proper Lions trip to New Zealand and Australia in 1930. The tourists set a pattern for British teams down under by being remembered as brilliant attackers who nevertheless lost the test series. Flanker Ivor Jones of Llanelli, yet another Welsh selectorial blind spot, won particularly glowing opinions. It is not Jones, though, who is most remembered but Lions manager James Baxter, the referee of Paris in 1913 and Swansea in 1921, now the most influential member of the RFU committee and therefore of the IRB. New Zealand were conciliatory before the tour, giving up the Auckland dispensations in 1929 and playing under IRB rules. Mr Baxter, a gunboat diplomat, was not impressed. Pausing only to insult Auckland's rugby league community ('every city needs its sewer'), he launched into the wing-forward, labelling him 'contrary to the spirit of rugby football' and 'nothing more or less than a cheat'. While some New Zealanders agreed, they were less keen to be lectured in resoundingly English tones. New Zealand selector Ted McKenzie struck back after the final test, accusing the tourists of deliberate obstruction and jersey-pulling. Between New Zealand and France, rugby was not short of controversies as it entered the 1930s.

## CHAPTER SEVEN

# Scrums, Bans, Nudity and Sandbags

'The greatest team ever to leave New Zealand? The 1937 Springboks'

New Zealand saying

'Owing to the unsatisfactory condition of the game of Rugby Football as managed in France, neither our Unions nor the clubs and Unions under its jurisdiction will be able to arrange or fulfil fixtures with France or French clubs, at home or away, after the end of the season, unless and until we are satisfied that the control and conduct of the game has been placed on a satisfactory basis in all essentials'

Letter from the home unions to the French Rugby Federation (1931)

The 1930s was a stormy, apprehensive decade, concluding in world conflict. That tension periodically found its way onto the pitch. In New Zealand in 1932, Merivale played Christchurch amid the bitterness of a city tramway strike. Most Merivale players were on strike, while several Christchurch players enrolled as special constables. There was trouble between specials and strikers the night before the game, which was predictably brutal, the Christchurch captain saying he had never taken such a beating. Amid verbal violence, a bottle thrown outside the ground hit a spectator on the head. He later died. Christchurch left in a police Black Maria, taking 'a young troublemaker' who was subjected to a kangaroo court and a blow on the backside from each player.

Four years later, more ideological tensions were released by the French championship final, a week after the election of the Communist-Socialist Popular Front government led by Leon Blum. Montferrand – creation of the Michelin tyre dynasty – played

Narbonne, Blum's constituency. Narbonne won 6–3, initiating a Montferrand sequence of championship-final failures which still continues. The decisive try was scored by wing Francis Vals, later a major figure in the Socialist Party. The players celebrated by singing the *Internationale*.

France and New Zealand had become rugby's storm centres. New Zealand, though, conceded quietly and in part voluntarily in the controversy over the wing-forward and its by-product, the seven-man scrum. Their undoing was their pursuit of IRB membership. In 1931, they agreed, along with the home unions, that future matches should be played under the rules of the IRB. Unrepresented, this left them vulnerable as the IRB continued its endless battle with the scrummage. Whether it was malice aforethought – James Baxter's membership of the IRB might support this conclusion – or, as one Kiwi journalist suggested, 'disregarding the New Zealand formation', it ruled in 1932 that the ball could not be played until it had passed three front-row feet. The effect was unquestionable. A two-man front row was no longer practicable.

New Zealand could have fought this. Players and journalists argued that Ivor Jones had shown that a quick back row playing only a nominal part in scrums could be as obstructive and destructive as any Gallaher. The new rule proved almost unworkable in Britain, forcing IRB clarifications. This, though, was the New Zealand which still thought itself as 'A Better Britain', tied culturally and economically to London and which would say in 1939, through Labour premier Michael Savage, 'Where Britain goes, we go' and join immediately in declaring war on Germany.

British sporting leaders were meeting challenges with the outraged rigidity of those threatened by changing times. In 1931, rugby ejected the French. Cricket nearly did the same to Australia in 1933, outraged at Australian effrontery in describing bodyline bowling as 'unsporting'. British soccer had, echoing 1895, pulled out of FIFA in 1928 over broken-time payments, excluding itself from the first three World Cups. New Zealand wanted an All Black tour of Britain in the 1930s – Reade Masters, who had wanted to keep the seven-man scrum, wrote in 1935 in the first *New Zealand Rugby Almanac* that the concession's one redeeming feature was 'providing a glorious tour to the British Isles this season for some

29 fortunate players'. By 1935, the hooking rule had been re-amended, and there was no formal requirement for a three-man front row until 1951, so New Zealand might, as Masters urged, have resumed old practices. There was also, though, the memory of the two-man front row being exposed by South Africa's 3–4–1 in 1928. On 14 April 1932, an NZRFU vote ended the era of the two-man front row and the detached wing-forward.

As a society, New Zealand had never had it so good as in the mid to late 1930s. The Labour government elected in 1935 continued the national pattern of political innovation, creating the first welfare state a decade ahead of Britain. In 1939, an American economist calculated that New Zealand had the highest real-terms living standards in the world. On the rugby pitch, in a rare inversion, it had rarely had it so bad.

The 1935 team, led by Jack Manchester, found Britain and Ireland in an era of parity. Each of the four countries won the title in turn between 1933 and 1936. Scotland won fewer matches than anyone, nine, in eight seasons of four-team competition, yet still claimed Triple Crowns in 1933 and 1938. Manchester's team was not, by any except All Black standards, a failure. It lost only three matches out of twenty-eight but was roundly condemned and accused of over-socialising. The likelier explanation, according to Terry McLean, whose older brother Hugh was on the tour and an All Black for much of the decade, was lack of 'pushing power', as New Zealand worked through the implications – psychological as much as mechanical – of changing ingrained patterns.

Wales was still heavily bruised economically but recovering politically, the South Wales Miners' Federation showing renewed vitality after the brutal defeats of the 1920s. This renewal also applied on the field. Welsh rugby's one decent legacy from that miserable decade was the Secondary Schools Rugby Union set up in 1923. Every Welsh back against the 1935 All Blacks had played secondary schools rugby. While there were always exceptions – when Wales next played New Zealand in 1953 they had three forwards who had been to public school plus another who sounded as though he had and, in a glorious inversion of stereotype, the only coal miner was the All Black outside-half – this broad pattern of graduate backs, workers and policemen in the pack would serve Wales for much of the next half-century.

Some had more recent school rugby experience than others. New Zealand encountered scrum-half Haydn Tanner at Swansea, partnered by his cousin and fellow Gowerton Grammar School pupil Willie Davies. Swansea exploited All Black vulnerability by taking the option, available until 1939, of scrums instead of lineouts, Tanner displayed the speed and elasticity of youth combined with the judgement of a veteran and centre Claude Davey, 'a demoniac . . . volcanic force', scored two first-half tries.

Manchester's urging 'We can't lose this match; we're New Zealand!' prompted a teammate's response: 'Look at the bloody scoreboard, Skip.' Finally, it read Swansea 11 New Zealand 3, to this day the largest Welsh victory over the All Blacks. It made the 'All Whites' the first team to beat all three southern nations.

Davey, as captain, and Tanner both featured in the international, which Wales dominated and did their best to lose before winning 13–12. Giant centre Wilfred Wooller, said to be '10 ft. tall and take steps 10 yards long', had also been capped as a schoolboy, albeit a 20 year old returned to resit his Cambridge entrance, when Wales finally broke the Twickenham bogey in 1933. He kicked ahead, outstripped New Zealand cover and was thwarted by the bounce only for wing Geoffrey Rees-Jones, following up, to catch and score. Memorable in itself, but also a precise copy, with the same order of events and participants, of one of Wales's two earlier tries.

Further evidence of Welsh recovery was seen in the numbers travelling to away internationals. The biennial trip to Murrayfield exerted a particular fascination, with 18,000 Welsh rugby fans travelling in 1938. In 1934, a group of miners from Tylorstown who had chartered a plane to travel to the match got lost and ended up watching football in Portsmouth. They did better in 1935, reaching Belfast, where Ireland invariably hosted Wales, Ravenhill's spacious terraces being thought better suited to Wales's working-class fans than the larger grandstands of Lansdowne Road.

England entertained New Zealand in the middle of a run that produced only forty-six points in eight championship matches and not a single double-figure score but was still enough for a Triple Crown in 1937. Yorkshire journalist Jim Kilburn had initially dismissed a team led by all-rounder 'Tuppy' Owen-Smith, who played cricket for his native South Africa, as 'not incompetent but lacking initiative'. Low scoring gave way to an extraordinary 36-point explosion in Dublin in 1938, the highest score in the championship between Poulton-Palmer's swansong in 1914 and France's savage beating of 1972-vintage England.

Nothing that happened in Dublin was more extraordinary than the events at Twickenham in January 1936. Alexander Obolensky, an exceptionally quick wing born in pre-revolutionary St Petersburg, scored the only tries of a short England career as England won 13–0. The second was the collector's piece, an angled crossfield run defying all orthodoxy which took him from the right wing to cross only a few yards from the left-hand corner flag. Spiro Zavos has suggested that its sheer unorthodoxy was New Zealand's undoing:

New Zealand teams invariably play to a system. There is an Aristotelian logic about their game, whether in attack or defence. This makes them vulnerable on the rare occasions when they are confronted with something different from what they have planned to deal with.

Unexpectedness and context, a newsreel film record and Obolensky's romantic life story ingrained both try and scorer in collective memory. Objectively a minor figure, he is better remembered than any other player of his time. He was still awaiting naturalisation, causing the Prince of Wales (very soon, and briefly, to be Edward VIII) to ask him by what right he presumed to play for England. Scion of an ancient Russian family, Obolensky was probably the only person among 70,000 at Twickenham who regarded himself as the Prince's social equal and replied with hauteur, 'I attend Oxford University . . . *sir*.' A few months later, the Prince's younger brother (soon to be George VI), ill-briefed for his role as chief guest at an England match, would ask a nonplussed 'Jenny' Greenwood, by now RFU president, 'Do you pay your players well?' That might have earned a hollow laugh from former England full-back Tom Brown, suspended *sine die* three years earlier for talking to a league club. He did not play a match but accepted travelling expenses and was banned for the somewhat Orwellian offence of 'discussing the advantages of Rugby League'. Brown's family say that he never saw a game of league until he bought his first television in 1954. When Major Stanley, the wartime connoisseur of rugby-league talent, invited players from his invitation teams to his 70th birthday celebrations, Brown was the only one of 15 Bristol players eligible not invited.

George VI was fortunate his faux pas was at Twickenham rather than Murrayfield. Some years earlier, his father George V asked Aikman Smith why players were not numbered – Wales and England's practice since 1921. Aikman Smith, monarch of Murrayfield whatever pertained elsewhere, retorted that 'this is a game for gentlemen, not a cattle market'. Aikman Smith died in 1931, taken ill on the train taking the Scottish team to their match against Wales. The All Blacks' return to play Scotland after a 30-year hiatus found them in the middle of the desperate run, two wins in four seasons, that separated their Triple Crowns of 1933 and 1938. Murrayfield, though, was still a thing of wonder – Kilburn was impressed not only by its size, but the noise accompanying Scottish forward drives:

> a low-pitched growl ... swells into a full-throated roar in which the one word 'feet' is distinguishable ... with every yard progressed by the players the roar grows louder and stronger, yet always deepening, so that there is no impression of imminent climax ... this is a sound as long-drawn and steady as the sound of a waterfall, which for all its crashing and thundering has a constant note.

It was, however, insufficient to intimidate the All Blacks, who won 18–8 with wing Pat Caughey, an executive in the family department store in Auckland, scoring a hat-trick. Scotland's happiest hour came in 1938 at Twickenham. It was the first rugby match to be televised, albeit to a miniscule London-area audience offered a postcard-sized image. An England team fresh from that record beating of Ireland were themselves dismantled by Scotland's outside-half Wilson Shaw, who scored twice – five tries to one a better reflection of the game than a 21–16 scoreline.

For the first time since 1899, Ireland had greeted the All Blacks as outright champions, but they also went down with New Zealand having something to spare in a match refereed by Billy Jeffares, son (and successor-to-be) of IRFU secretary Rupert Jeffares. Ulster achieved what the national team would not until 1973, holding the visitors to a draw at Ravenhill.

In 1937, New Zealand entertained South Africa for the first time in 16 years. The Springboks had made few friends but certainly influenced people on their 1931–32 tour of Britain, relying on forward control and the remorseless kicking of Osler. Collins wrote that they seemed bent on 'a lesson in the art and mystery of cross-punting', while Sewell thought Osler's performance as an outside-half 'a conspicuous failure'. Yet O.L. Owen of *The Times* noted his ability to 'plant the ball exactly in the spot most awkward for the other side'. For the second time, South Africa beat all four home nations and conjured some memorable moments. Gerry Brand, the latest of their monster kickers, landed an 85-yard penalty at Twickenham while Phil Nel initiated a dribbling rush on the Springbok line at Swansea that ended with lock Ferdie Bergh touching down at the other end. Osler himself, of whom it had been said 'he could never *make* his three-quarters or ever seemed to want to', admitted that he was below his best but insisted that he was playing to his team's strengths. His point was made most effectively on the worst day of his career, the second of a five-test series – a borrowing from cricket soon returned minus interest – against Australia in 1933. After kicking the Wallabies to destruction in the first test, he ran in the second. Equipped with a tough but speedy pack in which Aub Hodgson matched Cerutti for rugged combativeness, the Wallabies won 21–6. Point made, Osler tightened up again to ensure the Boks won the next two matches before dropping the last.

Non-white South African rugby revived after struggling in the 1920s – there had been no post-war Rhodes Cup until 1928, and several Cape Town clubs went under, although Roslyns and Violets survived to greet a new wave in the 1930s. Among the newcomers, Young Stars and Caledonian Roses from 1936 staged an annual Charity Rag match which rapidly became a significant social event, attracting stylish and festive crowds of up to 10,000. The Rhodes Cup again became a regular event.

The 1938 tournament in Cape Town inspired an internal tour the following year by a representative team – green-blazered and calling themselves Springboks – which went well enough for talk of an overseas tour, but it was aborted by the war. The foundation of the South African Bantu Rugby Union – this time in Port Elizabeth rather than Kimberley, but with its first tournament there – in 1935 was evidence of growing interest among the black population. The Cape Town Malays, 'row upon row of fezzes' in their designated stands at Newlands, were reckoned by Springbok Danie Craven to be the most knowledgeable supporters in the world. Possession of a fez was not always, though, an asset. The non-white unions were influenced by the increasing segregation of the time – the Native Representation Act of 1936 removed the last few black voters. Huge amounts of City and Suburban Union energy were devoted in 1937 to determining whether Gustav Ferreira, alleged to have been seen in a fez, was a Muslim and therefore ineligible. Found guilty as charged, he was banned.

Afrikaner consciousness continued to grow. The Bible was translated into Afrikaans in 1933 and the National Party formed in the same year, while the centenary re-enactment of the Great Trek in 1938 and the construction of the Voortrekker Monument near Pretoria continued and speeded momentum. So too did the rugby output of Stellenbosch University under the direction of A.F. 'Oubaas' Markotter, an obsessive who declared 'my politics and religion are rugby' and was prone to striking players but had an extraordinary gift for spotting and developing talent. Stellenbosch produced 130 players for Western Province and 53 Springboks in his 45 years as coach. His star pupil was Craven, whom he had helped send to Britain as a surprise – and wholly justified – first choice as scrum-half in 1931–32. Craven was still around in 1937 with other high-quality holdovers like Nel, now captain, Brand and 'Boy' Louw, whose gift for mangled English – congratulating teammate Dai Owen Williams on being chosen to play against Wales 'because his father was a whale' – his second language, has slightly obscured the smart, ruthless and versatile forward capped in four different positions. Craven matched that achievement in four consecutive matches against Australia. He played centre then scrum-half in the final two tests in 1933, then fly-half and number 8 in the two tests played in 1937 (with an appearance at full-back against Queensland in between) as the Boks passed through Australia, renewing acquaintance with Hodgson in another contender for 'roughest test of all time', en route to New Zealand.

New Zealand won the first test, but South Africa levelled at Christchurch. In the decider, South Africa, who received a telegram from Roos reading '*skrum, skrum, skrum*', did just that, emulating the example set by Swansea in 1935 in choosing scrums instead of lineouts. Craven, famous for introducing the dive-pass into international rugby, exploited All Black fear of it after half-time with South Africa already 8–3 up. He waved outside-half Tony Harris wider and wider, drawing opposite number Dave Trevathan with him. He then flicked out a short pass to wing Freddie Turner, running at an angle through the gap, creating a try for centre Louis Babrow, an observant Jew who squared playing on Yom Kippur with his conscience by reasoning, 'I'm a South African Jew, and the match will finish before Yom Kippur starts in South Africa.' South Africa's victory by 17–6 is less obviously impressive than the Durban whitewash of 1928, but it was on New Zealand soil and contained five tries against none by the All Blacks.

Almost the only relief afforded New Zealand came from regular meetings with the restored Australians, played from 1931 for the Bledisloe Cup, presented by a none-too-popular governor-general who knew little about rugby but recognised a good populist gesture. The Cup spent most of its time in New Zealand custody, as the All Blacks won eight out of eleven matches, but it had a two-year cross-Tasman trip from 1934, when Australia won one match and drew the other, their last home series win over New Zealand for 45 years.

At one level, Australian rugby remained narrowly based. Bodis has classified 58 of the 96 men who played for Australia between 1929 and 1938 as upper middle class, and only two as working class. At other levels, it was diversifying. The Queenslanders were back in numbers, reflecting the strength of a state team coached and selected by King Rennick, previously the inspiration of the remarkable Toowoomba rugby league teams of the 1920s. There were Victorians – the team of 1938 was the last until 1996 to represent three states – including Edward 'Weary' Dunlop, who, during the first test victory of 1934, showed something of the spirit that would make him the medical hero of the Changi prisoner-of-war camp. His nose was broken but he continued, at half-time splinting the break by breaking a toothbrush handle into two parts and stuffing them up his nostrils. Australia also fielded their first aboriginal player in 1938. Some sources believe this historical first was claimed by John 'Blondie' Howard, who played the first two tests of the series, but there are doubts over his ethnicity. There are none about Cecil Ramalli, son of an aborigine mother and an Indian father who started working life as a camel driver and ended it running a 27,000-acre sheep property. He played the second and third tests.

At least New Zealand's decade finished on a note of good cheer, brought by the Fijian tourists of 1939, returning a visit by the Maoris a year earlier. Laqeretabua had played his last match in 1938, but the successor generation, still mostly barefoot, dazzled Kiwi fans as they won seven and drew the other of their eight matches. The tour culminated in a 14–4 defeat of the Maoris, which the *Waikato Times* reckoned the best display of rugby seen in Hamilton for years, with the Fijians 'Almost uncanny in handling the ball, lightning in the pace of their sprinting, relentless in their dive-tackling . . . and all the time pursuing methods of bright, open football.'

The All Blacks did not play France in 1935, because they had been excommunicated four years earlier. France's difficulties were brought to a head by six clubs: Stade Français, Stade Bordelais, Toulouse, Bayonne, Perpignan and Racing Club. Joined by several other clubs, they set up the Union Française de Rugby Amateur (UFRA), 'devoted to the ideals of fair play and friendship' in January 1931. While the UFRA lasted only 15 months, it prompted the home unions into action, seeking information from the Federation and the new group. The new group's complaints about foul play and thinly veiled professionalism helped seal France's excommunication from international rugby, pronounced on 13 February.

Coming in mid-season, it left England with a diplomatically tricky trip to Paris. The English team were booed onto the pitch, Freethy – in his last international – disallowed two English tries and France won 14–13. England's players misbehaved at the dinner, Stoop made an interminable speech and the evening was saved by England captain Carl Aarvold, who was, in journalist E.W. Swanton's words, 'not only gracious in defeat, but fluent in French, a rare combination'.

Domestically, France saw a shift in regional balance, with unprecedented success for the south-east. Toulon beat Lyon in the 1931 final, Lyon won for the next two seasons and Vienne took a title in 1937. There was also a serious challenge from rugby league after 1934, with Jean Galia, a veteran of the Quillan club (which fell away when Bourrel spent four months in a coma following a car crash), as its leading light. By 1939, the French Rugby League had 434 clubs, compared to the FFR's 471 (down from 784 in 1930), its championship-final gate receipts were marginally ahead and it had beaten England away, a feat as yet beyond union.

Internationally, France turned in the only direction it could, to Continental Europe. This meant a decade of matches against nations of limited appeal either as opponents or politically: Fascist Italy, authoritarian-monarchy Romania, and Germany, Nazi from 1933. It led, though, to the formation in 1934 of the French-led Fédération Internationale de Rugby Amateur (FIRA), in time a countervailing force against the anglophone introversion of the IRB. Other founder members were Germany, Italy, Romania, Czechoslovakia (whose union was founded in 1926), Belgium (1931), the Netherlands (1932), Sweden (1931) and, in one of their periods of dispute with the central Spanish body, Catalonia.

In Italy, the game regained official favour when pro-rugby Achille Starace replaced volata-enthusiast Augusto Turati as Fascist Party secretary in 1931. In the following year, the Federation was reformed as the Federazione Italiana de Palla Ovale (Oval Ball), while the game was introduced into military academies and a university championship started. The word 'rugby' and the original FIR title were reinstated in 1933. Italian enthusiasm for international links prompted a letter to the home unions in 1932 suggesting the creation of an international body like those already in existence in football, motor racing and motorcycling:

Owing to the non-existence of an International Federation . . . the spreading of the sport of Rugby is handicapped, being impossible to properly coordinate the technical side of the game and difficult to arrange international matches, besides many other important reasons.

They suggested a meeting to set up a federation, offering, to the IRB's great amusement, to host it in Italy. The IRB denied being such a body itself – defining its duties as framing laws and controlling games under the four home unions – and told the Italians that they did 'not see the formation of such a body as either workable or desirable'.

Germany, though, ranked second to France for most of the 1930s, beating them in Frankfurt in 1938 and generally having the edge on the other nations in FIRA tournaments. Perhaps the most notable was held in conjunction with the 1936 Berlin Olympics. Italy and Romania were eliminated in the semi-finals, and France then beat Germany 19–14 in the final. It was, Ian Buchanan has pointed out, by some margin the best-organised Olympic rugby tournament, but it was classified only as a demonstration sport, leaving the USA their quiz-question status as the reigning champions. At the other end of the political spectrum, the Soviet Union's first national championship was won by Moscow Dynamo in 1934. In Morocco, where French colonists had been playing since the 1920s, the first native players arrived with two young men joining the Casablanca club in 1935.

Elsewhere, Canada and Japan responded to geographical logic with the first intercontinental tours between non-traditional nations, Japan going to British Columbia in 1930 and the Canadians reciprocating in 1932. Geography also made picking a proper Canadian team highly difficult, so selection committees for British Columbia, the prairies and the east nominated quotas. Meeting in Vancouver, they had a training session and three practice matches before leaving but had lost four balls overboard and been struck down by seasickness before reaching Honolulu. Even so, the Canadians won five of their first six matches before going down 38–5 to All-Japan in front of a crowd of 25,000, a defeat ascribed to 'excessive entertaining, too many games in a short period and the inspired play of the Japanese before the assembled nobility of Japan'. Two years later, Australian universities lost to Keio and Waseda before crowds of around 20,000.

In the United States, rugby continued to sit outside official structures in the universities. As Tim Chandler has pointed out, this lost it resources and status but kept it free of the domination of coaches and athletic departments and gave it an anti-authoritarian appeal. New York RFC was founded in 1929 and received RFU affiliation in 1932, two years before the Eastern Rugby Union was set up. A Southern California union formed in 1933 with a committee including actor Boris Karloff – in private life an English cricket enthusiast named Pratt – was hit by the embezzlement of most of its funds. The Midwest Union formed in 1932 was both active and colourful – while a powerful Chicago Rugby Club team featuring several top-class American footballers demoralised local opposition into inactivity, St Louis saw its first games in 1933 on a pitch where 'the grass . . . was so high that play was greatly impeded. The park authorities could not be persuaded to cut it for some time' and John Hoogewerf, a professor at St Louis University, concluded his pre-match talk with the instruction 'If your shorts are ripped off while running with the ball, keep running, for many a naked man has scored a try.'

Naked men were less welcome in Argentina, where San Isidro, finally displaced as champions in 1931, were suspended after players stripped at an after-match dinner in 1934. Jurado returned from disfavour to captain Argentina's first tour three years later, a hop across the Andes to neighbouring Chile, whose union was formed in 1935, to help celebrate the 400th anniversary of Valparaiso. Argentina won both matches. The Argentina v. Foreigners match was dropped in 1935 due to increasing difficulties raising the foreign team, but names like Gordon Buckley, Keith Bush and Victor Harris-Smith in the outstanding Old Georgians teams of the late 1930s – coached by 'Catamarca' Ocampo, who had translated Wakefield's *Rugger* and Gallaher and Stead's *The Complete Rugby Footballer in the New Zealand System* into Spanish and from them distilled the principles of scrummaging that would serve Argentina remarkably well – suggested life in the *extranjero* yet.

The war ended the British game's spell of four-team domesticity, a 9–6 England victory in the 1939 Calcutta Cup match giving them a three-way share of the title with Ireland and Wales. Had there been a 1940 championship, France would have been back in – finally readmitted in July 1939 after they had agreed, by a 315–154 vote at their annual congress, to abolish their club championship – a move they had been warned in March was not an absolute prerequisite of readmission but would certainly help. Whether the French would have agreed to this, or the home unions to their reinstatement, if anyone had really believed in July 1939 that there would be a 1940 season is a matter of doubt. Carwyn James and John Reason

# EARLY DAYS

Hand-off: England captain Frederic Alderson breaks out of defence against Scotland at Raeburn Place in 1892.

Wallace adds to his collection: All Black full-back Billy Wallace scores one of his 27 tries on the 1905–06 tour of Britain with Gloucester helpless to halt him. (© New Zealand Museum of Rugby)

# BEFORE THE GREAT WAR

Welsh Gold: The Wales team that played France in 1910, including
Trew (holding ball) and Owen (on ground, left).

*Victoire Française*: Captain François Communeau forms the centrepiece
of a magazine photo spread celebrating France's first ever victory,
over Scotland in 1911.

# PARIS IN THE '20s

America the unexpected: Action from the 1924 Olympic
final, in which USA beat hosts and favourites France.

Irish fire: An Irish forward drives for the line against
France in Paris 1925.

# MID-CENTURY MARVELS

'Absolutely buggered': Peter Jones completes his match-winning score for New Zealand against South Africa in 1956. (© *New Zealand Herald*)

The Miracle of Lourdes: Jean Prat (right) leads his Lourdes team out for the 1957 French championship final against Racing Club de France, captained by his long-time national team colleague Gerard Dufau (left). (© Offside/*L'Equipe*)

# FORCES OF NATURE

Colin Meads, personification of All Blackness, on the charge against
Wales, complete with high-class supporting cast – (L to R) Allan Stewart,
Wilson Whineray, Waka Nathan and Kel Tremain. Dewi Bebb is the
solitary Welshman. (© New Zealand Museum of Rugby)

Gareth Edwards hands off All Black Bob Burgess for the 1971 British
Lions, watched by a distinguished audience – (L to R) Mike Gibson,
Barry John and J.P.R. Williams. (© *Dominion Post*)

# FLYING KIWIS

Air raid: Anti-apartheid protestor Marx Jones makes one of his 62 passes over Eden Park as the All Blacks and Springboks play on in the final test of their 1981 series. (© *New Zealand Herald*)

'Not exactly your conventional winger': Jonah Lomu scores against Scotland. (© New Zealand Rugby Union)

# DEVELOPING WORLD

Germany (white shirts) look for the ball in their World Cup qualifier against Spain (red) at Heidelberg in 1998. (© Huw Richards)

Mexican players contest possession, 1999. (© Huw Richards)

# MASTERS OF THE UNIVERSE

Monarch of all he surveys: England's World Cup-winning captain
Martin Johnson dominates a lineout in the semi-final
against France. (© Offside/*L'Equipe*)

South African fans celebrate their 2007 World Cup victory in Paris.
(© John Richards)

suggest that if the demands made by the home unions in March had been carried through in France, there would have been nobody left eligible to play.

War came at the start of September, traditionally the start of the season. While the problems of a few rugby players did not amount to much in a demonstrably crazy world, the visiting Wallabies, who had left Australia on 21 July for their first tour of Britain for 30 years and arrived in time to do little more than hear Neville Chamberlain's speech and fill sandbags for civil defence while waiting for the boat home – a not entirely reassuring prospect given the sinking of the *Athenia* by a submarine on the first day of the war – were entitled to feel unlucky. Nine of them never would play test rugby.

## CHAPTER EIGHT

# Once More Unto the Breach

'In wartime, there was considerable virtue in men who played
rugby like professionals to win and not, like public schoolboys,
for exercise'

John Mulgan (1947)

This was different. There was little exultation. Joining up was a
weary acceptance of duty, informed by knowledge of where the
innocent enthusiasm of 1914 had led. The reaction of sporting
bodies was also coloured by memories 25 years old. British soccer
closed more rapidly than rugby, suspending its league programmes
on 8 September, while the RFU waited until the 15th and the Welsh
until the 25th to issue suspension notices.

Twickenham was requisitioned, the East car park used as
allotments, the West as a coal dump and offices, changing-rooms
and referee's room taken over by civil defence. The West Stand
was damaged by a bomb blast in 1944 and the ground returned to
the RFU in September 1945. Murrayfield became a supply depot,
Cardiff Arms Park's North Stand was devastated and its terraces
damaged by a bomb in 1941 and the Reddings, Moseley RFC's
ground, became a potato patch.

Rugby did not stop, though. An unofficial season was under way
almost as soon as the official one had been cancelled. The ban
on rugby league players was lifted in England and Wales on 14
November 1939, although the Scottish Rugby Union pointedly
retained it. In February 1940, cross-channel rapprochement was
made combative flesh by a British Army team beating France
36–3 in Paris. Wooller, in his last match, scored a hat-trick. A
charity international for the Red Cross was played the following
month at Cardiff in front of 40,000 spectators, England beating

146

Wales 18–9. This was still the time of the so-called 'phoney war'.

Distressing reality was signalled by the first death of an international player. Obolensky – following through the implications of voting to 'serve King and country', when the Oxford Union had famously voted against – was killed in a flying accident at the end of March 1940. He had admitted he found landing the toughest part of flying, while persistent rumour suggests that he was – with the over-confidence of the physically gifted – practising ill-judged aerobatics. Either way, his early death sealed a romantic legend.

By the autumn of 1940, with the worst British fears of invasion stilled but France conquered, there were enough New Zealand troops in Britain for an Expeditionary Force XV to start a programme of matches. Later in the war, New Zealand was invaded, but not in the manner feared. As James Belich has put it, 'New Zealand expected 100,000 Japanese. Instead, it got 100,000 Americans.' They proved amenable to local custom. Journalist Fred Boshier later wrote of a team of Marines who entered local competitions in Wellington. They had no kicking game, and struggled predictably with the ball on the ground, but were a different proposition with it in their hands:

> The single-handed spiral throw which is standard drill in gridiron football moves the ball in a flash halfway across the field. Also the criss-cross running with the ball slipped from one player to another, or with the transfer no more than a feint, added up to possibilities which a country like New Zealand might have investigated to the full.

New Zealand went to war willingly and united. Not so South Africa. A number of Springboks distinguished themselves in the war, including 'Boy' Louw, who served in the Western Desert, and Danie Craven, who created a physical training battalion in the South African Army. A sizeable proportion of the Afrikaner population was, though, opposed. The Western Province Rugby Union split in 1943, when some clubs, with Stellenbosch students particularly vociferous, objected to playing matches for war charities.

In occupied France, the collaborationist Vichy regime headed by Marshal Pétain displayed a loathing of professional sport worthy of the Scottish Rugby Union. All professionalism was anathema, and rugby league was suppressed, the decree signed personally by Pétain on 19 December 1941. With the help of sports minister Jean Borotra, the Wimbledon champion known as 'the Bounding Basque', rugby union was, as Phil Dine has said, 'settling old scores' from the battles of the 1930s. Borotra's first step towards suppression was his decision to ask Paul Voivenel – author of the 'King of Matches' account from 1914 and now a noisily enthusiastic Pétainist propagandist – to prepare a report on the relationship between the codes. Voivenel denied the legitimacy of league, arguing that it was a job rather than a game, even if not played for money. Borotra was succeeded in 1942 by Joseph 'Jep' Pascot, a Perpignan outside-half capped seven times in the 1920s, the last in that embarrassing 1927 defeat by Germany. His own club were immediate beneficiaries of enforced reunification, winning the revived French championship in 1944 with the assistance of an astonishingly gifted league player named Puig-Aubert.

French rugby union was not without committed resisters, although Jean-Louis Gay-Lescot's research suggests they were a distinct minority. Jacques Chaban-Delmas, who played for France in the pre-war FIRA tournaments, launched a political career that would make him prime minister of France (a Romanian opponent in 1937, Ion Papa, also became prime minister of his country) as a resistance leader and close associate of Charles de Gaulle. Referee Gilbert Brutus died under torture, without talking. One of many legends surrounding Alfred Roques, the Cahors prop so integral to French success in the late '50s and early '60s, was that he provided food to resisters by carrying the carcasses of entire bullocks on his back across hill country.

Eight French internationals, including Geo Andre, died. Allan Muhr, the American who played in France's first three matches in 1906 and 1907, was arrested by the Gestapo and died in a concentration camp. They were among 70 international players who are known to have fallen – the smaller number than in the First World War reflecting that, while millions of innocent bystanders died, there were fewer directly military casualties. Fourteen played for England – Obolensky was followed by Gerry Gerrard of Bath, a fellow three-quarter against the All Blacks in 1936. Wing George Hart, left out of that match for staying too late at a New Year's party, was one of two All Blacks who died. Among the fallen were also fifteen Scots, seven Irishmen, three Welshmen – including Maurice Turnbull, who had also played cricket for England – ten Australians and three Romanians. The nation hit hardest was Germany, which lost sixteen international players, including three of the team who beat France in 1938: Helmut Bonecke, Fritz Dopke and Karl Hubsch.

In Britain, club fortunes varied. Swansea and Gloucester closed down. Coventry won 72 consecutive matches between 1941 and 1945. Service internationals began in 1942. When Wales beat England in March 1942 at Swansea, 14 of their points were scored by league players, while 23 of England's 29 points against Scotland a year later came from the same source. Bleddyn Williams, a prodigious teenage Welsh talent at the time, has forever since paid tribute to the help he received from league players like Risman and Willie Davies, Tanner's half-back confrère of 1935, who had joined Bradford Northern. Spectators at Swansea were amazed by the sight of Risman attacking from full-back. League players found the matches rewarding as well. Risman, presenting his expenses as an amateur after one Wales match, was nonplussed to be told they were wrong and mildly amazed to be handed £8 rather than the £4 he had claimed. Two inter-code matches were played, at Headingley in January 1943 and Bradford in April 1944. Both were played under union rules, but league won on each occasion. Two RFU secretaries-to-be, Robin Prescott and Bob Weighill, were among the losers at Bradford.

As in the first war, Commonwealth troops added greatly to both the war effort and forces rugby. Former naval commander Bob Stuart, returning to Britain as captain of the All Blacks in 1953, said in his first after-match speech that he had 'many pleasant associations with Brighton and Hove, and I hope they are all married now'. Bob Scott, the outstanding player in that team, said that his real rugby education came in the quality of rugby played by the thousands of young men thrown together in the forces. Where New Zealanders encountered South Africans, whether in the streets of Cairo, Italian farmlands or a London pub, it was common for impromptu scrummages to form. In a more formal trial of strength, South African Services won a proto-Tri Nations in the autumn and winter of 1944–5, with three wins to two by the Royal Australian Air Force and one by New Zealand Forces. In 1945, a South African Sixth Division team including Springbok captain-to-be Stephen Fry embarked on a four-month tour through nine countries, losing only twice and drawing a crowd of 18,000 when they played a student team in Paris.

The liberation of Paris had been celebrated on Armistice Day, 11 November 1944, by the rekindling of the flame of remembrance at the Arc de Triomphe in the presence of de Gaulle and Churchill and a match between the RAF and French Services at the Parc des Princes. French captain Chaban-Delmas, emerging from undercover, scored two tries, but the RAF won 26–6 in front of 20,000. French reintegration continued with a New Year's Day victory over the British Army in Paris, then a first visit to Britain in 14 years a week before VE Day to play Empire Services at Richmond.

The 1945–46 season was one of transition. Its most remarkable events took place in Japan, which had been traumatised by defeat and two atomic bombs. Rugby in the country had survived a campaign against Western sports in the 1930s – defensively rebranding itself *tokyu*, 'fighting ball' – and had continued until 1943, when the military control of pitches, the absence of young men fighting abroad and the general disruption became too much. It revived with staggering rapidity after the war ended on 15 August. Shigeru 'Shiggy' Konno, the Japanese game's dominant post-war figure, recalled being in Hokkaido at the beginning of September 1945. A newspaper advertisement invited rugby players to a meeting. More than 50 turned up, and a match was arranged. A schools match was played in Kyoto as early as 23 September, while Kobe Steel was encouraging the game among its workers – prefiguring the increasing role of companies in Japanese rugby – by the end of 1945, believing it would be good for morale and encourage cooperation.

A full Five Nations programme of Victory Internationals was played during the season. Yet perhaps the most significant domestic contest was outside the tournament – Ireland's win in the fifth and last of a series of matches against the Army that had started in 1942 featured two young doctors, an outside-half from Ulster named Jack Kyle and a hooker from Dublin called Karl Mullen.

The most remembered action of the season concerned the New Zealand Armed Forces team, the Kiwis. Assembled on the initiative of New Zealand Division commander Bernard Freyberg, who had played for Horowhenua before the First World War, they were instructed to play bright, attacking rugby regardless of the outcome. While the New Zealand Division were regarded as efficient rather than punctiliously obedient soldiers, they applied this order to the letter under the leadership of 1938 All Black Charles Saxton, whose motto was that 'rugby is 14 men combining to put the 15th clear'. They beat England 18–3, then Wales 11–3 at the bomb-damaged Arms Park. Wing Jim Sherratt took a pass shin-high 65 yards out and somehow contrived both to maintain his hold and outpace Welsh cover, roared home by the commentary of Winston McCarthy, whose voice – likened by Tony O'Reilly to 'the mating call of two pieces of sandpaper' – formed a soundtrack for post-war New Zealand much as cricket's John Arlott did for England. The Kiwis lost to Scotland, but nearly 30 years later journalist John Billot credited them with 'audience appeal exceeding all the New Zealand teams who have followed them to Wales'. Sixteen of them, including Sherratt and Scott, who had played league until he was 19 and was close to returning home from his billet in Austria when his reinstatement came through, would become All Blacks.

**CHAPTER NINE**

# From Muller to Mias

'Hennie Muller? Dear, dear ...'

John Gwilliam (2002)

'Like finding the South Africans or All Blacks on one's doorstep'

H.B. Toft on French success (1959)

New Zealand entered the post-war era with optimism. Aside from the dash and dazzle of the Kiwis, a fearsome Otago provincial team was refining the ruck under the guidance of coach Vic Cavanagh. Devised for the soft grounds of the South Island, it involved inviting the tackle then, when the ball went to ground, driving in unison over it (and anyone down there too) in order to, in Winston McCarthy's words, 'start all over again until the defences were breached'. Opponents were battered physically and psychologically. Bleddyn Williams would recall of the beating of the 1950s Lions by Otago, 'I had never seen anything like their rucking in my life before, and neither had any of our forwards,' and suggested that the psychological impact contributed to New Zealand's victory in the test series.

Otago held the Ranfurly Shield between 1947 and 1950 and supplied 11 members to the All Black team who toured South Africa in 1949. New Zealand were so confident of their strength that they simultaneously sent another team to Australia, a consolation prize for those who had just missed the main trip and also for the team's Maori players. They had been excluded once more at the behest of South Africa, where the National Party, which would systematise segregation into apartheid in the following years, had been elected in 1948. The team sent to South Africa was, like its predecessor of

1928, widely advertised as New Zealand's best ever. Once again, the predictions were wildly off-target. South Africa won the series 4–0, and two defeats in Australia gave New Zealand a melancholy distinction as the first country to play – and to lose – two tests on the same day.

There were several reasons for failure in South Africa. (Decadence in Kiwi manhood can be discounted, even if the Ponsonby club introduced warm showers in 1947.) The All Blacks had been chosen the season before – ample time to lose form or gain weight. Cavanagh should have been coach, but he fell victim to NZRFU politics. Selector Alec McDonald, a veteran of 1905 still rooted in the 2–3–2 era, got the job but was ignored by the players. Long overnight railway journeys, a potent South African weapon, left players tired and irritated – although not nearly as irked as by home-town refereeing.

South Africa's scrummaging power was complemented by the new technique of hookers binding loosely to their props and swinging towards the entrance to the scrum, making it all but impossible for their opposite number to contest possession. Former All Black coach J.J. Stewart saw this as the beginning of the end for the scrum as a contest, while flankers packed very wide, enabling extremely quick ball. The Springboks had also refined the lineout, placing blockers behind and in front of the jumper. Craven, by now Springbok coach, offered the tourists a much-publicised coaching session on scrummaging. All Black prop Kevin Skinner remains angry more than half a century later, dismissing it as a publicity stunt and arguing that a front row of himself, Has Catley and Johnny Simpson – still remembered as one of New Zealand's finest – was more than holding its own by the end of the series.

Skinner also believes that New Zealand would have won with neutral referees. The scoring details present a case to answer. New Zealand scored more tries than their opponents in three of the four matches, and four tries to three in total, yet lost all four. The penalty count was ten to two in favour of South Africa. Scott points out that the penalties he attempted tended to be from long distance while Springbok Aaron 'Okey' Geffin, a Jewish prop who had perfected his skills in a prisoner-of-war camp in Poland, was normally kicking close to the All Black posts, evidence of an edge in pressure and possession.

What nobody denies is the effectiveness of South Africa's back-row tactics, incarnated in the astonishingly quick and ruthless Hennie Muller, of whom McCarthy wrote, 'He was here, there, everywhere, both on attack and defence.' In particular, he exploited the lack of limitations on lineout positioning to stand opposite the All Black five-eighths and run at them aggressively. Instead of worrying about their opposite numbers, Stewart wrote, midfield attackers now faced a player:

Whose every intention was to arrive on him at the same time as the ball, to tackle him in the hardest way humanly possible and to initiate a ruck over him, or toe the ball ahead once it had spilled from his hands, or to pick up the ball and run with it or pass it. And this player was never more than one to three yards away.

Terry McLean may, uncharacteristically, have been exaggerating when he wrote of this as:

The great watershed of international rugby. On the rear slope lay the great backs and back-plays. On the forward slope lay intense forward effort, domination of ground by touch-kicking and deliberate stifling of back-line initative by the posting of loose forwards operating from cruelly advantageous positions.

The 1930s had hardly been a festival of open rugby – Wales won the championship in 1936 by scoring only sixteen points, with all of their three tries in a single match. Nevertheless, a pattern was set for the 1950s – low-scoring, discontinuous matches dominated by aggressive loose forwards like Muller and Wales's Clem Thomas, who remembered having 'a license to kill outside-halfs' and was jokingly accused of practising his profession – butcher – on the rugby field. Stewart recalled, 'It was virtually impossible to make progress from set play by carrying the ball and passing it among the backs.' There were, in Stewart's words, 'almost annual rule changes', but this only made penalty goals more frequent. There had been more than four tries for every penalty in the none-too-expansive '30s. By the late 1950s, the ratio was less than one and a half to one.

There is an inherent drama in low-scoring matches – every

score matters – and there were outbreaks of brilliant open play, but a decade characterised politically by comfortable, prosperous conservatism – Sid Holland in New Zealand, Robert Menzies in Australia, Eisenhower in the USA and Tory domination in Britain – was one of defensive, low-risk rugby.

South Africa beat all four home nations in 1951–52, adding France for good measure, and made the most conspicuous breach of the low-scoring rule: a legendary, demoralising 44–0 demolition of Scotland. They were followed two years later by the All Blacks, the first tour party to travel by air. The increasing ease and availability of air travel, with Canadian Pacific introducing jets from Vancouver to Auckland in 1954, would transform not only rugby touring but New Zealand life as a whole. All Black captain Bob Stuart was horrified by his first sight of a British club match: 'We were amazed by how much offside play and killing the ball were tolerated. It meant you could not get the ball fairly at the breakdown and that outside-halfs were battered to hell.' His team had a powerful pack, in which Skinner and lock Richard 'Tiny' White – a genial, articulate middleman between the unsmiling Brownlie and Meads in New Zealand's succession of mobile ball-handling giants – attained legendary status and pacy, astute flanker Bill Clark barely fell short. Scott, 'several principles in himself', according to a reporter who perceived a team still seeking its first principles, combined attacking instincts with the innate spatial awareness of a great footballer and a ferocious competitiveness that reduced him to tears over major defeats. Hennie Muller called him 'the greatest footballer I have played against in any position'. In keeping with the times, the All Blacks scored only four tries, none by backs, in five test matches.

Post-war European rugby was first dominated by Ireland. While comedian Dave Allen had a point in remonstrating with an Englishman who blamed the war and rationing for defeat in Dublin in 1949, 'They knock the crap out of the German Army and couldn't out of 15 Irishmen,' Irish and South African success suggests that countries which were spared rationing, and whose players had fought from choice rather than conscription, had an advantage. Ireland also had, as ever, a highly serviceable pack – Mullen as hooker and captain and open-side Jim McCarthy were considerably more than that – and the extraordinary all-round gifts of Jack Kyle at outside-half. He was a quietly religious, literate man – he enchanted McLean by taking a copy of *The Rubaiyat of Omar Khayyam* on the 1950 Lions tour of New Zealand – whose unobtrusiveness was a trap that caught adversaries of the quality of Wales's Cliff Morgan, debutant against Ireland in 1951: 'Just when I had been lulled into a false sense of security, Jack suddenly took off and went past to score a try, which saved the game.' He could dazzle as well, in 1953 scoring a try with 'a fiesta of sidesteps' so brilliant that French defenders applauded him.

Ireland's ascendancy brought their only Grand Slam to date in 1948, followed by championships in 1949 and 1951. It gave way to Wales, who were to average three wins per year from 1950 to 1956. Led by Bleddyn Williams, the jinking prodigy turned elder statesman, and including his Cromwellian, cerebral predecessor John Gwilliam and lineout specialist Roy John, who was said 'to do the Indian rope trick without the rope', Wales beat New Zealand in 1953 for the third time in four visits. Wales trailed for much of the match but drew level at 8–8 then won in a straight contest between the world's leading wingers when Ken Jones, an Olympic sprinter with football skills, beat opposite number Ron Jarden to a cross-kick from Clem Thomas. Had the bounce favoured Jarden, he would probably have scored.

The post-war years produced huge crowds for spectator sport in Britain. Pre-professional rugby union rarely recorded precise gates, but there is no doubt it was a part of this trend. The brilliant Cardiff team built around Bleddyn Williams attracted massive audiences, peaking at 48,500 in 1951 for the derby against Newport and 40,000 at Swansea in 1952. English club gates were smaller – an admittedly retrospective survey in the late 1950s suggested that clubs like Bristol, Leicester and Gloucester attracted crowds of around 5,000. The balance of power this created was reflected in the 1951–52 season when *Rugger* magazine calculated, 'Welsh clubs won 46 of 54 meetings between leading clubs, including all 25 in Wales.'

There was a vital difference in structure. In England, the largest crowds, and the route to international and administrative preferment, came via the counties. In 1947, more than 15,000 saw Gloucestershire v. Middlesex and 19,000 Lancashire, beginning a run of three consecutive titles, against Leicestershire.

How well this served England is debatable. Clem Thomas remembered leading Welsh players falling about laughing at English selections. Northampton flanker Don White recalled with amazement being rebuked by chairman of selectors Carson Catcheside for giving a team talk before a trial match. He was told, 'That was a professional approach. We have chosen these players and we have thrown them in at the deep end. We want to see if they sink or swim.'

Selectors were often heavily influenced by the varsity match, played in December while both trials and deliberations were at their peak. This was admittedly a strong period in university rugby, with national servicemen and overseas students strengthening Oxford and Cambridge. England's recruitment of Rhodes scholars prompted ironic shouts of 'Come on the Home and Colonials' on their last visit to Swansea in 1951. Wales's matches were concentrated in Cardiff after 1954, the same year that Belfast was dropped when the IRFU (and, perhaps surprisingly, its Ulster branch) accepted player protests at being expected to play under the Union Jack and with God Save the Queen as their anthem.

Bleddyn Williams returned from the Lions tour of 1950 publicly convinced that Welsh – and British – rugby must adopt some New Zealand customs and disciplines. The WRU approved coaching courses run by the Central Council for Physical Recreation in 1950, and the first RFU-approved coaching manual, written by Humphrey Ellis, came out two years later.

The most influential university was neither Oxford nor Cambridge but Loughborough, as players graduating from its physical education course exerted increasing influence, both as teachers and at their clubs. Jeff Butterfield, a brilliant centre who made his debut for England in 1953, would supply the 1955 Lions in South Africa – British rugby's peak of brilliance in this decade – with advice on conditioning as valuable as his own playing contribution to an extraordinary back division. One wing was Tony O'Reilly, who had, in the words of Ireland teammate Andrew Mulligan, 'the build of a farmer but topped by the head of a barrister and tailed by the hands of a pianist and the feet of a Nureyev'. Lock Rhys Williams, Wales's finest forward between their two recognised Golden Ages, noted that while O'Reilly was only eighteen, he 'at times appeared to be at least ten years more mature than the rest of us'. At scrum-half, Butterfield's durable Northampton clubmate Dickie Jeeps, uncapped but chosen on the recommendation of Haydn Tanner, provided service to the archetypal Welsh outside-half Cliff Morgan, who was memorably portrayed by Gareth Williams and Dai Smith 'with the ball held at arm's length in front of him, his tongue out almost as far, his bow legs pumping like pistons, eyes rolling, nostrils flaring and a range of facial expressions seldom seen north of Milan'.

A drawn series begun with a cliffhanging 23–22 win at Ellis Park, Johannesburg, in front of a world-record 95,000 crowd was the single break in a 70-year pattern of failure by British teams in the southern hemisphere.

Jeeps waited until 1957 to become an England regular. Butterfield was still there, and England had an inspiring leader in the rugged Sale hooker Eric Evans, another Loughborough graduate, and a remarkable wing in Coventry's Peter Jackson. That year brought England's only Grand Slam between 1924 and 1980, while the following season was Jackson's, highlighted by a winning score to end a brutal match against Australia. Butterfield, laid out four times, remembered of Jackson, 'He jinked. He swerved. He gained half a yard. He changed pace. He went this way and that, and there were green shirts flailing all over the place.' During a 75-yard scoring run against France, Jackson stopped dead to allow a tackler to career past.

Scotland's lot, though, was one of unrelenting misery, with 17 straight defeats between 1951 and 1955. They had players of consequence, such as flanker Doug Elliott, who between 1947 and 1954 'often stood alone between Scotland and disaster', and the powerful, athletic Border prop Hugh Mcleod, whose long international career started in 1954, but Norman Mair, good hooker turned better writer, believed the Springbok debacle turned decline into collapse: 'We panicked right through. We went for a heavy pack one minute, then a light, mobile pack the next. We just dithered.' Scottish administrators remained in a time warp, as late as 1957 advocating the 3–2–3 scrummage formation that other, more successful, nations had long discarded. Old asset had become modern millstone as former pupils displayed the conservatism of men who spent their lives with the same men they had played against and with as schoolboys.

While defeats by Wales and Cardiff – the latter more convincing than that of the national team – dominate British memories of the 1953 All Blacks, their really important loss was to France. Wales have not beaten New Zealand in 17 meetings since. For France, it was a landmark in the process of turning European rugby's punchbag of the first half of the twentieth century into the dominant force of the second. New Zealanders were shocked – Lindsay Knight has written that it was 'remembered as a tragedy', although the Australians, whose skipper Bill McLean thought France the best team that his 1947–48 touring team played ('just a little bit quicker than our boys, always did the unusual') might have warned them. Jarden, too, was bemused, recalling 'a swarm of swarthy, muscular figures, all of whom looked exactly the same and all of whom appeared to be capable of running like backs'. Jean Prat of Lourdes scored the try in France's 3–0 victory. He, more than anyone, personified the forces effecting that transformation. Prat, and Lourdes, came to wider public notice in the first post-liberation final, which was lost to Agen.

Post-Vichy reprisals were limited, the decision made to punish only the worst cases of collaboration. League regained independence, although not for years the right to call itself 'rugby', and enjoyed a remarkable first post-war decade. Puig-Aubert's team achieved a spectacular victory in Australia in 1951–52 then reached the first World Cup final in 1954, an event which, like soccer's European Cup, started in 1955, was French-inspired. The code did not, though, receive restitution or even an admission of wrongs against it. More than 60 years on, a government report on rugby in wartime, victim of France's most recent swing from left to right, sits in a Paris filing cabinet awaiting the next political oscillation.

Union retained the benefits of its favoured status under Vichy and even state approval – the first attendance at a match by a president of the Republic was in 1949. It also retained sufficient old habits to renew concern across the Channel. France was close to being expelled again in early 1952 – Richard Escot has written that only Welsh support saved it. The home unions demanded the suppression of the French national championship as the price of continued contact. The FFR would have complied but was blocked by a club revolt led by Perpignan. Expulsion was finally staved off by a palace revolution, with former international scrum-half Rene Crabos taking over from Paul Eluere as FFR president in July 1952 and making an initial statement that was clearly intended for cross-channel consumption: 'We are entering a new era, that of amateurism.' Crabos submitted reports to the IRB in 1953 and 1954 and had to fend off fresh anxiety in 1957.

France had its own definition of amateurism. Alex Potter and Georges Duthen described the system of 'social aid':

A player getting married may be helped to find a flat. A loan may be granted on easy terms to a player establishing or developing a business. Aid may be given to a hard-up student to remain at a university, to a young doctor, dentist or solicitor to start a practice. Jobs are sought for unemployed players, or better jobs for fellows worthy of them.

Roger Martin, a Lourdes player of the 1950s, told Escot, 'To have a great rugby club, you need everything. And money has always been, with the quality of player, a part of the picture.' He recalled receiving around £800 in prize money one year and a weekly payment on top of income from work: 'The advantage with the rugby money was that it was not declared.' Lourdes imported players from other clubs, but their success in the 1950s was built around Jean Prat and brother Maurice, a centre, who could not have been more local – Lourdes's stadium was built on land purchased from their father in 1927.

A back-row forward who dropped goals – he landed five in a fifty-one-match international career and was a regular place-kicker to boot – Jean Prat recalled:

The French game at the time was fairly disorganised. Each player did just about whatever they wanted, and in rugby that is not acceptable. It should be a collective game. It was precisely because I wanted to institute this kind of game that I took on the captaincy of Lourdes, and the success we had there led to me being entrusted with the French team.

Those successes encompassed six championships in the decade from 1948, including a hat-trick from 1956 to 1958. Only one French team between 1945 and 1958 lacked a Lourdes player – they supplied seven in 1958. Prat missed only one international between 1945 and 1955.

Those years were a litany of French firsts: victories at Swansea (1948), Twickenham (1951) and Murrayfield (1952), followed by wins over New Zealand (1954) and South Africa (1958). The first shared title came in 1954. An outright win plus Grand Slam – a French coinage in answer to the home unions' Triple Crown – looked likely after three games in 1955, only for an inspired display by veteran Welsh forward Rees Stephens to thwart them and bring about another shared title. That was France's first televised match, a fresh stimulus to interest as the number of TV sets in homes grew from less than 1,000 in 1950 to 8.4 million by 1968. The idiosyncratic, folksy Roger Couderc became as familiar in France – albeit with less technical expertise, once exclaiming 'I don't think I'll ever understand these offside laws' – as Bill McLaren did in Britain. An outright championship was a matter of time. One thing only eluded France: membership of the IRB.

This had finally been conceded to Australia, New Zealand and South Africa in 1948, the RFU accepting parity, two seats, with other home unions to accommodate the single representatives of the new members. One immediate consequence, as a condition of membership, was the formation of the Australian Rugby Union in November 1949. The Australians immediately asked, citing league competition, for renewed dispensations – notably the 25-yard rule for direct kicks to touch and a ban on advancing beyond the centre line of the scrum before the ball was out – which were confirmed in 1951. By 1952, New Zealand were pressing for equal representation.

Having finally achieved representation, the new members were not successful – or perhaps, in the way of those who have themselves achieved a goal, no longer bothered – in interesting the IRB in the wider world. When British Columbia requested affiliation in 1949 (the Canadian Union had lapsed), they were told that IRB by-laws could not be changed for 'a Dominion in which Rugby Football is not established on a national basis'. Little encouragement was offered to Czechoslovakia (1946), Chile (1947) or Romania (1953) when they contacted the IRB. In 1958, when the new members achieved parity, it was agreed that 'informal conferences held from time to time with France were adequate' – not a view shared by the French – and that there should be a 'go slow' policy in relation to 'foreign fixtures' with new countries such as Romania.

The British Columbians could have done with some help. Club rugby in Vancouver was helped by a wave of British immigrants, while international contact continued. The World Trophy was resumed in 1947, fraternity-house stays before matches at Berkeley a shock even to such dedicated party animals as rugby players, many reporting 'a harrowing experience' characterised by sleep deprivation. Canada received, in 1957, the first overseas tour by the Barbarians, who explained 'they asked first'. Australasian touring teams carried on passing through on the way back from Britain, the 1958 Wallabies going down 11–6. There were, though, losses elsewhere in Canada. In particular, Halifax, a stronghold with 12 clubs in 1930, was wiped out in a generation after the introduction of Canadian football in 1936. The Canadian Navy pushed its football code vigorously during the war, the young men of the town preferring an apparently indigenous game to one that looked like an imperial relic.

Too bad Canadian rugby was not centred on Quebec. Then it might have looked to France. A cynic might see FIRA, resuscitated in 1951, as a French insurance scheme against a second expulsion, but it did far more to encourage newer rugby nations than the IRB. France resumed fixtures against Italy in 1948 and Germany in 1955, beginning an annual, increasingly competitive series against Romania from 1957.

Italy was the strongest of the other nations. Restarting after the war with 64 clubs 'but a thousand problems', it had been aided by rapid French contact, a Lyon select team visiting in April 1946. Italy's modern rugby geography had evolved, concentrated in prosperous north-eastern cities – Padua, Rovigo, Treviso, L'Aquila – that were not large enough to support successful soccer clubs. Rovigo was known as the 'town on the scrum', while in L'Aquila:

> Success in rugby often leads to success in other spheres of life, providing the men who play for the local team with the social capital to success in other walks of life in the town … men who are directly involved with the rugby club are able to cash in on their prowess to rise up the social ladder.

The great limitation remained the absence of schools rugby. When Italy, Romania and West Germany all came to Britain in the autumn of 1956, *Rugger* magazine's correspondent reckoned the Italians 'ahead of the other Continental countries in technical skill and experience of tactical play', if still well short of full international quality. (Romania, meanwhile, were of particular interest as the first visitors from behind the 'iron curtain'.) Another writer rated both Italy and Romania at around 12 points per match behind France but with a similar advantage over West Germany, Spain and Czechoslovakia.

The Romanians, fittest of the three, beat Gloucester and drew with Leicester, while drawing raised eyebrows by issuing glucose tablets before matches, but were heavily forward-orientated: 'The role of the three-quarter line appeared to be to send long punts upfield for the pack to follow up.' The Germans too were fit and competent up front but lacking attacking ideas. Romanian post-war rugby was able to draw on existing traditions but with clubs attached to industries and state institutions. Common to the Romanians' and Germans' tour programmes were matches against Swansea and Harlequins, who both also visited Romania, the former in 1954 and the latter two years later. A Quins official made after-dinner-speaking history by misunderstanding the import of words printed on a public convenience and opening his speech 'Urinals and Water Closets', and 45,000 people watched the Harlequins play a Romania A team. In spite of the potential evident in such enthusiasm, Romania were regarded warily by the IRB, which warned darkly in 1955 that the game there was 'not on amateur lines' – a conclusion reaffirmed in 1956 and used in support of the 'go slow' policy in 1958.

As in the 1930s, the IRB was sceptical about FIRA's fondness for international multi-team tournaments. It refused to endorse a tournament accompanying the Rome Olympics of 1960, with the Australian delegate – more aware than others of struggles to maintain the game – in a minority. The most striking of these events, attached to Moscow's World Student Games in 1957, reintroduced Russia into the mainstream. The final was a brutal contest between Llanelli, whose outside-half Carwyn James had learnt Russian while training as a decoder during national service, and Romanian champions Grivita Rosie. James remembered, 'After a fortnight in which the Russians made copious notes about everything that Llanelli did, their parting words were, "Come back in 20 years and we'll play you."'

French Africa too developed in the post-war years. Morocco established its own federation in 1956, and within four years the native-born outnumbered the French players. The first game was played in the Ivory Coast in 1946, two teams of expatriates organised by Mme Andre Benois, who fashioned a makeshift ball out of an inner tube.

France took their missionary work as far as Argentina in 1949 and were puzzled when the Argentinian test full-back looked remarkably like the chap who had played against them for England only a few months earlier – for the simple reason that he was. Barry Holmes of St George's club had gone to Cambridge as a student, winning Blues in 1947 and 1948 and playing so well that he won selection for all four England matches in 1949. Returning home that year, he started playing again for St George's and was chosen for Argentina. The French 'talked among themselves, noted and discussed this. Everything was rapidly settled, but the faces of surprise remained,' although they were composed enough to win two tightly contested matches. A few weeks later, Holmes died from typhoid, aged 22. Another death, that of Eva Perón, wife of Argentina's military dictator, disrupted Argentina's next major tour, by Ireland in 1952. The Irishmen took refuge in Chile but might also have found worthwhile opposition across the River Plate in Uruguay, where Carlos Cat, a San Isidro star of the 1920s, had after years of trying achieved a post-war rugby resurrection in his native country. 'Rugby criollo' was introduced in 1949 into the Carrasco Polo club. Carrasco provided two of the five teams in the first Uruguayan championship the following year, and the Uruguayan Rugby Union was founded in 1951, sending a team to the first South American championship, where it lost 62–0 to Argentina but beat Chile. One consequence of Uruguay's rebirth was that Argentina could no longer claim the River Plate to itself, so its union became the Unión Argentina de Rugby (UAR) in November 1951.

Eva Perón's death was not the only problem for the newly renamed union. Bills for Ireland's flights remained unpaid, aborting a visit by an Oxford University team. Still, the students were not short of travel, providing valuable stimulus in Japan with visits in 1952 and 1956, and going jointly with Cambridge (who went by themselves in 1953) in 1959. Japan also entertained the Junior All Blacks, who were beginning to make use of readily available air travel, in 1958. Two years earlier, a trip to Ceylon (as Sri Lanka was still called) was used as a chance to test young New Zealanders – including a lock named Colin Meads – away from the comforts of home.

Frequent cross-Tasman exchanges continued, although the Bledisloe Cup stayed on the New Zealand shore once a stronger All Black touring team took revenge for the indignities of 1949 with a three-match sweep in 1951. A drawn series the following year was the best Australia would do in five meetings during the 1950s. If this was a flat time for Australia – whose most important development was probably the legalisation of poker machines in 1956, foreshadowing new income for clubs – the same was not true of the country's players. Amid its mass of private-school products was Nick Shehadie, Lebanese-descended product of a decidedly unprivate school in a tough Sydney district, whose Wallabies career from 1947 to 1958, including two tours of Britain – a rare achievement in the once-a-decade era – was prelude to much longer service in rugby, and public, life.

Even so, both Australian and New Zealand audiences preferred visits by the Fijians, who were particularly beloved by hard-pressed Australian treasurers. In 1952, they attracted 42,000, the largest union crowd in 45 years, to the Sydney Cricket Ground. They won to square a two-match series, a feat they repeated in 1954. In New Zealand, they played the Maoris rather than the full test team but made such an impression in 1951 that three players – captain George Cavalevu, number 8 Rusiate Vuruya and wing Joe Levula – were among the *Rugby Almanack of New Zealand*'s five players of the year. It rated Levula, who attracted lucrative league offers in Australia, as the best wing in the world, ahead of Ken Jones and Ron Jarden, while Vuruya inspired comparison with Hennie Muller. If much of their charm was quick-thinking heterodoxy on the field – a 20-yard over-the-head pass switching directions and reviving an apparently unproductive move in Sydney in 1952 – they were different off it as well. Rugby teams often make an impression on female hotel staff, but generally not by insisting on helping them to tidy up. They were all also, with one exception, devout Methodists – with that creed's rejection of alcohol – who held daily prayer meetings.

Memorable though Fiji were, only one tour defined the 1950s for New Zealand: the Springboks in 1956. Rugby is often equated with war – to be fair, many of those who make the comparison have, like Wakefield, Bob Stuart and 'Boy' Louw, experienced the real thing – but has rarely felt more like it than during this tour. While Second World War imagery during the British Lions tour in 2005 was informed by postmodern irony, the atmosphere in 1956 was genuinely felt. It was, moreover, a war of revenge for the deeply felt wrongs of 1949.

The 1950s, Jock Phillips has argued, saw the 'triumph of the New Zealand male stereotype' and its 'holy trinity' of rugby, racing and beer. Twice as much beer was consumed in New Zealand in 1958 than in 1945. Warwick Roger, whose tour memoir *Old Heroes* is the nearest thing rugby has produced to baseball's *Boys of Summer*, recalls 'a rather flat mental and social landscape'. Yet amid the seriousness – 'a national crusade', in Roger's memory – was a strong sense of festivity. The film-maker John O'Shea recalled the intense excitement of the three-month tour:

> I was in Berlin when the wall fell and that had a similar sort of feeling. Or maybe the carnival in Rio, where the Latin Americans take most of their clothes off to enjoy themselves. Here we did it in our gumboots and our sou'westers and gabardine raincoats and hats, with bottles of beer.

It was the last time in New Zealand that the Springboks induced strong feelings simply as rugby players, rather than as representatives of an aberrant political system. As O'Reilly said of touring South Africa in 1955, 'The racial schism was about to be formalised, but . . . in the unthinking way of football players on tour, we gave little thought to the consequences.' Segregation was hardening and the Afrikaner Broederbond was continuing its long march through cultural and economic institutions including the SARFB. Craven, never a *broeder*, managed the Springboks. Dan de Villiers, a Johannesburg referee disliked by most of the team, was nominally his assistant but in practice he was the team's Broederbond political commissar – a standard tour role from now on.

Back in South Africa, the main non-white development was the institution from 1950 of regular interracial tests between the Coloured and Bantu Unions. The Bantus won the first 14–3. Abderahman Booley suggested that, without segregation, at least eight non-white players might have been Springbok candidates in the early 1950s.

As well as the New Zealand tour, 1956 saw the first serious proposal for a sports boycott, by Trevor Huddleston, a British clergyman working in South Africa. In his book *Naught for Your Comfort*, he wrote, 'Because the Union is so good at sport, such isolation would strike its self-assurance very severely . . . it might be an extraordinarily effective blow to the racialism which has brought it into being.'

Sporting relations were undoubtedly deteriorating. In 1955, the Orange Free State Union banned non-white spectators from matches against the Lions in Bloemfontein, while the French tourists three years later attracted 'vibrant sympathy' from the non-white sections.

New Zealand passion was evident from the first match of the 1956 tour, when 31,000 people crammed into a Hamilton stadium whose capacity was supposed to be 3,000 less. Waikato scored in the first minute, following up the kick-off with crunching tackles, led 14–0 at half-time and hung on to win 14–10 in spite of playing more than half the match with 14 men. Large numbers slept outside grounds to be sure of witnessing test matches whose war-like atmosphere grew steadily. Skinner – who, as every South African remembers, had also been New Zealand heavyweight champion – was recalled for the third test to counteract Springbok dominance of the scrums. In the fourth, White was kicked in the spine by a South African forward. New Zealand won the series 3–1, victory clinched when forward Peter Jones scored from a 40-yard run almost as legendary as his post-match announcement, to a rapt but slightly straight-laced nation, that he was 'absolutely buggered'. It was South Africa's first series defeat since 1903. At the end, Craven went to the Eden Park microphone to concede, 'It's all yours, New Zealand.' As Roger points out, there is hardly a smile among hundreds of New Zealanders in the famous photograph of Craven speaking. The mood was relief and exhaustion, rather than the joy that might be expected after so famous a victory.

Another South African concession speech was required two years later when France, warmly welcomed as a change of touring diet, went to the Union and won. The French had regressed after the disappointment of 1955 and Prat's retirement, winning only two of their next ten championship matches. Six consecutive defeats from the start of the 1957 season culminated in a 14–0 home hammering by England the following year marked by Jackson's legerdemain, cries of '*démission aux sélecteurs*' and a hail of seat cushions. In the year that saw General de Gaulle end an eleven-year purdah by claiming the presidency, Mazamet medic Lucien Mias was recalled from his internal exile after four years. Michel Celaya stayed captain, but Mias was the controlling intelligence. Mias was known as 'Doctor Pack' for his theories on forward play, influenced by the experience of France's 25–3 humiliation by the 1951–52 Springboks, whose practical expression took Mazamet to its only championship final in 1958. He reimposed Prat's disciplines and added his own. He said that the team he rejoined was 'a collection of captains. We had no sense of really belonging to each other,' and that the French post-war style had been misconceived: 'It wasn't rugby. It was just a game with a ball – it was handball or basketball, if you like. It wasn't rugby, because rugby is a game that requires physical contact.' Mias's preferred device used the ball-handling instincts of French forwards in the 'percussion' move, in which they peeled off from the lineout to drive into the opposing midfield, with the backs ready to take advantage when their opposite numbers were sucked in to defend. It did no harm that the child-welfare programmes introduced by the Popular Front were bearing very substantial fruit in large, powerful forwards such as lineout specialist Bernard Mommejat.

While the 1958 championship was beyond recall, France beat the touring Australians, then won for the first time in Cardiff, before finishing with a win over Ireland – Mommejat's first championship match and Maurice Prat's last. Before the South African tour, FFR president Crabos asked that they 'be good sports and try and win a match or two'. They duly won one and drew the other in a two-test series, more than matching South Africa up front, a triumph immortalised in one of the disappointingly few French rugby books translated into English, Denis Lalanne's *Great Fight of the French XV.*

They returned to a new season and several rule changes by

the IRB. Allowing the goal-kicker to place the ball himself for a conversion was a profound relief to players – generally scrum-halfs – who were previously required to place the ball, then lie on the ground holding it until the critical moment, risking a nasty blow and the kicker's wrath if they got it wrong. Far more significant, though, was the abolition of the requirement that the ball be played with a foot before it could be picked up after a tackle. Doing so was hard-wired into players' instincts. Michael Green recalled what happened in his first game under the new rules:

> We all carried on as before at the first tackle, scrabbling for the ball with our feet, until the team intellectual tentatively picked it up and scored.
> 'You cheating bastard!' shouted the opposing captain.
> 'I am playing to the new laws,' said our man.
> Back came the reply: 'What new laws?' He meant it too.

At a more exalted level, Clem Thomas found that 'Now a constructive wing-forward can start a new move immediately', while astute northeast of England chronicler John Pargeter reported that the change 'speeded up play more than even the greatest optimist had dared to hope and has made it possible to switch defence into attack with almost alarming rapidity'. These reflections did not necessarily delight the lawmakers. A running theme in IRB deliberations was that they legislated for the whole game, not just the elite, and that rule changes must not make the game too demanding for the weekend player.

It had, though, the entirely logical effect of establishing a new elite. The 1959 championship was won by the country most identified with constructive ball-handling forwards: France. The victory was less glorious than the French might have hoped – two wins and a draw was less than they had managed in sharing the championships of 1954 and 1955. The title already clinched, they lost to Ireland in their final match. No matter, though, the title had finally crossed the Channel. Mias retired to his medical practice and his garden, having, as Lalanne would write, 'in two seasons made up for more than 60 years of backwardness in forward play'. The rest of the world would just have to get used to it.

# CHAPTER TEN

# Not-So Swinging '60s

'Competitive rugby? Oh, no, we don't hold with it at all. There's no such thing as competitive rugby in our country. It's bad for the game, bad for the spirit of it. Apart from the Munster Cup, the Ulster Cup, the Leinster Cup, the seven-a-side tournaments, the International Championship, the West Wales League and, in England, the County Championship, the "Cuppers" at the varsities, the Hospitals Cup and things like the Yorkshire Cup, the Northumberland Cup and so on, we have no competitive rugby at all. No, it would never do!'

British Lion Noel Murphy in New Zealand (1959)

'He had six different signals, and they all meant kick'

Scottish spectator on Clive Rowlands (1963)

France's 1959 title was a harbinger of things to come. Over the next 40 seasons, France would average one championship point per season more than nearest rivals Wales and England – which sounds very little until you remember that eight points was the maximum per season. That maximum was all that eluded France in the first three seasons of the 1960s. England held them to draws in 1960, earning a share in the title, and in 1961. A first defeat in eleven matches and three seasons came at Cardiff in 1962 but could not prevent a third outright title in four years.

This was a team of diverse talents. In the front row were the picaresque Alfred Roques, who played soccer until he was 26, trained on a litre and a half of wine per day and was reputed once to have tackled a bolting stallion, and Brive's Amédée Domenech, a strong enough character to have defied the formidable Mias. Outside-half Pierre Albaladejo, destined to become TV commentator Roger

Couderc's straight man, earned the title 'Monsieur Drop' with a barrage of eleven drop goals in six tests in 1960 and 1961, none more remarkable than the one landed against his Dax team by scrum-half Pierre Danos, reportedly six yards from the tryline and only three yards from touch, to clinch Béziers its first (but far from last) championship in 1961. In an era of brotherhoods, the Camberaberos, Guy (5 ft 6 in., 10 st. 3lb) and Lilian (5 ft 4 in., 10 st. 3 lb), at half-back made a force of similarly diminutive La Voulte (population 4,500), while the next first-time champions, Mont de Marsan in 1963, drew dash and style from the centre play of the Boniface brothers – Andre and the ill-fated Guy, labelled 'the James Dean of French rugby' by Denis Tillinac after his death in a road crash on New Year's Day 1968.

Their one setback was losing all three tests in New Zealand in 1961, encountering playing conditions excessive even by Wellington standards. Lalanne wrote of 'the turbine-like whistling of the hurricane', corner-flags bent almost flat, large parts of the bizarre Millard stand, later nominated by Tom Scott as the perfect venue for the world hang-gliding championships, cordoned off for safety, and a match that was 'a series of grotesque and pathetic scenes'.

The French also had to contend with a comparable force of nature: Colin Meads. As scrum-half Chris Laidlaw wrote after ten years of extremely close observation, the All Black lock had 'no detectable weaknesses'. As a child, he was taught to knit to give flexibility to hands curved by first scarlet then rheumatic fever, but there was nothing wrong with his health or hands as an adult. Immense power – he won lineouts by wrenching the ball away from opponents – was supplemented with awareness and footballing skills. He created a try for Waka Nathan by taking a quick lineout against the 1966 Lions and dropped a goal on his King Country debut. James and Reason said, 'It was as if God had distilled in him the essence of competition' – a competitiveness that occasionally took him beyond the bounds of the acceptable and made him an ogreish figure to other nations. His achievements over an extraordinarily long career – he played for the All Blacks from 1957 to 1971, a total of 133 matches, including 55 tests – would by themselves have made him legendary. He also, though, distilled the essence of All Black-ness, or at least the commonest perception of what an All Black should be. To start with, he was a farmer – never as dominant a group as legend has it, but still an essential element in the archetype. He was famously photographed, a fluke due to the animal being unwell, carrying a sheep under one arm. He was the regular, unassuming bloke, as Laidlaw observed, 'a non-lover of publicity' whose 'pleasure is the simple enjoyment he gets out of the game'. If anything, his standing as the incarnation of a nation's self-image has grown since he retired – reports during the Lions tour of 2005 spoke without irony of visiting fans having 'an audience' with him.

Meads personified the New Zealand style of the time, himself explaining how the dashing French were beaten: 'heads down, bottoms up and drive, drive for 80 minutes'. McLean, whose patriotism was never the one-eyed variety, described the approach as follows:

Marauding play by number-eight forwards, chest-to-chest defensive stations by opposing backlines, constant use of the touch-lines by inside- and outside-halfs, and a general aim to promote mistakes by spoiling play ... it was cruelly efficient, markedly successful, quite abominably dull.

Nor were they an entirely happy group. Laidlaw writes of player cliques and divisions between senior and new All Blacks: 'Youngsters were continually reminded of this division. They offered little in the way of advice. They were blatantly impervious to the fate of any player whose game was faltering.' Young first-five Earle Kirton was blamed for the 3–0 defeat at Newport in 1963, even though senior players like captain Wilson Whineray and Meads also had forgettable games.

Yet they were the dominant team of the decade, winning forty-two games and losing only five between 1961 and 1970. They were undefeated in 17 matches between 1961 and 1964, then won 17 straight – still a record – from 1965 to 1969. They were undefeated away between 1964 and 1970. One reason was that the All Blacks had some astonishing forwards in the 1960s, with Meads joined by younger brother Stan, a remarkably gifted prop in Ken Gray and ball-handling back rowers like Kel Tremain and Nathan. One back rower, Red Conway, was so determined to tour South Africa in 1960 that he had an injured finger amputated rather than risk medical delays. Goal-kicker Don Clarke, a full-back bigger than most forwards, accumulated the then-awesome total of two hundred and seven points in thirty-one tests, his influence peaking in 1959 when he landed six penalties to beat a Lions team who had scored four tries 18–17.

In 1967, New Zealand saw a change of style under coach Fred Allen, nicknamed 'The Needle' for his skill in winding up players. Allen captained the ill-fated 1949 All Blacks but looked back further to the running game of his earlier touring team, the Kiwis of 1945–46. Knowing his forwards would win copious possession, Allen opted for an open style encapsulated by his rehabilitation of the creative Kirton and selection of Laidlaw, whose spin-pass influenced a generation of scrum-halfs, over the combative ninth-forward Sid Going. The captaincy had passed to Brian Lochore – according to Laidlaw, 'a team man in the truest sense'.

Rule changes aided Allen's approach. In 1964, all players not involved in the lineout were moved ten yards behind the point of the throw-in, and the offside line at scrummages was defined by the hindmost foot in the scrum. With midfield traffic jams consequently unblocked, there was now space to run. Laidlaw recalled Meads's amazement when Allen explained his tactics: 'You mean we're going to run the ball *all* the time?'

Like the Invincibles of 1924–25, the 1967 team were denied a Grand Slam by circumstances beyond their control. As an agricultural nation, they could not complain when Ireland closed its borders to repel the foot-and-mouth epidemic ravaging Britain. They peaked against England, scoring 18 points in the first half-hour, and their misfortune is that the enduring memory of the tour is of Meads's sending-off, only the second in international rugby, after he kicked out dangerously close to Scottish outside-half David Chisholm.

The tour broke with precedent by lasting only eighteen matches and taking place only four years after the last. It filled a gap left when New Zealand at last insisted on taking Maoris to South Africa. The Republic's government, which in 1962 formally banned mixed-race teams, overruled the country's rugby board in order to forbid the tour scheduled for 1967. Awareness of apartheid was growing in New Zealand. When General Howard Kippenberger denounced NZRFU passivity in 1948, telling Wellington's first anti-apartheid rally, 'If it is good enough for Maoris to fight, bleed and die on the battlefields of North Africa, it is good enough for them to play rugby on the sports fields of South Africa,' his was a comparatively isolated voice.

But, by 1960, a 'No Maoris, no Tour' petition begun by Wellington lawyer Ronald O'Regan attracted 162,000 signatures, and the NZRFU was sent up in song by American satirist Tom Lehrer, on tour in New Zealand:

> No it doesn't really matter what New Zealand may have lost
> As long as Kiwi rugby players are supreme
> And just think how glad they'd make us if they came back with the title
> Of the world's greatest non-pigmented rugby team.

International perceptions of South Africa were brutally jolted by the Sharpeville massacre in March 1960, when 69 peaceful black demonstrators were killed by armed police. Internal pressure was growing on South African sport. In 1958, the South African Sports Association (later to be the South African Non-Racial Olympic Committee (SANROC)) was formed, with the poet Dennis Brutus as secretary. Within a year, it had condemned the Springbok badge as an emblem of racism, declared opposition to all racially organised sport and dissuaded West Indian cricketer Frank Worrell from bringing a team to South Africa. By 1961, Brutus was 'banned' – a punishment forbidding meetings with more than three people. He was successively arrested, shot, placed under five years' house arrest and sent into exile.

In 1959, the Bantu Rugby Board dropped its title as racially pejorative – becoming the South Africa African Rugby Board. Two years later, its president, Louis Leo Mtshizana, called on unions to 'emerge from our racial kraals and form a truly representative organisation'. Discussions over a merger with the two coloured unions – Cuthbert Loriston led a breakaway group called the South African Rugby Football Federation (SARFF) in 1959 – stalled in 1963, the year when Mtshizana was banned. Clearances of non-white districts under the Group Areas Act, notably Cape Town's District Six in 1964, meant that grounds were lost and clubs seriously disrupted.

On the ruling side, the Broederbond continued to extend its

grip. Craven was too strong to displace from the presidency of the SARFB, but from 1959 all of his vice-presidents were *broeders*, as were a succession of tour managers – Kobus Louw, a vice-president of the union who managed the tour of New Zealand in 1965, was secretary of the Department of Coloured Affairs and later a cabinet minister. In the same year, Louw vetoed the selection of Doug Hopwood, a gifted number 8, as captain. His choice was former skipper Avril Malan, not only a *broeder* but younger brother of Magnus Malan, later chief of the South African Defence Force and minister of defence, who said, 'You can take a rugby player and within half an hour make a soldier of him.' This was also the year when Afrikaners captured the presidency of the powerful Transvaal Rugby Union after an intense campaign. Albert Grundlingh has written:

Nothing was left to chance; on the eve of the election it was arranged that a 'doubtful' member, who it was suspected might vote against the Afrikaner faction, be sent out of town on business on the crucial day to ensure that he would not be able to cast his vote.

Travelling Springbok teams were increasingly subject to demonstrations. A 1965 short tour featured a large demonstration in Dublin, Irish players throwing eggs at the protesters, and narrow defeats by Ireland, the first ever, and Scotland. Tommy Bedford, a player kept out of the captaincy because the *broeders* suspected him (correctly) of having liberal opinions, recalled arriving in Britain with a 1969 Springbok team coached by Malan and captained by Dawie de Villiers, later a National MP and Cabinet minister: 'Instead of proudly stepping out at Heathrow wearing our Springbok blazers, we were smuggled out in a coach to a golfing hotel. You feel you haven't got a friend in the world.' Vigilantes pitched into demonstrators at Swansea, where the final injury tally of two hundred demonstrators and ten police left little doubt about the balance of violence. Centre Mannetjies Roux consolidated his position as a hero amongst the supporters of apartheid by kicking a demonstrator at Coventry in the backside. British fans already had a different view of him after his late tackle in 1960 on Cardiff's Alun Priday and the challenge that put England's dashing outside-half Richard Sharp out of the 1962 Lions tour.

International pressure mounted. In 1964, South Africa was suspended from the International Olympic Committee (IOC) and excluded from the Tokyo games. A proposal in 1967 that the WRU cut links, proposed by Brynamman and Llangennech, lost only by 192 votes to 120. In two months in 1970, South Africa was thrown out of tennis's Davis Cup and the IOC and began a 21-year exile from test cricket when its tour of England was cancelled. In 1971, the United Nations backed a sports boycott against the country.

Rugby's political importance, both as a sport that had not cut off contact with South Africa and as the cherished game of the National Party's core Afrikaner voters, mounted. In 1965, President Henrik Verwoerd underlined South Africa's rejection of multiracial sport by his Loskop Dam speech, affirming that 'When other countries visit us, they will respect our customs . . . everyone knows what they are.' His successor, wartime pro-Nazi B.J. Vorster, restated this policy in 1967 and implemented it in 1968 by cancelling England's cricket tour following the selection of non-white South African-born batsman Basil D'Oliveira. While the ineptitude (or worse) of the English cricket authorities and D'Oliveira's Cape Town origins created unusual circumstances, though, it is hard to resist Grundlingh's conclusion that cricket, essentially an English sport, did not matter much to the Afrikaner-dominated National Party government. Rugby – and in particular the scheduled 1970 All Blacks tour – did.

In 1969, South Africa sent P.H. Phillips, an extremely senior diplomat, to New Zealand as consul-general. New Zealand had few trade links with South Africa, and only rugby explained so senior an appointment. In September 1969, it was announced that Maori players would be admitted to the tour. There was no change, though, in South Africa's domestic selection policies.

Ken Gray, New Zealand's best prop, retired: 'Very simply, I decided I would not play against a racially selected South African side.'

Four non-white players were chosen in a Kiwi party smuggled into Wellington airport in 1970 to avoid demonstrators. One junior team marked their disapproval by playing in black armbands. Three of the 'honorary whites' – Sid Going, Blair Furlong and Buff Milner – were Maoris. The one who made the greatest impact in South

Africa, teenage wing Bryan Williams, was a Samoan, forerunner of the islanders who would change New Zealand rugby. South Africa won the tests 3–1, for which Laidlaw blamed the coaching of Ivan Vodanovich – 'tactics were cast aside as unnecessary complexities' – and South African hospitality, particularly in Johannesburg, where the Transvaal Rugby Union 'provided a suite in the All Black hotel complete with girls, music and a cache of booze'. Williams, like many brilliant runners finding South Africa's hard grounds and altitude perfect for his game, was acclaimed as the best winger in the world and a hero to the non-white enclosures. At Kimberley, black fans were attacked by whites after running on post-match to chair Williams.

New Zealand continued to find Australia less troublesome, both on and off the field. The All Blacks went on stomping on the Aussies, an activity which never palls for the Kiwi male. Australia did better elsewhere, drawing 2–2 in South Africa in 1963 and beating Wales in 1966 for what was then regarded as the first time – the 1927 victory by the Waratahs was yet to be given test status. They adopted gold jerseys in 1962, a year after finding a scrum-half often characterised in terms of precious metals. After three matches against Fiji, 21-year-old Ken Catchpole captained the tour of South Africa and was hailed by selector Wally Meagher – half-back for the to-be-upgraded Waratahs – as 'the greatest scrum-half we've ever had'. Catchpole came from a Rules family but received a classic rugby education. He attended Coogee Prep then Scot's College before joining his home district club Randwick, which, under the influence of Meagher and Cyril Towers, was Australia's greatest nursery of attacking talent. Few opinions differed from Meagher's. Laidlaw regarded Catchpole as the 'supreme exponent of all the skills . . . quicker of thought, action and reaction'. The speed and consistency of a pass based on faultless positioning helped partner Phil Hawthorne develop into an outstanding outside-half. Both players were lost to Australia in 1968 – Catchpole's career ended by injury when Meads, in one of his less attractive moments, pulled his leg when he was trapped in a ruck, while Hawthorne followed the well-worn Wallabies path to league, taking a record fee from St George. Australia's truly significant contribution to world rugby in the 1960s came in 1968, as the ban on kicking directly to touch outside the 25-yard line – universally known as 'the Australian dispensation' – was tried worldwide as an experimental law.

Home-union contact with the southern giants in the 1960s was uniformly chastening. The 1959 Lions had been popular in New Zealand for brilliant attacking play, although many Kiwis had been uneasy at the refereeing which permitted Clarke's kicking triumph at Dunedin. A final test victory had been clinched by a superb solo try from England outside-half Bev Risman – son of Gus, and soon himself to switch to league – after earlier scores by O'Reilly and Jackson, wing-geniuses of widely varying type.

There was, though, no disguising the failure of the Lions teams who went to South Africa in 1962 and 1968 and New Zealand in 1966. Two draws, one on each South African tour, were the sole return from twelve tests (the tests won in Australia in 1966 were regarded strictly as a warm-up for the main event). The 1960 Springboks beat all four home nations, while only Scotland's draw in 1964 and Irish foot-and-mouth in 1967 thwarted two All Blacks teams. The undercooked Springboks who lost to Ireland and Scotland on a short tour in 1965 offered just a modicum of relief.

Southern observers were happy to explain the British problem. Springbok Tommy Bedford, a Rhodes scholar at Oxford University, argued in 1967, 'The fact that you play friendlies is reflected in your national team. You can hardly complain about your lack of success in international matches if, through the structures of your game, there is little incentive to win.'

A year later, Fred Allen asserted that British players were 'just not as dedicated as our chaps . . . clubs don't take the game seriously enough. They haven't devoted enough time to coaching. They don't seem to devote enough time to the finer points and fundamentals of the game.' Ronnie Dawson and David Brooks, coach and manager of the 1968 Lions who scored one try in four tests in South Africa, agreed, saying the only alternative to competition and coaching was to go on losing.

Wales – rarely accused of insufficient seriousness – had already acted on coaching after receiving their own salutary shock from their first short tour, to South Africa in 1964. A 24–3 beating at Durban, the worst since Inverleith 40 years before, and the inquiry that followed were the catalyst for Wales's wholehearted adoption of coaching. The 1965 AGM of the WRU approved the creation of a full-time national coaching organiser. Further impetus was supplied by the whitewashing of the 1966 Lions in New Zealand – John Robins, a Loughborough-trained Welsh international, went as coach (officially assistant-manager) but was marginalised when the captain, Scottish soldier Mike Campbell-Lamerton, saw him as a challenge to the prerogatives of captaincy. Ray Williams was appointed coaching organiser in June 1967, followed three months later by David Nash as honorary national team coach. There was another glitch to come, when the management team for the Argentina tour in 1968 excluded the coach. Nash resigned, along with Alun Thomas, chair of the coaching committee. The 1968 AGM produced a rethink and the appointment of Clive Rowlands, who took Wales first to Argentina and subsequently to achievements not seen in the previous half-century. Regular national-squad sessions were introduced in 1968.

Rowlands' leadership skills – in a style that reminded Dai Smith and Gareth Williams of Phil Silvers' immortal screen creation *Sergeant Bilko* – had been demonstrated in 14 matches, every one as captain, between 1963 and 1965, sharing the title in 1964 and winning outright in 1965. Outside him, should he choose to pass, was the darting, league-destined brilliance of Newport outside-half David Watkins. Wing Dewi Bebb, a rare North Walian, carried on family nationalist traditions by scoring six tries in eight appearances against England. In the pack were two fine Abertillery back rowers, the pacy Haydn Morgan and number 8 Alun Pask, whose football skills and positional sense made him a highly effective emergency full-back as the Triple Crown was clinched against Ireland in 1965.

Wales's economy was changing, the number of coal miners dropping by more than half to 41,000 as 137 pits were reduced to 54. Activity migrated from valleys to coast, but confidence and prosperity – expressed politically in the creation of a secretary of state for Wales in 1964 – was reflected in the WRU's decision in 1967 to turn the creaking old Arms Park into a national stadium. It was partly funded by £50 debentures that guaranteed the right to buy two tickets for each international. Still a lot of money in 1960s Wales, the £50 outlay gave its purchasers social cachet and no little envy.

A proposal for a league was rejected in 1968, the clubs happy with a status quo that allowed them to choose their own fixtures, but limited competition had been introduced in 1964 by the creation of a Floodlit Alliance – midweek games between ten clubs leading to a final in which, in the first year, Cardiff beat Llanelli. There would have been twelve, and a cross-border element, but the RFU stopped Newport, a member of both unions, and Bristol, a leading spirit in setting up the Alliance, taking part. Happy, as the acerbic John Reason would point out, to support competition between the armed forces, hospitals and counties, the RFU was firmly set against it for clubs. Players from Coventry, England's outstanding club team, won seven county championships between 1958 and 1966 lightly disguised as Warwickshire. The club supplied an average of 12 players to each winning county team.

Adrian Smith points to Coventry, a city where secondary as well as grammar schools played rugby and the best young players were channelled to Coundon Road via a network of old boys' clubs, as 'a microcosm of the meritocratic society 1960s Britain strived for but never attained'. The 1960s saw grammar-school products outnumber the English-private-education teams for the first time, although the old order still had its ways of fighting back – Llanelli Grammar School dropped out of the public schools sevens tournament in 1964 after winning three consecutive titles because they had grown so tired of the jibes of their social superiors but sporting inferiors. Nor were clubs rewarded for their excellence. Smith explains, 'Coventry had no league or cup triumphs to underpin the club's reputation and thereby attract fresh support', handicapping it hopelessly in competition with Coventry City FC, who rose from the Fourth to the First Division, adding 12,000 to average crowds in an era of general decline, over almost the same period.

English clubs were affiliated to the RFU merely as individuals, with committee membership based on county organisation, and had no representative body of their own. This finally began to change in late 1968 with meetings chaired by Ronnie Boon of London Welsh. A group of 25 proposed a national league, which the RFU rejected out of hand, declaring the idea 'against the interests of amateurism'. This snub prompted the creation of the Association of Gate-Taking Clubs as a formal club pressure group.

England broke even in the Five Nations during the 1960s, winning and losing 15 matches while taking part in 10 draws. Success was concentrated early in the decade with a shared championship in 1960 and an outright win in 1963, the Grand Slam denied only by the competition's last 0–0 draw in Dublin. If the most durable player was Bedford flanker Budge Rogers, who finally erased Wakefield's appearance record, the undoubted star, particularly in 1963 when his brilliant try turned a closely fought Calcutta Cup match at Twickenham, was the Cornish outside-half Richard Sharp. Credited by Cliff Morgan with 'grace, pace and coordination', his name was borrowed (with one very small amendment) by author Bernard Cornwell for his spectacularly successful series of Napoleonic War novels.

Ireland enjoyed little about the 1960s – the defeat of South Africa in 1965 the saving grace of the first half – but was improving by the end with second places in 1968 and 1969. The problem, as so often, was lack of depth, with little quality in some positions. There was, though, a small group of players with both durability and star quality, who were major influences well into the following decade. Ray McLoughlin was living proof that one can be both world-class prop and a man of sensitivity and acute intellect. Tom Kiernan, Lions captain in 1968, supplied defensive solidity and accurate goal-kicking on his way to being the first Irishman to play 50 internationals, a total later eclipsed by both charismatic Ballymena giant Willie John McBride and Mike Gibson, an elegant midfielder whose manifold gifts included total recall of every incident in a match.

Until the late 1950s, the Irish claimed the only eponymous international player: James Ireland, capped twice in the 1870s. He was emulated, though, from 1957, by Ken Scotland, another full-back from Heriots, a pioneer of instep-style place-kicking with pronounced attacking instincts and the hands of a man who also kept wicket for his country. Kiernan, his rival as Europe's best in the early 1960s, said it was a privilege to be on the same field. Scotland's misfortune was that, winning the last of 28 caps in 1965, he played just before the Australian dispensation liberated full-backs for a much freer role. His own union asked for its opposition to be minuted when the IRB allowed the Australians to use the dispensation in matches against the 1957 All Black tourists, but there was evidence – as British rugby attempted to cope with commercialism, competition and coaching – that Scotland was becoming a little less reflexively conservative. In 1963, the Scottish Rugby Union proposed that individual unions be allowed to experiment with dispensation laws during the coming season. Four years earlier, it had accepted Charles Hepburn's gift of undersoil heating for Murrayfield – a pragmatic, even far-sighted act given the ferocity of Scottish winters but still, given that Hepburn was a commercial distiller, unexpected from the guardians of amateur purity. In 1960, Scotland were the first home union to go on one of the short off-season tours that became common in non-Lions years, losing a single test to South Africa 18–10 in Port Elizabeth. Five years on from this, the Scottish Rugby Union president David Thorn suggested that there might be virtues in competition as he presented the *Sunday Telegraph* pennant to London Scottish: 'Friendly matches are all very well, but unofficial league tables such as this are providing the sort of needle that rugby union needs.'

Corpses doubtless revolved in Edinburgh graveyards, but the sky did not fall, and there were still reminders of old instincts. In 1965, the Scottish Rugby Union joined with the other home unions in forcing Wales to repay £2,500 that they had accepted from Horniman's Tea to fund a youth cup competition, the Irish arguing that 'a great matter of principle was at stake'. A puzzled Vivian Jenkins noted in *Rugby World* that Welsh schools had been playing for the Dewar Shield for the last 30 years.

Scotland fielded players of quality like Scotland, McLeod and the similarly durable Fife prop David Rollo – both won 40 caps – giraffe-like lineout specialist Peter Stagg and, for a happy mid-decade spell of 13 matches, the Melrose half-back pairing of David Chisholm and Alex Hastie. The horrors of the 1950s were past and the title was shared with Wales in 1964, the only season between 1938 and 1984 when Scotland won more than two matches.

Divisions of class and accent remained. When McLeod, a Hawick man to his formidable bones, gave instructions as pack leader, one Anglo-Scot remarked, 'I didn't understand a word of it, but it all sounded damned impressive.' There was increasing realisation that Scotland's school-based club structures were now its greatest handicap. As one Scottish writer of the time put it to a Welsh colleague, 'Break up Swansea, Llanelli and Cardiff, make your players play for their old schools, and see what happens.'

While the 1960 Springboks and 1963 All Blacks won more matches than friends with their muscular play, Britain's next visitors, Fiji, who visited Wales in 1964, had the same impact as in New Zealand and Australia the previous decade. One player had walked 60 miles from his home to play in the tour trials. Denied full test status by the IRB at its most disapprovingly prescriptive, the matches attracted such large crowds – totalling more than 100,000 in 5 games – that the WRU, which had budgeted for a loss, made a tidy profit. Playing a Wales XV containing 10 of the players who won the Triple Crown later that season, the Fijians were reduced to 14 men for 70 minutes, trailed by 28–9 and roared back with 3 tries in the final 12 minutes to lose only 28–22. Prop Severo Walisoliso scored a hat-trick.

The Canadians of two years earlier also fell victim to IRB inflexibility. Asked to ban anyone who had played Canadian Football, they explained patiently that it was a different game but were still required to introduce a ban on anyone who played it professionally. Refused permission to pay players the 10 shillings daily allowance permitted under IRB rules because it was not a major tour, they asked for a reduction from ten weeks to six, and were refused again. Eleven players out of twenty-six chosen, on a regional quota basis because of the expense of trials, declined because of the length of the tour. They were not short of colour – 41-year-old captain 'Buzz' Moore had played representative games before the war, while outside-half Ted Hunt won a national lacrosse championship and ski-jumped in the 1954 Olympics – but they had little hope of success. They won only one of sixteen matches, though managing a 3–3 draw with the Barbarians.

A better time was had by the Canadian Balmy Beach club who toured Britain in 1958 and announced on a later visit, 'We came in 1958 and lost heavily. We're back, and you can judge if we've learnt anything.' Canadian rugby, happily, was not to be deterred by the IRB. In 1965, the Rugby Union of Canada, in abeyance since 1939, was reformed.

To the south, US rugby won considerable publicity when Peter

Dawkins of West Point, winner of the 1958 Heisman Trophy for the best college American footballer, went to Oxford on a Rhodes scholarship and won three Blues, demonstrating some of the gridiron passing skills that had made an impression on wartime New Zealanders. Several years later, a New York writer reported that rugby-style jerseys had become fashionable thanks to the film *This Sporting Life*, naturally unaware that it was about rugby league. A regular 'Bermuda Rugby Week' competition popular with US teams was dropped by the sponsoring Bermuda Trade Development Board following complaints of rowdyism, but 1959 also saw the launch of the New York Rugby Club's 'Thanksgiving Weekend Sevens', forerunner of many such weekend festivals.

Further south still, Argentina was beginning to make a serious impression on the established rugby nations. Lessons left by Marcel Laurent, coach of the powerful French team that won all three tests on its visit in 1960 – 'You need to remember that attack is the best form of defence, and it is less boring to attack than defend' – were taken to heart. Arriving five years later in South Africa, they announced, 'We've come to learn,' but left their hosts wondering who was teaching whom. Winning 11 games out of 16, including an 11–6 win over the Junior Springboks in Johannesburg, Argentina left senior South African journalist Reg Sweet enthusing over a game he saw as modelled on the French, with 'probably the best handling in the game . . . exemplary pace and an almost uncanny ability to improvise', while liaison officer Izak van Heerden, who assisted with coaching, spoke of 'the quickest learners I have ever handled . . . the most intelligent players I know'. They even acquired a nickname in the classic manner – 'Pumas' was coined by a journalist who misidentified the jaguarete on their jerseys. It was a name that established nations rapidly learnt to respect. A Wales team on the verge of dominating Europe went to Argentina in 1968, followed in the next two years by Scotland and Ireland. Only Scotland, who drew their series 1–1, won a test. Wales lost one and drew one, while the Irish dropped both. Ireland's manager reported back, 'It is now evident that nothing less than a full international side can hope to take on the Pumas at home on equal terms.' Pumas lock-forward Aitor Otano, carried off in triumph as captain at Ellis Park in 1965, played all six matches, while centre Arturo Rodriguez Jurado, son and namesake of the interwar captain, played four in the early stages of an international career which earned him twenty-four caps in ten years. Compared with his father's eight in nine, this showed how far opportunities were expanding.

The established nations – France, as ever, apart – gave less encouragement to aspirants from Europe. A secession to rugby league by leading Italian clubs, protesting at the stockpiling of top players by Padua Fiamme Oro, champions from 1958 to 1961, was cited by the IRB as justification for its 'go slow' policy and for rejecting a request by the 1960 Springboks to visit Italy. Even so, Italy were strong enough in 1963 to come within six minutes of beating France at Grenoble, where two of their players, prop Sergio Lanfranchi and second row Franco Piccinini, helped the city's club to that year's championship semi-final. Francesco Zani was rated by some as the best number 8 in France and retrospectively chosen as Player of the Year by the French *Rugby Guide* when he won a championship with Agen in 1965.

Romania were still further on the outer fringes, yet good enough to be unbeaten in four meetings with France between 1961 and 1964, winning at home and drawing away, and to win again in 1968. Full-back Alexandre Penciu, an army telephone engineer who had impressed international opponents in the 1950s, was rated better than any full-back in France after the 6–6 draw at Toulouse in 1962. Second place behind France on the Continent was confirmed in 1970 when, after three matches during the 1960s had gone with home advantage, Romania beat Italy 14–3 at Rovigo, in northern Italy. Romania applied to join the Five Nations in 1966, but getting anyone to play them was a problem. The IRB's anathema was reaffirmed in 1965 and 1967. Australia's 1966 tourists were forbidden to accept an invitation to Bucharest. This induced a furious outburst from France's rugby journal of record *Midi Olympique*, saying that the IRB's attitude ensured that 'The finest game in the world is restricted to a small minority instead of spreading as it deserves.'

At least Czechoslovakia – from where Swansea returned in 1966 reporting that rugby there was 'if anything, more amateur than it is in the British Isles. We saw clubhouses, modest by our standards, which players and officials had built themselves' – came off the blacklist in 1967, and a visiting French team was among the phenomena of the 'Prague Spring' that preceded the following year's Soviet invasion.

The less contentious Netherlands prospered. Dutch rugby had been played since 1918 but never by more than a handful of teams. In 1952, the complaint had been that it was boring always playing the same opponents, but the game grew fast in the '60s. The number of players quadrupled between 1963, when buying shorts for the national team was still a challenge, and 1969, when there were 2,500 players, regular Sunday-night television coverage and a national rugby centre opened by Danie Craven, although still no crowds.

The game was still finding fresh territories. It was introduced into Norway, where climatic problems dwarf even those of Canada, by oil workers in 1965 and into Hungary by Italian diplomats three years later. In 1961, a French news agency reported five teams, one all-African, in the Ivory Coast, showing the pioneer spirit:

> A team in Abidjan, the capital, playing at Bonoke, leaves at 7 or 8 p.m. after Saturday's work, travels about 160 miles by motor-coach along tracks and often in clouds of dirt, arrives about 2 a.m., plays at 4 p.m. and is back in Abidjan at 4 a.m. on Monday and working again at 7 a.m. Grounds are hard, but all the players are fast and have unusual stamina. Many are Africans, fine swimmers and star canoeists. Bare-footed trotting by the hour in the bush is prominent in their training.

The decade ended on an upturn in European rugby. Although France remembers much about 1968 with mixed feelings – an echo of old revolutions with barricades, protesting students and riot police in the streets – for the narrower world of rugby it is redolent of triumph. Christian Carrere – 'elegance made flanker', for Denis Tillinac – was chaired from the Arms Park as a team featuring both Camberaberos at half-back and a new generation of tough, gifted forwards led by Walter Spanghero and the phenomenally talented Benoit Dauga secured France's first Grand Slam. Once again, rule changes presaged a shift in the balance of power. As the touch-kicking dispensation arrived in 1968–69, a formidable Welsh team came together. Full-back John (as yet the only one, so not yet J.P.R.) Williams had apparently been designed with the new rule in mind.

Wales played to audiences limited by the demolition of the old North Stand, its successor not yet in place. Something equally formidable was under construction on the field, as Wales beat England 30–9 in the final match of the season, wing Maurice Richards the first player since Ian Smith to score four tries in a championship match, to take the title.

## CHAPTER ELEVEN

# Triumph of the Welfare
# State Rugby Player

'They ought to build a bloody cathedral on the spot'

Spike Milligan, on Gareth Edwards's try for Wales against Scotland

(1972)

'It continues to be an unfortunate fact that too many coaches
and players are skilled at seeking ways of frustrating the
intentions of the Board'

IRB Laws Committee (1975)

The promise evident in Wales's 1969 season was fulfilled as they
dominated Europe for a decade, challenged only by France. There
was a hiatus – the uncompleted 1972 season, when Wales won three
games but, like Scotland, chose not to travel to Dublin because of
security concerns, was followed by the only ever five-way tie in 1973
and Ireland's first title in a quarter of a century in 1974. But Wales's
record over the 11 seasons starting in 1969 speaks volumes: 33 wins
and only 7 defeats, 3 by France, in 43 matches. Only France, in
1974, escaped Cardiff undefeated, drawing 16–16.

The hiatus defined a division between two Welsh teams. The
earlier was Clive Rowlands', driven by his tactical ingenuity and
exhortatory rhetoric invoking *calon* (heart). He found a leader, and
successor, in John Dawes, captain of the remarkable London Welsh
team built on the capital's Welsh schoolmasters. As a centre, Dawes
was unspectacular – the kind who is often criticised, as he was after
his first appearances for Wales in the mid-1960s, not a maker of
slashing breaks but a subtle enabler, a straightener of lines and
superb timer of passes who made everyone around him look better
and captained in much the same way. Randwick, where, as Max

Howell recalled, centres are judged on how well their wings do, would have rated him highly.

The back row – pacy, hirsute open-side John Taylor, grafting Dai Morris and Mervyn Davies, whose prehensile tackling and domination of the back of the lineout redefined standards for number 8s – reflected the analytical work of Ray Williams in recasting back rowers as creators. The star, though, was outside-half Barry John, a languidly deceptive runner and hugely gifted footballer. Once, when miked up for television during a match against Swansea – rarely accommodating opponents, least of all against Cardiff – he performed on demand a series of scoring feats, starting with a try in a nominated corner, then a drop goal and, though not then his team's usual kicker, a penalty. Asked what he intended to do in a certain set of circumstances, he said, 'How can I tell you? I don't know myself till I get the ball.'

The transition from Barry John, early retirement precipitated by the pressures of being the most recognisable player in a televised age, to the darting sidestepper Phil Bennett, marked the shift between the two teams. The second was also identified with the Pontypool front row – thanks not least to comedian Max Boyce, whose songs and monologues form, along with Bill McLaren's match commentaries, this period's soundtrack. Leonine, Egyptian-born prop Graham Price is on a very short list of the greatest Welsh forwards – an all-rounder quick enough to score a long-distance try on his debut in Paris in 1975 and so dominant a scrummager that it sometimes worked against him. When scrums went awry, some referees judged him guilty, assuming he could do whatever he wanted.

That this team generally played with less flamboyance – epitomised by powerful centres Ray Gravelle and Steve Fenwick – than its immediate predecessor reflected the latest swing of the attack–defence pendulum. Making rules for rugby is like traffic management – solving one problem tends to exacerbate another. By the mid-1970s, the game was closing up, characterised by long loose mauls, in which Geoff Wheel's ability to rip the ball free made him Wales's key possession-winner, shambolic lineouts and midfield players who sought contact rather than the gap. While the rugby of the late 1970s was much more attractive than that played 10 or 20 years before, Five Nations matches for the first time started producing more penalty goals than tries.

Continuity across Wales's second golden age was represented by three backs. J.P.R. Williams (a second John Williams, the sprint hurdler J.J., joined Wales from 1973) was a full-back with the ball skills of a junior Wimbledon champion and the aggression of a front rower. Wing Gerald Davies had sufficient sense of perspective that he gave up international rugby for one season to ensure that the experience of studying at Cambridge University was not wasted upon him and a sidestep so devastating that one referee complained that he disappeared when he got the ball.

Scrum-half Gareth Edwards routinely tops surveys of the greatest player of all time, whether the jury are experts or the general public. Opponents could have quoted Stanley Baldwin's verdict on Lloyd George: 'a dynamic force is a terrible thing'. An extraordinary combination of physical attributes, including pace, power, the balance and elasticity of a gymnast and a low centre of gravity, were complemented by formidable football skills and a driving will to win. If his long-range try against Scotland in 1972, ending with his rising, face blackened, from the mud at corner-flag, remained the definitive demonstration of these unique talents, he also had both the pragmatism and the skill needed to single-handedly kick Wales to victory amid a Twickenham deluge on the day in 1978 when he became the first Welshman to earn 50 caps.

The Wales players of this era were fortunate in both age and location. They were old enough to have been formed in the minimal time and space of pre-1964 matches before entering the adult game with the terms of trade changed in their favour. They also benefited from social change in post-war Wales. John, Edwards and Gerald Davies were born into mining familes in south-west Wales between 1945 and 1947, grew up in the new dawn of publicly owned pits and free healthcare and fulfilled parental dreams of escaping the pit via the classic Welsh working-class route into teaching. West Indian Marxist C.L.R. James thought the 'welfare-state cricketer' a dull, safety-first practitioner, but the welfare-state rugby player was a being of unprecedented brilliance, exploring the fresh possibilities of a game liberated by the rule changes of 1964 and 1968 (the touch-kicking dispensation was made permanent in 1970) and the 'cricket catch' knock-on rule that was introduced in 1972. Superb as their record was, the warmth with which these players are remembered by the fans of most nations relates not to results but panache, wit and their simple sense of joy at playing the game. Pierre Albaladejo's exclamation as a particularly dazzling first-half passage settled a third consecutive Wales v. France Grand Slam decider in 1978 spoke for many: 'this may be the best rugby ever played'.

They were also watched by far larger numbers than previous outstanding British teams. By 1971, 91 per cent of British households had a television. Coverage demystified the game for people who had not gone to rugby-playing schools. While he never quite acquired the cult status of rugby league's much-impersonated Eddie Waring, the Border tones and mannerisms of BBC commentator Bill McLaren became as familiar in Britain as Couderc in France and McCarthy in New Zealand. He had a taste for rolling out full names – 'John Peter Rhys Williams' – and proclaiming that people would be 'dancing in the streets' of whichever town a try-scorer or successful kicker hailed from. McLaren had played well enough to win a Scottish trial before being struck down by tuberculosis in the late 1940s and had a qualified teacher's urge to elucidate and explain.

Rugby benefitted not only from greater accessibility and comprehension, with Wales providing a superb advertisement for the game, but from economic prosperity. Full employment and increased mobility – there were five times as many cars on the road in 1970 than in 1950 – helped drive rapid grass-roots expansion. The number of clubs affiliated to the RFU grew from 971 to 1,769 in a decade from 1965, while Scottish Rugby Union affiliations rose from 110 to 207. If there was less expansion in Wales, it was because, with 162 clubs already serving a population less than one-fifteenth England's in 1965, there was much less room for growth.

There was a single, rather large, asterisk on the Welsh record. They could not, even at this peak of brilliance, beat New Zealand. In 1969, a young team, subjected to an absurd travel and playing schedule, was flattened by one of the last outings of the All Blacks' '60s steamroller. Early dominance and desperate late tackles got the New Zealanders home, just, at the Arms Park in 1972–73, and Wales were frustrated again in 1978 by a late penalty awarded for a Welsh indiscretion at a lineout also featuring an ostentatiously cynical premeditated dive out of the line by All Black lock Andy Haden. There was a further defeat in 1975, inflicted on a full-strength team which the WRU, for reasons comprehensible only to itself, chose to call merely a Wales XV and deny test status.

When playing alongside the rest of Britain and Ireland, though, it was another story. There was a Welsh core to both the 1971 Lions team, led by Dawes and coached by the astute, analytical, humane Llanelli polymath Carwyn James – whom John Taylor would remember as 'working harder on individual players than any other coach I have seen' – which dazzled New Zealand and the 1974 edition which demolished South Africa. That core was surrounded by vital contributions from others. Laidlaw reckoned Mike Gibson's performances in 1971 sealed his rating as 'the greatest back of the decade'. Ray McLoughlin's analytical abilities, perfectly meshing with those of his coach, underpinned a strong scrummage, and the understated skills of England's Peter Dixon balanced a fine back row. If the length-of-the-field second-minute try initiated by the sidestepping of Bennett and concluded by an unstoppable burst from Edwards is the single most remembered and replayed moment of that tour's extraordinary coda – the 1973 Barbarians v. All Blacks match at Cardiff – then England hooker John Pullin provided a vital link and wing David Duckham, revelling in receiving more passes in an afternoon than in several international seasons, contributed as much as anyone to the subsequent brilliance of the Barbarians' 23–11 win.

In 1974, the ageless McBride, on his fifth Lions tour, contributed both charismatic leadership and the earthier qualities of the top-class lock. That his pack won 70 per cent possession owed something to Springbok disarray but more to players like dynamic Irish open-side Fergus Slattery, who linked attacks and hit rucks like the best New Zealanders, granitic England prop Fran Cotton and Scotland's Gordon Brown, the perfect second-row complement to McBride. At full-back, Andy Irvine showed himself the latest and greatest in the remarkable Heriots line, competing with J.J. Williams to see who could wreak greater, more vivacious attacking havoc to delight both the non-white fans in the stadiums and the political prisoners of the apartheid regime on Robben Island, who were denied news but knew from the demeanour of their guards that the Springboks were doing badly.

# TRIUMPH OF THE WELFARE STATE RUGBY PLAYER

In 1971, New Zealand were beaten 2–1, with one draw – exactly as manager Doug Smith, a Scottish international who admitted he had changed his mind about the value of coaching, had predicted. Three years on, South Africa were swept aside in a manner which reminded one writer of Genghis Khan, a run of 21 consecutive Lions wins ended only by a final test draw after a home-town referee had ruled out a late try by Slattery. British rugby, driven by Welsh brilliance, could for the first time for the best part of a century claim to be the best in the world. Laidlaw's verdict that 'The Welsh Rugby Club is perhaps the most graphic example of a sporting institution providing the central focus of community life anywhere in the world' and that because of it 'devotion to the game is deeper and will last longer' than in New Zealand looked secure, even if the 1977 All Blacks v. Lions series saw reversion towards the status quo as a last-minute try in the final test denied the tourists, led by Bennett and coached by Dawes, a drawn series.

There was a price for Welsh brilliance. Part of it was paid by their neighbours. England won the annual meeting only once and failed to win the championship at all between 1963 and 1980. Infamously incoherent selection was epitomised by 15 scrum-halfs in as many years. Jan Webster of Moseley played brilliantly in England's best results of the decade – short-tour victories in South Africa in 1972 and New Zealand a year later – yet he only won eleven caps spread across four seasons. The forwards whose power took England to a 1980 Grand Slam, which made a national figure of affable captain Bill Beaumont and followed a total of only eleven wins over the previous nine seasons, had all been available for some years.

English rugby needed the boost. The RFU acceded to club pressures without fully accepting leagues, introducing the Knock-Out Cup in 1971–72, the season when Wales revived cup rugby for leading clubs, then Merit Tables in 1976. It discovered how important these were to club status and finances a year later when three northern clubs sued after being excluded. Limited commercialism was also accepted, with an agency employed to sell perimeter advertising at Twickenham in 1973 and the Knock-Out Cup sponsored by cigarette company John Player from 1975. Neither competition nor commerce was as yet an unqualified success. The Cup discovered strength in unexpected quarters

– Harlequins complained of being 'ambushed in a lay-by off the M6' after being beaten by the Wigan suburb Orrell – and gave Coventry some belated silverware to call their own. It did not lead to the bloodshed and mayhem some predicted. Nor, though, was it a crowd-puller. The 1979 final between Leicester and Moseley attracted only 18,000 fans. A year later, a debenture issue for a new stand at Twickenham failed miserably.

It was the Scots, modernising with a sudden decisiveness that recalled the Catholic Church's adoption of the vernacular mass under Pope John XXIII, who went for leagues first, because the clubs asked for them, introducing a comprehensive national system in 1973–74. Hawick won the first championship and the four after that before Heriots deposed them in 1979, not quite the old order triumph it looked. By the first league season, Watsonians were the only 'closed' club among six nominal former-pupil clubs in the 12-team First Division. One traditionalist said audibly, 'too much like soccer', as Hawick captain Norman Suddon received the first championship trophy, but as Norman Mair noted, the scene was indistinguishable from a final of the Borders' cherished sevens tournaments. One sending off in the top four divisions and a crowd of more than 6,000 for the title decider between Hawick and West of Scotland also augured well. Bill Dickinson, who made the case for leagues when he said, 'It isn't who you play for that really matters, but who you play against,' was appointed the first national coach, thinly disguised as 'adviser to the captain', in 1972.

Chronic travel-sickness was Scotland's 1970s affliction, with only two away wins denying real reward for nine consecutive wins at Murrayfield, including two over Wales, between 1971 and 1975. Scotland's sudden taste for innovation was also evident in celebrating the Scottish Rugby Union's centenary in 1973 by staging a world sevens tournament that was won, slightly to their own surprise, by England. While showcasing a distinctly Scottish version of the game – one that would steadily internationalise once the Hong Kong sevens were devised as the best party the game could offer in 1976 – the competition's success was also a gentle nudge towards a full World Cup competition.

Ireland had started the decade strongly and were frustrated in 1972 after beating both France and England away when Wales and Scotland concluded their safety could not be guaranteed in Dublin. England captain John Pullin won immortality in the annals of English self-deprecation a year later when, after his team had been cheered onto Lansdowne Road and soundly beaten, he began his after-dinner speech with the words 'we may not be much good, but at least we turn up'. Slightly ungratefully, Ireland won at Twickenham the following year, a 26–21 victory inspired by Gibson, whose international career still had five years to run and would be described by John Reason as 'beginning to resemble the seven ages of man'. This gave Ireland an unexpected title when Wales went down to the English. There was inevitably a dip after the mid-1970s with the all-but simultaneous retirement of McBride, bequeathing all-time records of 63 Ireland caps and 17 for the Lions, McLoughlin and hooker Ken Kennedy. New blood was, though, arriving. Moss Keane, a colossally strong Kerryman, was the first former Gaelic player capped following the lifting of the 'ban' on 'garrison games' in 1971. Always a stronghold of schools rugby, with provincial finals sometimes attracting five-figure crowds, Ireland played its first schools international in 1975. Gibson endured almost to the end of the decade, finishing with 69 caps, and Slattery well into the next, but by 1979 Irish rugby was preoccupied with a classic outside-half dispute. Tony Ward, a dashing attacker with a soccer background, looked set for years after being elected European Player of the Year for copious scoring in the 1978 championship, followed by an important part in the best Irish performance of the decade: the 12–0 defeat of the All Blacks by Munster, which has since been commemorated by a plaque at Thomond Park, Limerick, much mythology, a book and an award-winning play, *Alone It Stands*. Within a year, he was dropped for the comparably talented, if less mercurial, Ollie Campbell.

There was a price, too, for the squad sessions and preparation that underlay British rugby's improvement in the 1970s. Rugby union's commitment to amateurism was increasingly out of line with other major sports. Cricket abolished the distinction between amateurism and professionalism in 1963, tennis went open in 1967 and football followed cricket's example in 1974. Demands increased not only on players but on the families and employers whose support enabled so much unpaid activity. As early as July 1962, Vivian Jenkins had calculated that England players on that year's Lions tour and the following season's trip to New Zealand would have only one wholly rugby-free month between August 1961 and April 1964. One of those players, Coventry hooker Bert Godwin, revealed that going on a Lions tour cost him £400 in lost income and a further £8 for every trial or international.

That was before the mounting demands of the 1970s, with more short tours, squad sessions and clubs taking Merit Table and Cup matches increasingly seriously. David Perry, an England captain of the mid-1960s, said in 1973 that he couldn't imagine coping with modern demands: 'I don't think it right that clubs should insist on their players devoting so much to the game. I think the game is becoming professionalised, not perhaps in the financial sense, but in that many clubs are treating the players like professionals.'

Asked to tour New Zealand in place of the cancelled Springboks in 1973, Scotland had to decline, because players could not manage the time off. In 1979, John Watkins of Gloucester and England reckoned that he was losing three months' work per year – worth around £1,500. Elsewhere, as Carwyn James pointed out, employers were bearing the burden if they declined to dock the wages of those absent playing. Journalist Roy McKelvie suggested a variation of broken time, with employers reimbursed for time lost.

Players were becoming what athlete Chris Brasher had termed 'time professionals'. Stories proliferated of 'blindside remuneration' and cash payments for after-dinner speaking or opening new clubhouses. Yet there was almost no explicit demand for open professionalism. J.J. Williams was in the distinct minority when he argued in 1974 that 'We're virtually full-time players. The only difference between us and the soccer professionals is that we don't have to hang around the club all day . . . They'll have to pay us in the end, you know. Scrap all this nonsense and let us earn a bit from something we can do well.'

The game's rulers remained committed to 'all this nonsense'. There were some amendments, affecting specific professional groups. Andrew Mulligan, the Ireland and Lions scrum-half, argued successfully that writing about rugby was an essential part of his full-time profession as a journalist, while provision also had to be made for teachers. Specific reference to rugby league was removed from the regulations in 1973, but playing it – paid or not – continued to be anathema. The British Amateur Rugby League Association (BARLA), formed in 1973, launched a campaign for a 'free gangway', arguing that amateur players should move freely between the two codes. The case of former league player R.M. Reid, assistant director of physical education at Aberdeen University, prompted debate of almost Talmudic complexity over precisely what the phrase 'accepted educational duties' meant in terms of coaching and selecting university teams. When England lock Nigel Horton joined Toulouse in 1977, taking a post as a bar manager, he was warned that he was contravening the rule against benefits obtained 'directly or indirectly' if the club was involved in getting him the job.

France, as ever, had its own approach. Albert Ferrasse, latest in the FFR's succession of patriarchal presidents, answered that 'talk is one thing, proof is another' when pressed on allegations of professionalism in 1978. This was Béziers' time as completely as the 1950s had been Lourdes'. In fourteen seasons from 1971 to 1984, they won ten championships, losing another in extra time. Escot records that players were on a regular 3,000 francs (about £300) per month, paid on a Wednesday, plus bonuses, and that coach Raoul Barrière reckoned players at Perpignan and Narbonne were on more. Barrière argued, 'We were not pros; we had a pro approach, which is different. Remuneration was the means to obtaining performance, never a goal in itself. Money allowed players to train better, more often and for longer. That is how we conceived it. We were pros in action, not in salary.' If jobs were found for players, he said, it was no more than what leading English clubs were doing.

Where Béziers were undoubtedly ahead was in preparation, with intensive training backed by advice from a club dietician and regular medical testing. While Barrière the player struck Lalanne as 'a typical Frenchman, lost in a foreign country' on the 1958 tour of South Africa, he took notice of the power-based game played by his hosts and as a coach adapted it to domestic needs. While he wanted forwards to handle like backs, it was still more important that backs had the power and appetite for contact of forwards, giving 'total physical commitment'. Inevitably, so successful a formula influenced the national team, particularly under the captaincy of

Jacques Fouroux, a tiny Napoleonic figure goading a gigantic pack when France won the Grand Slam in 1977.

It was not to every French taste. Jean-Pierre Rives, the Toulouse flanker whose dash and bravery were even more noticeable than his frequently blood-bespattered blond hair, said in 1978 that Béziers matches were 'rubbish to watch and to play in' and were damaging rugby as a whole: 'We have made the move from just playing to winning rugby, but we have lost the excitement along the way. All the fun has gone out of our game and it is the same with international rugby.' To Jean Lacouture, it was 'the rugby of paratroopers'. Bans for two of Béziers' international forwards in 1978 – totemic bearded lock Alain Estève for 'repeated brutality' followed not long after by second-row partner Michael Palmie, who wound up in court and was banned from international rugby for life – showed the uglier side of their physical approach. That Palmie is now one of the most important officials in French rugby reflects a national taste for redemption taken to comical lengths in 1974 when it was suggested that a referee shortage might be remedied by recruiting players banned for life for violent play. Redemption of another sort was accomplished in 1978 when, 65 years after first asking, France were admitted to the IRB.

Violence was far from exclusively French. Tours of Australia generated ugly scenes, with England prop Mike Burton sent off in 1975 and Graham Price's jaw broken in 1978. Australian prop Steve Finnane, a successful barrister, earned an unattractive reputation with punching ability that once gave rise to a job offer from a leading Sydney gangster. It typified the occasionally schizoid character of Australian rugby that after miserable results – defeat by Tonga in 1973 prompted an appeal for Ray Williams to go and advise on coaching structures – and ugly incidents, it should finish the decade by reclaiming the Bledisloe Cup and with a schoolboy team built around the talents of four young Aborigines named Ella and half-back Wally Lewis enchanting British crowds and bamboozling opponents on an unbeaten tour in 1978. The long-memoried Vivian Jenkins reckoned them a throwback to the dashing Waratahs of exactly half a century earlier, while devoted admirers included former England wing Cyril Lowe, who at 86 watched them at every opportunity.

Nor did British teams play in the pacific spirit which led the 1950 Lions selectors to exclude Welsh flanker Ray Cale for being too physical – undoubtedly the strangest reason anyone has ever been denied a trip to New Zealand. The 1971 team coined the strategy of 'getting their retaliation in first', while their successors of 1974 were notorious for a '99' call signalling general mayhem.

In 1971, Barry John, whose tour performances – adding goal-kicking to other skills and promptly breaking records – launched him to the fame from which he would recoil, left New Zealand feeling that 'they had forgotten it was supposed to be for enjoyment'. Carwyn James, who embarked on a second tour – this time of Britain – with a newsreel film of tour highlights, regaled audiences with the story of the boy in his early teens who explained that he was not playing because he had already been concussed three times. In New Zealand, enjoyment has been closely connected to winning, a habit the All Blacks resumed, along with what some described as 'sensible rugby', on the 1972–73 tour of Britain. This time, the Grand Slam against the home nations was missed through a draw with Ireland, who scored a last-gasp equalising try through Tom Grace and barely missed the conversion. On the last traditional full-length All Black tour, with thirty-two matches in just under five months, they were vulnerable outside the tests to teams who were better organised and more prepared than on previous visits. If the losses to Carwyn James-coached Llanelli and the Barbarians are the best remembered, they also left extremely fond memories in north-west England and the West Midlands. Munster offered a hint of future glory with a 3–3 draw. New Zealand's sensible rugby was based around the powerful pack led by skipper Ian Kirkpatrick, a quick and intelligent flanker with a remarkable try-scoring record, and a back division of some talent kept on short commons by the conservative, but highly effective, play of the abrasive Going at scrum-half.

The Grand Slam would be achieved in 1978 by a team led by another fine open-side, Graham Mourie. His teammate Andy Haden noted that, while slower than most international open-sides, he was 'almost always first to the loose ball, such was his anticipation and intelligence', while McLean described him as blessed with 'fitness that is fathomless, courage that is inestimable and as sharp and cool a brain as ever graced the head of an international captain'. He took leadership seriously. His memoirs were called *Graham Mourie: Captain*, and Haden described the almost trance-like concentration he brought to composing team-talks. His team responded, coming from behind in three of the four tests.

The main development in domestic New Zealand rugby was the creation in 1976 of the National Provincial championship, intended, as journalist Don Cameron put it, 'to transform the old, traditional, patternless representative programme into a single, effective national league (although NZRFU officials shy away from the word)'.

The main issue throughout the 1970s was, though, what to do about South Africa. In 1973, Labour premier Norman Kirk cancelled the scheduled Springbok tour after police warnings of major demonstrations and probable disorder. A year later, he reversed Labour's traditional policy of non-intervention on sport, declaring that no sporting organisation practising apartheid should send teams to New Zealand. In 1975, Labour was ejected from office, National Party leader Rob Muldoon campaigning on a pro-South Africa platform. The All Blacks went to South Africa in 1976, arriving a week after armed police had fired on protesting schoolchildren in the township of Soweto in that decade's nearest equivalent to Sharpeville. They lost the test series 3–1 and played two non-white teams plus a mixed Invitation XV. Springbok flanker Jan Ellis refused to captain the Invitation team, saying, 'When in Rome, you do as the Romans tell you. Here in South Africa, the same thing holds, and I am a white South African.' The All Black tour prompted a boycott of that year's Montreal Olympics by 26 African nations protesting against New Zealand's presence.

Australian federal politics were bipartisan on the issue. In 1972, Gough Whitlam's Labour government banned racially selected teams. Four years later, Malcolm Fraser's Liberal-Country coalition reaffirmed this policy. The 1971 Springbok tour, leading to the declaration of an 18-day state of emergency by the Queensland government of the maverick right-winger Joh Bjelke-Petersen, was enough to convince conservatives that tours were much more trouble than they were worth. Cricketing isolation was confirmed in 1971–72 when an Australia tour by a Springbok team already selected and fitted for its blazers was called off.

There was considerable external support for South Africa. The notion of excluding them from the IRB was not entertained until the rebel tours of the late 1980s seriously disrupted other members. In March 1972, *Rugby World* carried an advertisement from 'Freedom Under the Law', a group which described itself as non-political and aimed to 'stop the agitators' game before they stop yours'. 'Non-political' implied accepting the official South African view. Bodis notes that J.B.G. Thomas's disavowal of politics in one of his tour books is followed, not many pages after, by a description of fears of communism coming over the border from Zambia, while All Black player Andy Haden's assertion that South Africa had no Communist Party may have surprised members serving sentences on Robben Island.

The notion of being non-political would have surprised the Broederbonders who staged an unsuccessful putsch against Danie Craven in 1971 as much as the executive of the South African Rugby Union (SARU – formerly the South African Coloured Rugby Board). The SARU renamed its Rhodes Cup the South African Cup in 1971, declined to join the Proteas touring team to England in 1972 because it would not 'play overseas whites for as long as it was not allowed to play local whites', then in the following year affiliated to the campaigning South African Council on Sport (SACOS). By 1975, the SARU, representing people that former Springbok captain Dawie de Villiers would assert in 1980 'had only known Western sports for the last ten years', had 150,000 players registered in its 16 unions. Post-apartheid SARU president Brian van Rooyen remembered, 'Black rugby . . . could be an instrument to help you vent your anger at the system. There were only two disciplines in which you could express these feelings – the Church and black rugby. The rest were banned.'

It was the SARU who proved most resistant to closer relations with the white union, while Cuthbert Loriston's Federation and the African Union fielded representative teams against tourists and on tour – an English coach who met the Protea team remembered them as 'subdued and overawed in the clubhouse. They were more like dogs cowering in the corner of their kennels,' showing fear which, as cricketer Basil D'Oliveira's memoirs show, was endemic to non-white South Africans entering unsegregated societies.

Loriston had predicted in 1972 that rugby would be integrated within five years. He was right in an extremely limited sense, as his union and the African Union joined the whites in forming the South African Rugby Board (SARB) in 1977, with Craven as president. A year later, the SARU voted against affiliating by twelve votes to nine, arguing that apartheid still made normal sport impossible. Twenty-five non-whites played in Springbok trials in 1977, while a South African Barbarians team with eight white, eight coloured and eight black players toured Britain in 1980. To enthusiasts for South Africa, it proved that apartheid was 'almost non-existent' – to opponents, the structure of the team made a nonsense of that idea. And as Albert Grundlingh has pointed out, nothing altered the underlying reality of South African life:

African, coloured and white could play together, perhaps enjoy a beer together, but that was where it ended; they had to return home by their racially segregated trains, sleep in their racially defined suburbs and townships, and the following morning go to their place of work where their positions were also largely determined by race.

When the Watson brothers from East Cape defied the laws and played inter-racial matches in 1976, retribution was fast. All were harassed by the security forces, their home was burnt down and Dan 'Cheeky' Watson lost an excellent chance of playing for the Springboks. There was a later reward, with echoes of Willie Llewellyn's immunity from looting at Tonypandy in 1910, when theirs was the only shop in downtown Port Elizabeth exempted from a black boycott in the mid-1980s. The Watsons remained almost the sole exception to white rugby's conformity under apartheid.

South Africa's declining presence on tour schedules did little harm to the opportunities for other nations. The favourable impression Argentina made on visiting home unions in the late 1960s was reinforced by reciprocal visits in the following decade. Non-cap status reflected inbuilt conservatism rather than any remaining doubts about Argentina's quality. Scotland escaped luckily with a 12–11 win in 1973, all their points from the boot, while Argentina scored two tries. Three years later, a full-strength Wales team – Gerald Davies and Gareth Edwards scored their tries – needed a controversial last-minute penalty to scrape a 20–19 victory, and in 1978 England had to settle for a 13–13 draw. If attention was drawn initially in 1973 by the splendidly mixed-heritage name of wing Eduardo Morgan, the man to watch then – and for the next decade and more – was outside-half Hugo Porta, in time to be rated by many serious critics as the best to play for any country. Porta joined the Banco Nación club at 15 and took them into the First Division in 1971, the year he was first capped and turned 20. Initially a scrum-half, he had been converted by club coach Angel Guastella, who would become national coach with Porta as captain in 1977 after a row over tactics (Porta complained that 'the scrum had become an end in itself') and the appointment of Arturo Rodriguez Jurado as captain had led to a split in the squad and the dismissal of the previous coach. John Reason would write that Porta 'could play closer to an opponent without being tackled than the top matador works with a bull', beating defences by subtle changes of stride and pace and, like all great outside-halfs, 'with the gift of improving the options of those outside him'.

Argentina were less successful, though rarely badly beaten, against France and New Zealand. They underlined their status as the top nation outside the traditional eight in 1973, when a visiting Romanian team was well beaten in two tests. The IRB bar on Romania was lifted in 1970, but with the proviso that matches should not have full cap status. For most of the decade, their international competition was provided by Continental nations, particularly once FIRA had instituted a formal championship in 1973–74. Matches against France were almost invariably the title decider, with the French finding their trips to Bucharest difficult – the giant pack who delivered the 1977 Grand Slam had started their international season before Christmas by going down 15–12, Romania scoring three tries. Their forward-orientated style was described by one observer as 'based on very sound scrummaging, utilising the eight-man shove on the opposition put-in and long throws, using peel moves in the lineout'. Acceptance by the home unions took longer, but a visit to Wales in 1979, who had to settle for yet another single-point victory, began a sequence of tours around the turn of the decade, with trips to Ireland and Scotland following in the next two years.

Italy stuttered occasionally as the Continent's third force, losing to Spain in 1977, but by the end of the decade was host to an impressive array of overseas players, its clubs making offers that Wallaby Dick Cocks described as 'round the world air tickets, rent, food, free drinks and maybe a little pocket money'. By 1978, there were five Auckland players, including Haden, in Italy, while French centre Jo Maso had been offered the equivalent of £12,000 to play there in 1971. At the strictly amateur end of the European market, the Swiss national team's coach driver and two journalists were capped when they arrived three short at an away match, and Austria's first rugby club, Vienna Celtic, founded in 1978 by expatriate Scot John Skinner and American Vietnam veteran Will Crisp, acquired a detailed knowledge of visa regulations – every away match was on the other side of the iron curtain – and a signature tune as another Scottish member piped them onto the pitch. Dutch players had intended to travel still further in 1973, but a tour of South Africa was called off when several student players pulled out in a protest against apartheid.

Japan's visit from England in 1971, and two closely fought tests, initiated regular contact with European national teams. Union chief Shiggy Konno admitted lack of height was a problem but noted it also made it easier for them to 'pick the ball up, pack down low in the scrum and generally move about more quickly. This is where our strength is, and we have to play to it.' Ingenuity also provided some compensation – England lock Bill Beaumont recalled jumping in the lineout on a Japanese put-in, only to see his opposite number cleanly fielding a low throw – but lack of weight could be as problematic as height, as a prop from Maesteg demonstrated by trundling around 15 yards to the line for Wales Clubs at Swansea in autumn 1976 with several Japanese defenders hanging off him at different angles.

There was serious progress in North America with the formation of the RFU of the United States in 1975 – logistical difficulties underlined by founding delegates travelling 8,000 miles between them to attend – and growth which saw the New York-based Eastern Rugby Union expand from 48 clubs in 1966 to 260 just under a decade later. By the end of the 1970s, there were around 1,000 clubs across the United States, with around 400 colleges playing, and newly secured sponsorship from Michelob beer for national competitions. Around 150 of those clubs were for women.

France, with a heritage based on *barette*, led the women's game in Europe, with a federation formed in 1970. There were also pioneering games in Spain, Holland, Italy and in Britain during the 1970s, with universities playing the same role as they had for men in the nineteenth century and for some of the same reasons. There were concentrations of young people in the universities, with sports facilities on tap, while feminism redefined the limits of what young women thought they could and should do. California was the cradle, with four universities fielding teams by 1972. Rapid growth through the decade was reflected in the organisation of a national competition by 1980.

That year also saw the British and Irish Lions touring South Africa, calling up an unprecedented number of injury replacements and losing the test series 3–1. New Zealand, though, was where the significant action was taking place. In 1979, the NZRFU offered a significant pointer to the near future by canvassing IRB opinion on the idea of a World Cup. The IRB had been offered a proposal as early as 1968, rejected without a second glance. A decade on, 'the idea found no support' – a view reaffirmed unanimously when sports promoters West Nally and IMG came up with proposals. By 1980, the New Zealanders were preoccupied with the following year's tour by South Africa and its potential repercussions. Both issues would resonate loudly into the following decade.

# CHAPTER TWELVE

# To Boldly Go

'Whether we like it or not, New Zealand is a major factor in
the survival of the present structure of South African sport'

Chris Laidlaw (1973)

'Rugby needs a transfusion of ideas and an injection of progress.
The suggestion of a World Cup contained both'

Andy Haden (1984)

When Dr Danie Craven was introduced to the New Zealand High
Commissioner in South Africa in 1992, he said, 'What your people
did to our boys in 1981 was unforgivable.' It did not occur to him
that New Zealanders might also have cause for complaint. New
Zealand suffered its worst civil disorder in living memory in 1981.
This was the year in which Robert Archer and Antoine Bouillon's
assertion that, in the struggle over apartheid in sport, 'the real
battle has been in rugby – and the real battlefield New Zealand'
took on literal truth.

Police appeared on New Zealand city streets equipped with what
David Lange, prime minister from 1984, called 'all the regalia of
certain fascist countries'. The Springboks match against Waikato at
Hamilton was cancelled, leaving demonstrators to run the gauntlet
of angry fans. A light plane, piloted by one Marx Jones, made 62
passes over Eden Park during the fourth and final test. There were
2,000 arrests, one-third of them women. Premier Muldoon and
police minister Ben Couch, by a typically New Zealand irony one of
the Maori All Blacks denied a trip to South Africa in 1949, can hardly
have failed to see it coming. They knew that police had predicted
mass demonstrations in 1973, when public opinion was generally
in favour of contact with South Africa. Polls in 1981 showed the

country spilt more or less in half – a difference symbolised by All Black full-back Alan Hewson, whose late third-test penalty decided the series, and his wife Pauline, who was strongly against the tour. Mourie refused to play against the tourists.

Protestors included All Black trialist Greg McGee, whose play *Foreskin's Lament*, with the eponymous Lament speaking of 'The Bokkies in '73 – the ones that didn't come, that never more will come', was hailed as a national theatrical breakthrough when it opened in 1981. Chris Laidlaw argued that his compatriots had learnt that 'there were issues that loomed larger than the God-given right to go and play rugby on Saturday and to play rugby with whomever you choose'. Rugby itself was, as Mourie predicted, deeply damaged. Sociologist Geoff Fougere wrote that rugby had served for most of the century as 'a mirror to our society', but that whatever the game's future success, the mirror had been smashed irrevocably. The liberal half of New Zealand, particularly women, recoiled. Six years later, visitors to universities were still being advised 'don't mention rugby'. Brian Lochore believed that it became more difficult for players to feel pride in being All Blacks.

Craven proclaimed that 'we are building a new South Africa on the rugby field'. It was definitely a white field – a survey in 1982 would show that whites, 15 per cent of the population, used 82 per cent of the rugby pitches. Critics argued that Craven's development schemes were cosmetic, pointing to projects like the remodelling of Ellis Park, Johannesburg, at a cost of £16.5 million, with 71,000 seats and 245 executive boxes rented for £8–10,000 annually, as a reflection of real priorities.

The limited amount that was being done was enough to scare Afrikaner fundamentalists. When Craven insisted on the inclusion of non-white schools in the Craven Week schools rugby festival in 1980, three all-white East Rand schools declined to send teams. Hard-line MP Andres Treurnicht's subsequent verbal attack on Craven was, Paul Dobson has suggested, the first public step in Treurnicht's estrangement from the National Party. He resigned two years later to set up the new Conservative Party.

South Africa retained cheerleaders and contact abroad. In 1981, the 'Campaign for Freedom in Sport' was launched under the leadership of former Irish international prop Syd Millar, best known a quarter of a century later as the chairman of the IRB. Millar raised the European XV who played the opening match at the new Ellis Park. In the following year, the SARB staged a world media congress at costs estimated at £375,000 or more to show off its development programmes. Four journalists chagrined their SARB hosts by declining a boat ride around the Cape in order to meet officials of SACOS. One of them, David Lawrenson, who reported that 'everything in South Africa is permeated by politics', noted the contrast between facilities in white schools, clubs and grounds and City Park, the main non-white ground in Cape Town.

> An average of twenty-one games per Saturday takes place on the three pitches and in between time the grounds are used by local schools not only for rugby but also athletics. In summer, there are baseball and netball.
>
> This vast over-use is reflected in the lack of grass over wide areas of the main pitch. It seems impossible for anyone to play rugby on it without being scarred for life, and yet, from 8.00 a.m. on a Saturday morning, players from junior level through to senior are keen to play. One wonders how good these players would be if they had halfway decent facilities.

A drip-feed of tours continued. Ireland came in 1981, and two of their players, John Robbie, who went on to a successful media career, and Freddie McLennan, liked it so much that they decided to settle. Three others – Moss Keane, Tony Ward and Dick Spring, who would be deputy prime minister of Ireland within six years – refused to go. Argentina were participants in the boycott, but their players lacked international contact, particularly once British unions stopped playing them after the Falklands War of 1982. 'Jaguars' teams, nominally representing South America but composed almost entirely of Argentinians warned by their union not to wear any symbol associating them with Argentina, visited in 1980, 1982 and 1984 – the 1982 team shaking South Africa with a 21–12 win at Bloemfontein, Porta scoring all the points. The last conventional tour was by England in 1984, which, like Ireland, came without three original selections – Stuart Barnes, Ralph Knibbs and Steve Bainbridge – and lost both matches, rather more heavily than the Irish.

In 1985, South Africa were due for the tour they really wanted

– the All Blacks – but were thwarted when two rugby-playing lawyers obtained a court ruling that the tour contravened NZRFU's constitutional duty to promote the interests of New Zealand rugby. Rumours of an unofficial tour began immediately and came to fruition a year later. All but two of the All Blacks squad, coached by Meads, toured South Africa as the New Zealand Cavaliers. David Kirk, one of the refuseniks, recalled the last provincial match before their departure:

> The Auckland All Blacks literally sprinted off the field, changed into jeans and T-shirts in front of the rest of us and, with scarcely a word, loaded themselves into a wartime minibus. They looked as though they were making an escape, as though they were doing something disreputable.

The NZRFU disowned the tour. So did Craven, who was in London for an IRB meeting. The tour was technically to celebrate Transvaal's centenary and organised by them. On Craven's return home, the SARB awarded Springbok caps for the four 'tests' played by the Cavaliers, who did not play a non-white team. Craven's credibility with his IRB colleagues never recovered. There was also the issue of how much was paid to the Cavaliers. Both Kirk, who did not go, and Dave Loveridge, who did, refer in their memoirs to payments of $NZ100,000 (£30–35,000). The tour management stated that the Cavaliers had been paid only the maximum permissible daily allowance of £15 per day. Journalist Stephen Jones recorded that he put this to a recent All Black: 'By the time he had stopped laughing, my own phone bill had increased £5.' The IRB accepted this with a straight face. The NZRFU emulated the RFU after Shaw and Shrewsbury's tour a century earlier by asking players for a sworn oath – an excellent device for asking questions to which you do not want to know the answer – that they had not been paid. At least two of the Cavaliers made land purchases shortly after the tour, while Meads spoke of receiving money from 'donors'. He kept his place as a national selector while the players involved were banned for two tests and recalled at the earliest opportunity for the last two of three tests against Australia. The NZRFU was duly punished for its lack of loyalty to players who had stayed loyal to it by losing the Bledisloe Cup.

The Cavaliers tour was another blow to the credibility of the rules on amateurism. Voices for outright professionalism were still few, but the southern hemisphere nations continued to seek amendments. In 1983, the daily 'personal and communication' allowance was fixed at £8, with Australia arguing for £20. It was increased to £15 in 1986. The following year saw the acceptance of broken-time payment for tours, for which Australia in particular had been pressing, with an additional amount of up to £15 per day allowed on tours longer than 21 days. This new rule, with the proviso that 'in no circumstances shall it exceed the normal earnings of the person entitled thereto', was instituted by an IRB vote of thirteen to three.

From 1983, each player was allowed payment for advertisements 'which are related to his full-time bona fide employment provided it does not refer or relate to his activities or involvement with the game'. The chief point of contention was books. New Zealand and Wales proposed in 1985 that it should be possible to keep royalties from a book without becoming a professional. This rule mostly affected players who had just retired, exiling men with much to offer in expertise and public appeal. Colin Meads had found a way around this in 1977 – a trust fund created for his family out of profits from his autobiography, which had sold 57,000 copies. Sid Going's attempt to do the same met with less favour from the IRB, while others who were professionalised under this rule in the early 1980s included Graham Mourie, Bill Beaumont, Fran Cotton, Gareth Edwards and the Scottish prop Ian McLauchlan. Wales and New Zealand found almost no support, losing the IRB vote 11–5. In 1986, a committee on amateurism was formed under the chairmanship of Harry McKibbin of Ireland. The committee minutes noted the underlying problem of 'vast differences of opinion' among member unions.

There was movement on rugby league. English IRB delegate Micky Steele-Bodger reported in 1980 that the RFU was in talks with BARLA and 'asked, rhetorically, whether the Board still believed that a man, who, although not receiving money, plays with or against a professional is guilty and whether the Board might consider some relaxation'. A year later, he spoke again of the need to remove 'guilt by association' from the rules, and it was agreed to remove prohibitions on 'an amateur club having any connection with a non-amateur rugby organisation'. The RFU also agreed free movement for students, provided they had not signed for a professional club or received payment, and the free gangway for amateurs was finally conceded in 1987. Direct contact with professional league remained completely beyond the pale. In 1985, Cardiff wing Steve Ford, whose elder brother Phil was a Great Britain rugby league player, had rugby league trials but chose not to sign, explaining that he had discovered he preferred playing union. An unintended consequence of union's hard line was that it had no answer to players who 'went north' and then extolled league as the better game. One possible response to Ford would have been to send him to explain to the first-team players of every major union club exactly what he had disliked about league. The other was to follow the rules and ban him. Ford was duly banned. More players might have been banned if the home unions had obtained the list that sportswear company Adidas was discovered in 1983 to have submitted to the Inland Revenue, disclosing payments to players for wearing their boots. The WRU promptly cut off this little earner by concluding an exclusive deal with Puma, while Andy Ripley, still playing for Rosslyn Park at 35, whimsically advertised his availability for hire by wearing boots from different manufacturers on his left and right feet.

A far greater threat to both amateurism and the game's existing order was posed by Australian entrepreneur David Lord's plans for professional rugby, leaked to the press in April 1983. Lord claimed to have 203 leading players signed up on contracts of £100,000 per year for an international rugby circus. Not everyone was convinced by Lord. While Escot argues that Lord's great advantage was privileging players increasingly impatient at the penny-pinching of officialdom, he also reports that Jean-Pierre Rives always thought he was bluffing. His plans were finally shelved in November.

The IRB, though, was concerned enough to call, at Australia's request, an emergency meeting in June 1983 to discuss the threat. Its suggestion for heading Lord off was to reconsider IRB opposition to a World Cup, reiterated as recently as March that year. The IRB remained unconvinced, but when the issue was raised again in 1984 it agreed to let the New Zealand and Australian unions, both of which had proposed a competition, to produce a joint feasibility study.

The crucial vote was at the 1985 AGM. Derek Wyatt suggests that the Cup proposal was carried by ten votes to six, with Australia, New Zealand, South Africa and France casting both of their two votes each in favour – Ferrasse had long been publicly convinced of the case for a World Cup. Ireland and Scotland were against, while Wales and England split. Wyatt believes that England's John Kendall-Carpenter, appointed chair of the five-man World Cup committee, and a Welsh delegate voted against the views of their unions. A decision was rapidly made to invite 16 participants rather than holding qualifiers. In 1987, it was decided that all of those participating in the Cup should be invited to become associate members of the IRB, albeit with no voting rights. Argentina, Canada, Italy, Japan, USA and Zimbabwe were admitted before the competition took place – Fiji, Tonga and Romania shortly afterwards. The conspicuous absentees were South Africa, leading Craven to warn that South Africa might turn professional if totally isolated, and Russia, which had progressed fast in the 1980s.

That Australia played so prominent a part reflects the transformation of its position. Sharing territory with by far the strongest rugby league in the world – the 1982 and 1986 Kangaroos set new standards for the game, Clem Thomas describing the 1982 team as ranking with the best to visit Britain in either code and capable, given two more men, of beating any British side at union – had a paradoxical effect on Australia. Competition forced it to be consistently progressive and open to new ideas, but the attrition of player losses to league left it weak in financial and playing terms. James and Reason wrote in 1979 that 'It has been evident for at least 20 years that, but for the constant drain of its best players to rugby league, Australian rugby union would be of a higher standard than either New Zealand or South Africa.'

Almost as soon as that sentence was published, Australia demonstrated what could happen if it retained enough talent, beating New Zealand 12–6 in Sydney to reclaim the Bledisloe Cup. The Sydney-based New Zealander Spiro Zavos suggests that the moment when the Wallabies 'grabbed the huge cup and ran around the SCG [Sydney Cricket Ground] brandishing it to their delirious supporters like a trophy of war' was when the often-disregarded Bledisloe took on iconic status. Nor was it a fluke. Australia came as co-hosts to the 1987 World Cup with a record of parity so far in the decade against its partner New Zealand – two series each, six wins apiece. Still more strikingly, their 1984 tour to Great Britain fulfilled the promise of that schoolboy team six years earlier, beating all four home nations. Among previous Wallabies teams, only the 1947–48 tourists had managed even three out of four.

Success came just in time for the best Australian players of the 1970s: scrum-half John Hipwell, for 14 years a worthy successor to Catchpole, and smart, mobile back rower Mark Loane. A new generation, though, was taking over. Not everything had changed – 1978 schools star Wally Lewis became the dominant figure in league, while as late as 1983 seven of the Wallabies team had been to the Greater Public Schools, four more to upmarket Catholic institutions.

Never before, though, had the Australian game had a player quite like outside-half Mark Ella, one of an Aboriginal family of twelve from La Perouse – sometimes called 'Sydney's Soweto'. The star of the schools team, he had adjusted seamlessly to the adult game and was capped in 1980. Coach Bob Dwyer, who analysed rugby with the cool precision of the trained engineer he was, recognised similar qualities in a 19 year old who subverted all stereotypes about indigenous sportsmen: 'He spoke with precision about how he played the position . . . this was a skilled operator talking, not some kind of free-spirited person.' Australian journalist Evan Whitton credited Ella with 'the timing of Bob Hope, the subtlety of [mime artist] Jean-Louis Barrault and a feeling for angles unrivalled by Euclid'. He was perfectly suited to the environment at Randwick, whose playing style would make a deep impression on England centre Clive Woodward, who moved to Australia to work in the mid 1980s: 'They stood so flat it was incredible. You could touch them, see the whites of their eyes, but you couldn't touch the ball because it was passed on so rapidly.'

Another 1980 newcomer was a smart, durable flanker named Simon Poidevin, with the top-class back rower's knack for being in the right place. By 1984, the Wallabies had been joined by Enrique 'Topo' Rodriguez, a formidable scrummaging prop persuaded to emigrate from Argentina, dynamic scrum-half Nick Farr-Jones, cool-handed inside-centre Michael Lynagh and a pyrotechnic Italian-Australian winger named David Campese. It said something about coach Alan Jones's personality that he overshadowed all of them on a tour in which Ella scored against all four home nations and his team's handling, angles and support-running overwhelmed opponents who, without defensive errors or missed tackles, might find themselves isolated against three attackers. A consummate showman and communicator, by turns incisive, witty and bombastic, who had formerly written speeches for Prime Minister Malcolm Fraser, Jones was, as New Zealand journalist Don Cameron wrote, something new in international rugby: 'He dominates everything about the team, nothing happens without him. Seldom has one man so completely dominated and controlled the destiny of a rugby team.' He was not to all tastes. Predecessor Bob Dwyer complained of being deposed amid 'squalid intrigue', while dislike of his coach's domineering style hastened Ella's retirement at 25. The less stylish but coolly efficient Lynagh inherited the number 10 shirt, and if Australia never quite charmed and bedazzled as they had in 1984, they still arrived at the first World Cup as Bledisloe Cup holders and among the favourites.

The shortening of tours meant the 1984 Wallabies did not go on to France for what would have been the toughest match of the whole venture. At club level, Béziers' dominance had lasted until 1984, giving way to Toulouse, who won for the next two years and would again in 1989. France's most vivid on-field presences, however, played for other clubs. Agen's Philippe Sella was quick enough to win his first caps on the wing and a good enough footballer to switch seamlessly to the centre, where he became an invariable presence for more than a decade, becoming in 1994 the first player to win 100 caps. Even he, though, paled slightly alongside the exuberant brilliance of Biarritz's Venezuelan-born full-back Serge Blanco, an audacious runner who summed up his own philosophy of the game: 'It is instantaneous. It is spontaneous. It is spiritual. It is instinctive. That is the real rugby.' France went to the World Cup as Five Nations champions, brandishing a third Grand Slam in nine years and a record of twelve wins to only two losses – both at Murrayfield, to which they were developing a distinct aversion – over the previous four seasons.

Australia's sequence of victories in 1984 continued a miserable British pattern begun by the 1980 Lions' 3–1 loss in South Africa and deepened three years later by an abject 4–0 failure in New Zealand. Grim defensiveness was also apparent in scoring trends in the Five Nations, with 54 penalties kicked, against 24 tries scored, in the 1983 championship. It was Scotland and Ireland who had the best memories of a somewhat cheerless period. The Scots broke Wales's fourteen-year unbeaten Five Nations home record in 1982, scoring five tries to one, drew with the All Blacks in 1983 and then in the following year claimed their first Triple Crown since 1938 and only their second Grand Slam ever. Success was rooted in coach Jim Telfer's conception of the Scottish game – 'doing the simple, basic skills well under pressure, especially in the tackle, the art of winning the ball on the ground and in close support of the man with the ball either in defence or attack' – leavened with strong elements of New Zealand rucking. In marked contrast to 1925, their success was Borders-led, the region supplying the coach, his assistant and 12 of the 20 players, although nobody was more important than the Dundonian David Leslie, whose agility of body and mind complemented Jim Calder and Iain Paxton in a classically balanced back row. The value of Border sevens heritage was readily apparent in hooker Colin Deans's athleticism and handling, while Iain Milne had succeeded Price as Britain's leading prop. As ever, Scottish success coincided with stability at half-back, quick service from Roy Laidlaw of Jed-Forest helping elegant John Rutherford from Selkirk become the most consistently dangerous attacker in British rugby for several years.

There were, though, underlying worries. School sport had always relied on the goodwill and commitment of teachers, but this was largely withdrawn in the 1980s as the profession found itself in an unsympathetic climate of spending cuts and attacks on the public-service unions. Scotland's heavily unionised state schools were particularly hard hit, and the number of pupils playing dropped from 15,000 to 6,000 in 4 years from 1987.

Ireland enjoyed their best period since the post-war years, with Triple Crowns and titles in 1982 and 1985. France denied them Grand Slams and shared the title with them in 1983. Hooker Ciaran Fitzgerald led in both Triple Crown years, though his experience captaining the Lions in 1983 was less happy. Slattery and Campbell were still around in 1982 and 1983, but the 1985 success was accompanied by generation change and an outstanding new back row. Only Phillip Matthews, who had the abrasive qualities of his Gloucester birthplace, went on to a long career. That ball-handling ex-Gaelic footballer number 8 Brian Spillane never reproduced the form of a brilliant first season and Nigel Carr's career was cruelly truncated by injuries from a bomb helps explain why Ireland enjoyed the second half of the 1980s much less than the first. The IRFU exploited early buoyancy in a hugely successful debenture issue which raised £2 million within a month in 1982 but failed to bring in the league system proposed in 1984, as clubs shied away from the idea.

England's debenture scheme may have needed rescuing by professional marketers in the early 1980s, but they had delivered leagues – a key recommendation in the Burgess report of 1980, one of a proliferation of inquiries seeking the reasons for English underachievement. Once minds were made up, they had moved with a vengeance. Players left a world of Merit Tables when they went to Australia for the World Cup and returned to a new structure incorporating 1,200 clubs – from first champions Leicester at the top to Armthorpe Rovers at the bottom of Yorkshire League Six – sponsored by brewers Courage for £1.65 million over 3 years and described by the RFU as the greatest change in the English game since the union's own foundation in 1871.

The RFU appointed its first marketing executive in 1985 and made his job easier a year later by finally putting its number in the London telephone directory. What did not change was underachievement by the national team, the 1980 Grand Slam a happy blip in a spell between 1964 and 1988 when England otherwise averaged little more than one championship win per season. There was, though, undoubtedly life in the club game, where Bath, underpinned by intense local pride, sports-science expertise from the city's university and the management skills of Jack Rowell, started winning trophies in 1984 and Wasps caused the odd raised eyebrow by the efficiency with which a bright generation of Cambridge University backs, including outside-half Rob Andrew and full-back Huw Davies, were attracted to Sudbury. Even so, some England players still preferred to play in Wales. Lock Maurice Colclough joined Swansea, while rugged number 8 John Scott spent most of his international career as a Cardiff player, explaining, 'Welsh players have a much harder attitude . . . they are far better prepared for international rugby because the gap between club and country is not the yawning one that exists in England.'

Even so, Wales, expectations geared by the 1970s, were scarcely happier. The glory years ended with the '70s – Gareth Edwards and Gerald Davies retired in 1978, a final championship was won as if from memory in 1979 and then came a drop back into the pack. There were still players of distinction, though. Bob Norster was a magnificent lineout technician, Terry Holmes one of the finest exponents of the ninth-forward school of scrum-half and Jonathan Davies a buzzingly vivacious outside-half. Wales's problems were social and economic. If the return of mass unemployment and the demise of coal and steel, highlighted by the year-long miners' strike in 1984–5, were the more noticeable factors, rugby was equally hit by the decline of the public services. There were few teachers left in senior rugby by the end of the 1980s, while working to rule and overtime bans took their toll on the schools game. By 1984, Gwendraeth School, whose former pupils included Carwyn James, Barry John and Jonathan Davies, had no first XV. The head teacher blamed 'a growing diversity of interests' among his pupils. With money short in Wales, the drift north, which had all but ended in the 1970s, started again, with Holmes in late 1985 the highest-profile departure. While Five Nations results were undistinguished, the low-point was in late 1983, a 24–6 hammering in Romania.

That was when the Romanians were being hailed as 'world champions of defence' by the French. But the victory in 1982 which prompted that description was the last over France for eight years, as the social and economic decay that would bring down the Ceausescu dictatorship at Christmas in 1989 began to bite. A particularly severe blow was Ireland and Scotland ending the reciprocal deal under which each country paid the visiting team's expenses. Forced to pay their own way to Dublin in 1986, the Romanians minimised expenses by travelling on an ancient aircraft and arriving less than 24 hours before kick-off, with no time to acclimatise or train. Their 60–0 defeat was the highest ever in a full-cap international

(Romania and Argentina had been elevated to full international status, somewhat belatedly, in 1981). Earlier in the year, they had lost 17–15 to Tunisia, a FIRA third division team representing a nation where rugby was introduced in 1972.

Regional supremacy was under challenge from the Russians, whose play led Lalanne to remark that, in beating a France B-team 12–6 in 1982, 'in the first 20 minutes they displayed more open rugby than the Romanians have done in 20 years'. A 16–14 defeat of Italy in 1987, their fifth in their last eight meetings, included a length-of-the-field try 'that would not have disgraced the All Blacks'. It had been started and finished by dashing outside-half Igor Mironov, with two interventions by Igor Nechaev, who was described by *Rugby World*'s reporter as 'a centre the size of a prop-forward with the speed of a wing-three-quarter'.

In the final decade of bipolar power, rugby in the other superpower was fast becoming a female activity. The US national women's team made its debut in 1987, beating Canada 22–3. European women's rugby, unencumbered by the logistical handicaps of North America, had, though, started playing internationals earlier than in the United States; the first ever was between France and the Netherlands at Utrecht in 1982. France won 4–0, but fell on their first trip across the Channel, losing 14–8 to Great Britain. The British team benefited from an outstanding crop of Loughborough players, among whom Karen Almond offered echoes of Australian league star Wally Lewis, as an outside-half who was taller than most forwards as well as the best footballer on the pitch. Jim Greenwood, a Scottish and Lions international whose *Total Rugby* and *Think Rugby* are among the most influential modern coaching texts, had coached the Loughborough players, then took charge of both England and Great Britain.

The first women's competition in Italy was held clandestinely in 1984. Overseas male players, by contrast, continued to openly regard Italy as a desirable destination. Japan, too, had begun to import players in the 1970s, with attractive company team offers to those who could manage three hours' daily training, often dominated by repetitive drills, on top of a working day. Alison Nish has noted the advantages enjoyed by university rugby players seeking jobs with corporations:

> It is thought that club members have been used to a hard regime and discipline which makes them likely to follow orders blindly, as they would a coach . . . Having survived the disciplined club environment, they are considered to be easier to mould into good company workers.

Deference was not, as overseas visitors were increasingly noting, ideal for producing effective rugby players. Hiteshi Oka, chair of the national coaching committee, recognised the problem late in 1986 when he promised to find ways to 'Free the spirit of Japanese players. I am trying to eliminate inhibition and set moves. Coaching in Japan is like teaching players how to play chess. We dismantle the game into parts to make it more accessible to the Japanese high-school student. The problem is they never manage to put it together again.'

A little bit more inhibition was exactly what Fijian coaches were seeking. In 1980, national team manager Ehutate Tavai complained that 'Fijians are undisciplined players who will run with the ball at the slightest opportunity, often despite instructions to the contrary.' The problems created were evident when every match was lost on the 1982–83 tour of Britain. Uninhibited running was no longer as effective against opposition that was increasingly well-organised and fit, while they were struggling in the ball-winning phases – one statement that they must 'learn to ruck' becoming famous outside rugby circles due to a typographical error. George Simpkins, a New Zealand coach invited to the islands in 1985, immediately diagnosed that his players were insufficiently interested in the set pieces and in particular lacked upper-body strength, so struggled badly in the scrums. Simpkins was still in charge in 1987 when his team went to New Zealand for the World Cup. It nearly did not make it, as communications were shut down by a military coup less than two weeks before the tournament was due to start. With no news getting out, the organisers were set to invite Western Samoa as late substitutes when Fijian journalist Sri Krishnamurthi went to the military headquarters and persuaded them to open a phone line so he could call *New Zealand Rugby News* and relay the message that Fiji were coming.

The 1987 World Cup was, by later standards, small and experimental. In New Zealand, where three of the four four-team pools were situated, it had the feeling of a glorious travelling party. Australia, with the fourth pool, felt somewhat left out. 'Great, but there was no bloody rugby,' responded one journalist based in Sydney for the preliminary stages when asked by his New Zealand-based colleague how he had enjoyed Australia. A firm post-tournament recommendation was that future cups be played in only one country.

The NZRFU's insistence on taking games to non-test venues, over the objections of some home unions, was fully justified, as communities like Napier responded enthusiastically to matches like Canada v. Tonga that would have attracted little more than a dismissive shrug in the rugby-sated test towns. Among the less-established rugby nations, Canada were the revelation, hammering the better-known Tongans – captain Hans de Goede's half-time talk, which was captured by radio microphones, included the words 'Come on, boys, we're making history' – then giving both Ireland and Wales tough matches. It was nevertheless Fiji, after narrowly squeezing out Italy and Argentina in the pool stages, who were closest to providing a genuine shock in the quarter-finals at Auckland. European champions France were scared witless by Fiji's running game. Had giant wing Severo Koroduadua, thundering down the left with the ball clutched in one massive hand, not squeezed too hard and fumbled just short of the line, Fiji might have won. France scraped through ignobly with two pieces of close-range *force majeure* by their pack. Afterwards, George Simpkins was asked what the established nations could do to help Fiji. 'Come and play us,' he said.

Home nation fortunes matched the somewhat dispirited state of the British game. Scotland, much the best of the four, were unlucky to meet New Zealand in the quarter-finals. Wales, advancing by way of abysmal matches against Ireland and England, met a hideous fate in the semi-finals against New Zealand, who dismembered them 49–6. They did, however, have the best British player in the competition, scrum-half Robert Jones, latest in a line of Welsh number 9s that has proved more consistent and durable than the famous outside-half factory and a perfect echo of Townsend Collins's description of his golden age predecessor for Swansea and Wales, Dickie Owen: 'Little, but stout-hearted, plucky to the last degree, great in defence but in attack more notable for what he enabled others to do than what he did himself.' Wales recuperated from that semi-final defeat by beating Australia for third place, cheered on by a Rotorua crowd mindful of old friendships and desirous of seeing one put over on Australia, and in particular Alan Jones.

Australia were consigned to Rotorua by a semi-final defeat at home in the first undeniably great World Cup match. Jones had announced that his team could now 'play Beethoven without a score', but it was the French who achieved the full range of orchestral variations in an epically fluctuating contest climaxed by a winning try from Blanco, whose joyful backward leap after touching down provided the tournament's most imperishable image. A ticket to face New Zealand in Auckland in the final on 20 June was hardly fair reward for so joyous a display.

This was New Zealand's World Cup, on and off the pitch. Never since has a winning World Cup team been so overwhelmingly superior. Opponents could have been given a twenty-point start, two extra men, or perhaps machetes for their back row, and the All Blacks would probably still have won. Their chief weapon was the remorseless driving power of a pack unequalled in the last 20 years.

Number 8 Wayne 'Buck' Shelford did a fair impersonation of the irresistible force while open-side Michael Jones's pace, athleticism and intelligence redefined the possibilities of the position as well as bringing the same sort of fluid elegance of movement to rugby that Michael Holding brought to cricket and Thierry Henry supplies in soccer. The backs were not as good, but they did not need to be. Outside-half Grant Fox was a steady organising hand whose goal-kicking routine was rapidly ingrained in the memory of everyone who watched the tournament as he metronomically converted try after try. Wing John Kirwan scored the most memorable try in the opening match against Italy, running a kick-off back through the entire Italian team to touch down.

Half of the squad – 13 – played for an Auckland team that was dominating domestic rugby. The previous record for retaining the Ranfurly Shield had been 26 matches, by Auckland between 1960 and 1963. This Auckland team would retain the Shield for 62 matches and just over 8 years, starting in September

1985. David Kirk, scrum-half for Auckland and the All Blacks, remembered:

> Auckland believed they could do better with the ball than anyone else. This was the new world of positive rugby. It was a world of technically superior players who were striving for a perfection that other teams didn't realise existed.

The All Blacks were also a blend of rehabilitated Cavaliers and the 'Baby Blacks' who had replaced them in 1986 – players like Kirk, Kirwan and young hooker Sean Fitzpatrick – and begun making rugby acceptable again across the range of New Zealand society and opinions. New Zealand's pleasure in a tournament that brought the world of rugby to its towns and stadiums, and the brilliant rugby played by its own team, continued that process. The mirror might never again be quite what it was, but there was at least a recognisable image again.

An old joke, still appreciated in Australia, advises travellers arriving in Auckland to put back their watches ten years. In rugby, visitors are better advised to advance their timepieces by that amount, and rarely more so than in 1987. Players like Scotland's John Rutherford, whose union had warned him that collecting a Player of the Year award would breach amateur regulations, could watch injured All Black captain Andy Dalton advertising tractors on television – the caption 'Andy Dalton – farmer' inserted to make the advert conform to IRB regulations. Bob Dwyer would later say that 'Professionalism is about more than paying money. New Zealand had been professional in their approach to the game from about 1986–87. Not in terms of payment, but in their attitude.' Intensive All Black preparation for the tournament was funded by sponsorship from Lion breweries worth around £800,000.

The team generated by these forces was unstoppable, its only passage of uncertainty the first few minutes of its first match against Italy, which ended in a 70–6 victory. Scotland captain Colin Deans's comment after losing to them in the quarter-final that 'we tackled and we tackled and we tackled until we couldn't tackle any more, and still they came at us' summed up their remorselessness. Their best opponents, like Scotland, could stay in contention for perhaps an hour. That was France's fate as well. The incomparable Michael Jones claimed a first-half score to give New Zealand a 9–0 interval lead, then tries by Kirk and Kirwan finished the job. Fox added 17 points for a tournament tally of 126 points as the All Blacks won 29–9. Captain Kirk went where no man had gone before, to collect the World Cup, and it was clear that rugby would never be quite the same again.

# CHAPTER THIRTEEN

# Resisting the Inevitable

'When the going gets weird, the weird turn pro'

Hunter S. Thompson

'They say the bigger they are, the harder they fall. I think that
the bigger they are, the more they hurt you'

Ian Hunter on Jonah Lomu (1995)

Two more World Cups were played with rugby union still formally
amateur. By 1995, it was evident that the ideology had run its course.
Vernon Pugh, chairing an IRB working party on amateurism,
reported in April that year:

> All recognised that the breaches of the current mechanism are so wholesale
> and often representative of a considered assessment of that which is believed
> to be right for the game that they are essentially incapable of consistent and
> effective disciplinary action. All agreed that the pressures within the game were
> such that, like it or not, the game would inevitably become fully professional, if
> it were not better regulated.

Louis Luyt, president of the SARB, put it bluntly in 1994: 'Contrary to
popular belief, our players are not paid cash for playing as such, but
are given cars and numerous perks which, as far as I'm concerned, is
professionalism, so who are we fooling here?' And France's former
coach and captain Jacques Fouroux said, 'Professionalism is here
already. Maybe not in Zimbabwe or Namibia, Spain or Morocco, but
everywhere else.'

The amateur principle was eroded to the point where it looked
hypocritical. This was true nowhere more than South Africa, where
as early as 1988 a player won a court judgment for not receiving

payments promised. A still greater concern was South Africa's inability to keep its money to itself. The SARB promised there would be no repetition of the Cavaliers, yet within a year the South Pacific Barbarians, allegedly on £20,000 per man, toured the Republic. The IRB's patience was finally exhausted, and it warned the SARB that any further rebel tours would lead to its expulsion.

New Zealand had also had enough. In 1988, the IRB allowed South Africa to invite players as individuals to form a World XV for its centenary celebrations the following year – a decision which RFU secretary Dudley Wood reported had 'South African delegates doing cartwheels'. New Zealand forbade its players to take part, one NZRFU council member saying 'there have been too many lies told'. Wales, France and Ireland followed suit, but Luyt promised, 'Next year, come what may, there will be international rugby at Ellis Park.' And so there was, assisted by Welsh officials, who put South Africa ahead of their own country and channelled invitations to ten players – all of whom were handsomely paid. The subsequent row cost the WRU its highly regarded secretary David East, who resigned in disgust, and much of its already dwindling credibility. Handling the investigation brought Pugh, a high-flying barrister, into rugby administration.

The following year saw some revision of the amateurism regulations. Players could now 'receive material benefits from any form of communication, written, oral or visual, provided that the reward does not derive from the game' and also 'participate in advertising or product endorsement provided it has no rugby connection'. Scotland, Ireland and England had voted against the initial proposal. The main debate was whether after-dinner speeches 'derived from the game'. The RFU thought that they did and refused to implement the new regulations. This led to England players protesting by refusing to give comments to the media after their match against Wales in 1991 – their first win in Cardiff since 1963, so comment was in demand – and a longer-term legacy of distrust and disaffection.

The NZRFU, losing players to financially buoyant Australian rugby league, was sufficiently angered by the home unions to consider supplying the IRB with details of offers made by British clubs to New Zealand players – fares, housing, pay of up to £330 per week plus perks. In 1992, South Africa's outside-half Naas Botha, one of many high-profile players in Italy, said that Northampton had offered him as much as his Italian club. Australia felt pressure from both league and Italy. David Campese's claim to be ahead of England's Will Carling as 'the first rugby millionaire' was based on spells in Italy, where his club was owned by media baron Silvio Berlusconi. Michael Lynagh followed Campese to Italy and in 1994 was joined by centre Jason Little, who had resisted league offers.

Hearsay and rumour proliferated. There was no question, Pugh reported in 1995, that 'The demands made of the players, the expectations of them and the fact of financial reward sit very uneasily with the traditional understanding of the amateur principles.' As early as 1989, journalist Stephen Jones pointed out:

> Every major union in the world let down its players in some respect in rugby's central bargain – that if the players are to be asked for more and more, week by week, and are still not to be paid, they must be treated wonderfully well.

England lock Paul Ackford calculated that he needed 74 days off police duties every year to fulfil rugby demands, while fellow policeman Wade Dooley said he lost overtime payments every time he played for England. England players hopeful of playing in the 1991 World Cup were warned by RFU technical administrator Don Rutherford that those not meeting necessary fitness standards would be 'ruthlessly eliminated'. Hooker Brian Moore was a recipient of the training programme: 'Eighteen months before the World Cup, a giant scroll almost a yard long was pushed through my letter box. That wall chart has dominated my life ever since.' Moore, whose legal brain and acerbic tongue might have ruffled officialdom in any era, noted that the chart was accompanied by a reminder of the regulations on amateurism.

Daily allowances were increased to £20 in 1991, while the broken-time payment rose to a maximum of £20, then £40. The All Blacks were rebuked for paying allowances at home against the Lions in 1993, but no action was taken because the rule was due to be changed. Players also had time-honoured ways of raising cash – Richard Escot noted in the 1980s that British players 'among themselves spoke all the time of money'. Stephen Jones wrote in 1993 that:

There is no longer a major test team which does not, for the right rate and on a rota basis, farm itself out to a range of sponsors' functions, club dinners and company lunches and photo opportunities; not a team which does not add to the communal pot by flogging off its allocation of tickets ... The All Blacks are particularly clued up.

It was clear before long that the 1990 settlement, too much for some but seen by others as a workable compromise between amateur principle and modern reality, would not hold. Pugh had risen rapidly after the leaking of his report on the World XV precipitated the overthrow of the WRU board and the sacking of IRB delegates Terry Vaux and Gwilym Treharne. He became chair of the union, IRB delegate and then IRB chair in 1994–95. He was asked to chair an inquiry into the regulations.

The report warned that the 'truth may be unpalatable'. Pugh later spoke publicly of 'a central hypocrisy . . . There's no way back, no way of living within the current regulations, because they are being totally flouted by unions who won't enforce the rules.' Only Argentina – where regulations were enforced so strictly that the CUBA club banned radio and TV reporters, Tucuman province was censured for allowing a small sponsor's logo on players' jerseys and 50 players had left for Italy – still played by the rules. One option was the status quo, with some amendments to regulations, but, the report argued, this would simply 'postpone decisions that will have to be addressed honestly and openly at some stage'. The second option – advocated vigorously by Australia, whose union notepaper carried sponsors' logos, and New Zealand – was 'lifting the veil' and accepting professionalism. The reality was that most players in the Five Nations and World Cup would be paid. The report concluded with 'another view', maintaining 'no pay for play', but accompanied by broken time, other indirect benefits and a season limited to seven months, with a restricted tour programme. Whatever the decision, Pugh warned 'the one thing not on our side is time'.

Tim Gresson of the NZRFU warned that 'the current situation cannot be reversed. Professionalism in rugby is too far down the track' and expressed bemusement at claims that players did not want payment: 'New Zealand test players currently are paid generous allowances.' Other unions remained unconvinced. Argentina had been given IRB membership, with one vote, along with Canada, Japan and Italy in 1990. It argued that 'Instead of appearing increasingly permissive and flexible, we should be stricter in the pursuit of our objectives.' The RFU said the phrase 'amateur game' had lost its meaning and suggested replacing it with 'non-vocational recreational sport'. It remained against pay for play, as did Ireland and Japan. It was agreed to resume debate at a special meeting in Paris in August 1995, after the World Cup.

One immediate consequence of World Cups was that the game settled into four-year cycles. The second World Cup, in 1991, ignoring the 1987 recommendation to play future tournaments in one country, was divided between five nations with four legal systems, three currencies and at least two languages.

While the RFU was first among equals, with the opening match and final at Twickenham, matches were also spread across Wales, Scotland, Ireland and France. Unlike in 1987, this edition was preceded by qualifiers. Sweden, led by aptly named lineout specialist Kari Tapper, began the process by beating Israel, Denmark and Switzerland in Tours, France. One new finalist emerged. Western Samoa won the Asia-Pacific tournament in Tokyo ahead of Japan, with Tonga eliminated. In last place were Korea, who had emerged as Japan's regional rival, winning the 1986 and 1988 Asian championships. The game there was firmly established among military servicemen but with only one company team – Korea Electric Power Company – in a fourteen-team league.

Samoa displayed traditional South Pacific virtues and deficiencies as late as a 1988 tour of Ireland and Wales when their props sidestepped better than they scrummaged. Island life was dominated from the 1950s by mass migration to New Zealand, leaving more male Samoans in Auckland than in Samoa. Where Samoa ended and New Zealand began was often hard to tell, but in 1991 New Zealand felt threatened as players on the fringe of All Black selection, such as centre Frank Bunce and prop Peter Fatialofa, a piano-mover who looked capable of lifting a Steinway one-handed, invoked Western Samoa qualifications. They did much more than make up the World Cup numbers, eliminating Wales in Cardiff with a devastating display of tackling. Welsh decline between the world cups had been such that this was not their lowest point. That had come a year earlier, when a hundred and thirty-four points were conceded over two weekends to New South Wales and Australia, followed by a public intra-squad punch-up. The brief promise of the bright young team who won the Triple Crown in 1988 was wrecked when the WRU panicked, sacking coach Tony Gray and manager Derek Quinnell, after an insanely scheduled trip to play the All Blacks at their intimidating peak. Losing Jonathan Davies to rugby league was a huge psychological blow, the departure of props Stuart Evans and Dai Young still more damaging on the field. Remaining world-class players Robert Jones and wing Ieuan Evans could at least contribute to the successful Lions tour of Australia in 1989: Jones's pass transformed England outside-half Rob Andrew from harassed inconsistency to calm control – even this would rebound on Wales, as Andrew's improvement became fundamental to English success in the 1990s. Evans scored the series-winning try when one of Campese's audacious experiments backfired. The tour, though, in keeping with the balance of the British game, was essentially an Anglo-Scottish enterprise, led by Scotland flanker Finlay Calder.

England finally answered the question asked by other nations during the post-war era: what happens if the English, with their overwhelming numbers, ever get their act together? Leagues helped, although a key player was Wade Dooley, a Blackpool police constable combining effectively with a detective-inspector, Paul Ackford, in the second row and whose club, Preston Grasshoppers, played outside the national divisions. Leagues brought with them professional coaches, often labelled directors of rugby. Barrie Corless was the first appointed, at Northampton in 1989, with Colin McFadyean the first to be fired two years later. English rugby's middle-class heartlands, particularly the finance industries that often found employment for players, did as well as Wales did badly out of Britain's long spell (1979–97) of Conservative government.

Favourable conditions still have to be exploited. England's appointment of Geoff Cooke as team manager in 1987 brought organisation, coherence and analytical skills, with insight from other sports – his other job was chief executive of the British Institute of Sports Coaches. Cooke's talents as selector were first apparent in 1979 when his North team beat New Zealand a week before an incoherently chosen England XV were well beaten. He settled his captain early on. In November 1988, centre Will Carling was 22, with a single international season behind him, but gifted with presence, confidence, a powerful square-set build and a talent for timing passes out of contact. Cooke imported consistency and continuity in selection around a core of tough, talented forwards like Moore, Peter Winterbottom – a destructive blond flanker who had been working on the family farm at the beginning of his international career, but whose assassin's eyes and competitive urge proved so well suited to the city dealing room that he joined after signing for Harlequins that he was rapidly headhunted by other firms – and prop Jason Leonard, who cheerfully defied stereotypes by being both a Harlequin (controversially persuaded away from Saracens) and a carpenter who turned up to training from whichever London area building site he was working on that day. Andrew had begun his international career misleadingly by counter-attacking from under his posts from his first touch against Romania in 1985, subsequently subordinating creative talents to his team's demand for a kicking outside-half. One consequence was that too little was seen of elegant centre Jeremy Guscott, England's first player of West Indian descent since James Peters, a Bath player since his first mini-rugby session aged seven. Wing Rory Underwood, half Burmese, all athlete, an RAF pilot and, like Andrew, a product of Barnard Castle school, was a ruthlessly quick finisher.

This gifted assemblage played brilliantly in the first three matches of 1990 but were undone in the final-day Grand Slam decider by the purposefully focused Scots on the afternoon that made 'Flower of Scotland' into a semi-official anthem. It was, in one sense, a false dawn. Scotland did not regain the Calcutta Cup for a decade, as England dominated European, and particularly British, rugby. That reverse, though, left England's most gifted team since the 1920s with a legacy of inhibition and risk-aversion.

Both teams went into the World Cup with genuine ambitions, although England's were immediately dented by the All Blacks. Michael Jones, two years after a ghastly knee injury, was first to every loose ball – plus some not so loose – and scored the only try. New Zealand reached the semi-finals, but never again looked convincing. United States captain Kevin Swords dominated them in the lineout, then both Italy and Canada – who beat Scotland and Argentina earlier in the year – gave them serious trouble. It was an unhappy ride. Grant Fox has suggested that once-constructive perfectionism had transmuted into inability to enjoy themselves, ill-temper and ultimately division. 'Bring Back Buck' signs brandished by fans would eventually become ironic, but in 1991 they expressed real shock at Wayne Shelford's brutal axing from team and captaincy a year earlier. Yoking together John Hart, a smooth Aucklander whose business-inflected vocabulary reflected a background in industrial conciliation, and traditionalist South Islander 'Grizz' Wyllie as joint coaches was a political compromise doomed to failure.

Semi-final opponents Australia had experienced a close-run thing in their Dublin quarter-final. The late Lynagh try to defeat Ireland, who played well above themselves and took the lead with three minutes left, was made and taken with the confident aplomb that marks the exceptional team. The semi-final underlined that impression. New Zealand, missing the religious Jones, who did not play on Sundays, were 13–0 down by half-time, dominated in a manner that offered no way back. Campese's performance recalled Australian journalist Wanda Jamrozsik's description of him as 'the rugby equivalent of quantum physics – he's there, he's not there, he's atomic', opening with a solo try. Willie Ofahangaue, a Tongan-born flanker whose style perfectly reflected his day job of piledriver, once more had New Zealand cursing the immigration officer who refused to readmit him when returning home in 1988 with an All Black schools team, provoking resettlement in Australia, as he and Poidevin controlled the breakdown. Australia's 16–6 victory did little justice to their superiority.

England and Scotland reached the other semi. Losing to New Zealand condemned England to a brutal route, with away matches on consecutive weekends in Paris and Edinburgh. Victory over France had been high in tension and concluded ignobly when France coach Daniel Dubroca assaulted referee David Bishop. Scotland had home advantage, memories of the previous year's triumph, an exceptional full-back (albeit a Watsonian rather than a Heriot) in the 6 ft 3 in. Gavin Hastings and a powerful pack with Calder, John Jeffrey and Derek White forming their latest formidably balanced back row and captain David Sole a feared scrummager. England matched them in a grindingly attritional contest. Two penalties by full-back Jonathan Webb, latest and nearly last in the tradition of test-rugby-playing doctors, equalled two for Scotland by Hastings. Rob Andrew dropped a goal, while Hastings missed a short-range penalty he would usually have landed if blindfolded and required to incorporate a back somersault into his set-up routine.

Bizarrely, England forsook the admittedly much criticised trench warfare which got them to the final and opted for a cavalry charge. It failed, as wild lurches in approach are wont to do. Australia's line remained inviolate – albeit assisted by a questionable failed interception-cum-deliberate-knock-on by Campese and an inspired piece of corner-flagging by young lock John Eales, who was already prone to feats rarely associated with his position. Australia were comfortable with their game, aware of their own capabilities and limitations and capable of adapting to circumstances. Prop Tony Daly scored their try, and captain Nick Farr-Jones lifted the cup after a 12–6 victory, completing a remarkable transformation in less than two decades of what had been the weakest and most vulnerable of the traditional rugby nations.

Part of that process was introducing rugby into the famed Australian Institute of Sport in 1988, with 35 to 40 players aged between 17 and 21 on scholarships working with an approach defined as 'professionalism in terms of attitude and support'. Bob Dwyer, who succeeded Alan Jones as coach, had picked a 45-man squad to prepare for the World Cup in late 1988, weeding out established players unlikely to last another three years and introducing newcomers like 18-year-old centre Jason Little, who played alongside fellow-Queenslander Tim Horan in the 1991 final. Appeal was beginning to stretch beyond traditional constituencies, although a survey in 1992 would find that 76 per cent of Australian union players had attended fee-paying schools. Farr-Jones, fearful of an embarrassingly low turnout, tried to have the team's ceremonial bus-ride through Sydney cancelled. He failed – and 100,000 people turned up to cheer.

It was England's second World Cup final defeat of the year, after earlier losing the first-ever women's final 19–6 to the United States in Cardiff – a disappointing reward for four officials who had remortgaged their houses to pay the team's costs. Russian players had sold souvenirs to cover their expenses. Revenge and the trophy would be taken three years later in Scotland, when England beat the Americans 38–23. New entries included Kazakhstan, but there was no southern hemisphere presence and several countries did not attend because of confusion over affiliation with national governing bodies.

Australia's men still looked good when their next World Cup started in 1995. They were Bledisloe Cup holders courtesy of a miraculous tackle by Zambian-born scrum-half George Gregan on New Zealand wing Jeff Wilson in a 20–16 victory in Sydney in 1994. Wilson had played the match-winning innings in a one-day cricket test against Australia and scored a hat-trick on his All Black debut before he was many weeks out of his teens. England had maintained both dominance and their grindingly conservative game plan in Europe, sustaining a remarkable ascendancy over France through seven consecutive meetings from 1989 to 1995. Their back division remained largely unchanged, but the pack had undergone extensive restructuring, with a recall for Leicester policeman Dean Richards, a number 8 adept in asphyxiating opposing ball, and a permanent place for club-mate Martin Johnson, a lock whose distinctive qualities were noticed early by Stephen Jones: 'It is something in his body language and body position. He has the gloomy, fierce, challenging look about him that Colin Meads had.' This was no coincidence – Johnson had spent a couple of formative seasons at Tihoi in Meads's own King Country, New Zealand, and had played for New Zealand Colts before returning home, reflecting, 'I couldn't believe how seriously every match in New Zealand was taken . . . it was a revelation . . . I went to New Zealand and returned a battle-hardened rugby player.'

Meads recalled, 'He was a very good lad. I was very disappointed when he went home.'

England won Grand Slams in 1991, 1992 and 1995 and dominated the Lions team, led by Gavin Hastings, that lost 2–1 to New Zealand in 1993. They were headed by another home union only in 1994 when Wales, in a short-lived recovery, squeezed them out on points difference. With a trophy presented that year for the Five Nations, shared titles were no longer regarded as practical. It was appropriate that Wales should be first to benefit this way. Of their ten previous shared titles, nine – including the five-way tie in 1973 – would have seen them outright champions if points difference had been in force.

Wales's leagues had not yet, though, had the hoped-for effect, in part because concentration on home-based competition as opposed to cross-border matches increasingly cut Welsh clubs off from old opponents, just as England's clubs became seriously worth playing. This particularly applied to Bath, who won four championships and four cups between 1990 and 1995, with doubles in 1992 and 1994. Border dominance continued unabated in Scotland, although Melrose had displaced Hawick as perennial champions. Ireland's leagues produced a duality of dominance – Ulster won nine consecutive provincial titles from 1985, but Munster, particularly Limerick, clubs dominated the All-Ireland leagues started in 1990. Limerick's advantage as the one Irish city where rugby is the game of the masses was underlined between 1991 and 1993, when three different clubs from the city and district – Young Munster, Garryowen and Shannon – won the championship in consecutive years.

These, though, were unhappy times for the Celtic trio. Scotland's one title challenge came in 1995 after a memorable win in Paris enabled by brilliant combination between Gavin Hastings and Gregor Townsend, a brilliant runner from Gala who had been in selectors' minds since his schooldays. As in 1990, there was a Grand Slam decider against England – at Twickenham and with a different outcome, as Andrew kicked all England's points in their 24–12 victory.

French success was limited by inability to beat England. At club level, there was an interregnum between two spells of Toulouse dominance, with the title being shared around. Grenoble fell short under Jacques Fouroux in 1993 in spite of an annual budget reported at £2 million. Drastic contrasts remained. There was the suave, ironic charm of Racing Club de France, who, in 1990, won Paris's first title since 1959, only the second since the First World War, while sending themselves up by wearing pink bow ties and sipping champagne at half-time. Franck Mesnel, leading spirit of 'The Show-Bizz', joked, 'Because we are Parisians . . . we are all homosexuals!' This was more than just playful subversion of traditional rugby masculinity. As Mesnel has also noted, you have to play well to get away with such antics. The pink bow tie would become the symbol of his Eden Park fashion empire, built on rugby-based shirt designs and with leading players as franchise holders. In the other corner was the demotic brutality of Bègles-Bordeaux, who triumphed in 1992 with a steamrollering pack known as 'the tortoise' and a functional scrum-half named Bernard Laporte.

Elsewhere in Europe, it was an achievement that rugby survived in Romania. National captain Florica Murariu was among five players who died in the revolution against Ceausescu at Christmas 1989. This was a little more than a year after Murariu led his country to victory over Wales at Cardiff. Federation secretary Radu Demian summed up their problems in 1990: 'There are clubs in the country where they simply can't afford to buy jerseys. We can't buy boots or balls because we can't spend any hard currency.' International assistance peaked with a Home Unions v. France charity match at Twickenham in 1990. In the same year, Romania managed to tour New Zealand, technical adviser Russ Cooper recalling that 'they had brought one ball with them, which the fly-half kicked every time it was passed to him' and that players refused to spend their daily tour allowance of $NZ30 (about £10): 'They saved every penny that was paid to them and took it all home.' The 1991 World Cup team flew out of Bucharest hours ahead of armed miners who were marching on the city. Results inevitably deteriorated. They lost to Spain in 1992, and the player numbers declined from a peak of 8,000 to 3,000 by 1994, but they qualified again for the 1995 World Cup, and Federation president Viorel Morariu, previously both national coach and captain, was confident enough to sell the game with the words 'Everybody can play soccer; not everybody is able to play rugby. This is a special game for special people.'

Romania qualified by beating Russia, which had undergone similar, if less bloodstained, times. In 1988, Russia reached the semi-finals of the Student World Cup, beating eventual winners New Zealand in a style described as 'skilled and athletic . . . they defeated New Zealand comprehensively at their own game. Not only was their hard, low-driving style reminiscent of the Antipodean approach – on the day, they were better at it.' Russia's senior team struck one late blow in the cold war, a 31–16 defeat of the USA in an 'ill-tempered, though spectacular' contest in Moscow in 1988 that saw players from both sides sent off.

From 100 clubs in the Soviet system in the mid-1980s, Russia was down to 16 by 1993, survivors divided between Moscow and Krasnoyarsk. This created logistical difficulties to dwarf Germany's concentration in two cities – Hanover and Heidelberg, which are 400 miles apart – or even Canada's distances. Nearly 2,000 miles separated the two cities, with return flights costing two to three times the average monthly wage. Still, Russia returned to international competition at a lower level in 1993, beating Belgium 11–8.

Georgia's secession from the disintegrating Soviet Union accounted for nearly half, 40 clubs, of the difference between the Soviet 1980s and the Russian '90s. This provenance bemused and embarrassed the IRB, which took two years to admit Georgia, after turning down an initial application for associate membership in 1990 while it clarified relations with the Soviet Federation. While eliminated from the 1995 qualifiers by Russia and Poland, Georgian performances in FIRA youth competitions suggested a brighter future.

Romania and Russia's decline reinstated Italy as Europe's second force – a status it might have reclaimed anyway, as it benefited from the expertise of bought-in international stars and an influx of Argentinians, many with antecedents that qualified them for Italy. Outside-half Diego Dominguez was hailed as Porta's natural successor when he played brilliantly in the Argentinian team that finished second in the 1988 Student World Cup. By 1991, he was playing in the Italy senior team that beat Romania.

In spite of their losses, Argentina remained number one in South America but with a newly dangerous rival to their north. Uruguay had minimal player numbers but an outstanding club, Carrasco Polo, transformed when the scientific training methods of Washington Amarillo replaced earlier habits of 'training hard, but then after matches going to the bar to eat and drink everything'. Carrasco's leading player, Diego Ormachaea, introduced to the game as a 15 year old in 1976, would still be playing for club and country more than 20 years later. In 1993, Carrasco beat a Buenos Aires team including 14 Pumas. Uruguay's national team, known since 1973 as Los Teros (the Lapwings), gave the Pumas a serious shock in the World Cup qualifiers, going down only 19–10 and challenging their traditional strength by taking four scrums against the head, one leading to a pushover try from Ormachaea.

In the Pacific, it was Tonga's turn to eliminate Fiji, but Japan maintained their World Cup dominance over Korea. Company rugby had boomed in Japan, as corporations realised that televised games turned the successful teams into a valuable advertising medium justifying serious investment. Australian wing Ian Williams, who played for Kobe Steel, reported late in 1994 that there were more than 100 overseas players in Japan, most receiving double the local wage solely to play rugby. He reckoned only half a dozen of them had 'real' jobs, while there was money 'below and above the table'. The Japanese Rugby Union remained firmly committed to amateurism, but Konno would admit in a 1995 memo to the IRB that 'I am not assured our instructions have been kept' by companies employing overseas players.

The debutants of World Cup 1995 came as a complete shock. The francophone West Africans of Ivory Coast squeezed past Zimbabwe, Morocco and Namibia in the African playoffs. Namibia had been the favourites but rested key players against the Ivorians and paid for their condescension. Expatriate French schoolmasters had helped develop the game, and half of their squad played in France. Nevertheless, it was an unquestionably indigenous team, with 25 of the 26 players Ivorian-born, many from Abidjan's harbour district. Eight of the ten senior clubs were also based in the capital, and even here there were implications of professionalism, with players receiving the equivalent of £1.25 for turning up to training sessions. Coach Claude Ezoua declared, 'We want to prove to the world that there is more to African rugby than just South Africa.'

There was particular reason to be conscious of South Africa in 1995 since, only three years after its readmission to international rugby, it was hosting the third World Cup. With indecent haste for some, the tournament was awarded in 1993, when the National Party still reigned and South Africa was beset by political violence. The decision had been predictable, though, from February 1990, when the African National Congress was legalised and Nelson Mandela released from jail. Aside from goodwill towards a new order in South Africa, many rugby officials – epitomised by RFU president Peter Yarranton's glutinous welcome to the Springboks on their return to Twickenham in late 1992 – had never understood why they had been isolated in the first place.

Formal contact with the ANC, initiated by Transvaal Rugby Union president Louis Luyt and assisted by opposition leader Frederick Van Zyl Slabbert and former Springbok Tommy Bedford, had begun in 1988. In the same year, a SARB delegation led by Craven and Luyt met ANC leaders including Thabo Mbeki, Alfred Nzo and Steve Tshwete in Harare. They were condemned both by SARB vice-president Fritz Eloff and the minister of education, F.W. de Klerk. The ANC agreed to support the readmission of non-racial rugby to international competition – earning its own rebuke from SACOS, which saw this as a break with agreed positions.

The interlinked processes of integration and readmission were tricky, not least because of rugby's political salience. Steve Tshwete, the ANC's sports chief and a former president, while in prison, of the Robben Island Rugby Board, described 'a delicate process where the rugby talks are bound to influence the political process in the country and vice versa'. Cricket moved much more quickly, achieving both a unified board and international readmission – with the Springboks renamed Proteas – in 1991.

Tshwete intervened several times in a tortuous merger process between SARB and SARU, which met for the first time as the South African RFU (SARFU), with Craven as president, in January 1992. Renewed rugby links were held out to the white electorate two months later as the likely prize for a 'yes' vote in a referendum on constitutional negotiations. International readmission in August that year produced precisely the sort of incident Tshwete had worried about. Luyt, responding to the crowd at Ellis Park, broke an agreement that the old South African national anthem 'Die Stem' should not be played before the match against New Zealand. It seemed possible that readmission might end there and then. The ANC, still entirely excluded from formal power but wielding immense moral and political power as the certain winner of any democratic election, warned the SARFU that 'they can make rugby a reconciler of people, or they can use it as a ritual that celebrates conquest and domination of black people' and threatened a renewed boycott. Australia, waiting for the following week's test in Cape Town, were ready to return home.

Agreement was reached. Australia were played in a less febrile atmosphere and the Springboks, who for the moment retained their name, went to England and France before the end of the year. The World Cup was awarded in January, shortly after Craven, a major figure in South African rugby for more than 60 years, had died. Steve Tshwete hailed him as a 'visionary', but memories still remained of his deviousness over rebel tours and of his reported statement that no black man should ever wear a Springbok jersey. Craven had denied saying it, claiming a security-service smear, but former England international Derek Wyatt recalled Craven telling him in 1980 that 'Black players should stick to soccer; that's their game. We don't want black players in our game.'

The game and country that Craven left behind continued to be contentious. In 1993, the SARFU's much-trumpeted development programme came under scrutiny – ANC official Ngconde Balfour calling it a smokescreen intended solely to enable the resumption of international tours. Bedford pointed out that an annual allocation of £1.2 million for non-white development looked less impressive when compared with £12 million for extending provincial stadiums. Two years later, Sports Congress officials in the impoverished Johannesburg district of Alexandra talked of dealing with different sports: 'The Transvaal Rugby Union came to us and said, "We are going to do this." Cricket people said, "Tell us what we should be doing."'

Political violence meant no insurer would touch the World Cup, and contingencies were planned. If the tournament was moved to before the end of September 1994, New Zealand would host it, while England and Wales would host it if it had to happen later. They were not to be necessary. South Africa staged its first democratic election on 27 April 1994 – Errol Tobias, the first black Springbok 14 years earlier, said he did not feel fully South African until that day – and voted Mandela and the ANC into office. A little over a year later, it welcomed the World Cup.

One consistent subsidiary concern had been whether the hosts would have a team capable of challenging for the trophy. Reinstatement shocked a nation that had assumed its teams were as impressive as its stadiums. The All Blacks' victory at Ellis Park was easier than the 27–24 scoreline suggested, and there was no mistaking the import of the 26–3 beating handed out by Australia the following week. In Europe, the Springboks split a two-match series with France but were well beaten, 33–16, by England. With huge, slow-moving forwards, over-reliance on the boot of outside-half Naas Botha and once-great centre Danie Gerber inevitably past his best at 34, the Springboks looked like dinosaurs. Coach John Williams, who admitted the rest of the world was playing a different game, was fired in January 1993, and few of his players would make it to the World Cup.

Controversy over methods and personnel ran through to the World Cup, with many South Africans convinced coach Kitch Christie had imported far too many of his Transvaal teams – in particular that skipper Francois Pienaar was nowhere near the best available back row. They had, though, shown serious quality the previous autumn, devastating Welsh champions Swansea, who had beaten world champions Australia two years earlier, 78–7 on their own ground. Greyhound-fast scrum-half Joost van der Westhuizen, elegantly incisive full-back Andre Joubert, lock Mark Andrews and omnipresent flanker Ruben Kruger all looked like world-beaters on that day.

No country has stamped itself on a World Cup quite like South Africa did in 1995; nor is any likely to, unless another is staged in a nation which is finding itself in the wake of a bizarrely aberrant political system. The scene was set in Cape Town with an opening ceremony that for once in a sporting lifetime genuinely lifted spirits, with Mandela acclaimed by the crowd. A magnificent Springbok performance ensued, beating holders and favourites Australia 27–18. Australia's dangerous midfield was snuffed out by swarming defence and a brilliant try scored by wing Pieter Hendricks, playing because South Africa's one non-white player, Chester Williams – whose eyes stared down from an advert that was one of the competition's abiding images – was injured. A thoughtful column in the *Sowetan* newspaper by Aggrey Klaaste, explaining his reactions as a black South African accustomed to wanting the Springboks to lose, as he and his Springbok-supporting sons watched the game together, set the tone, together with Mandela's evident enthusiasm and the paper's exultant 'Amabokoboko!' headline, for the emerging new South Africa's embrace, temporarily at least, of one of the defining institutions of the discredited old order.

There was insight into the complexities of Afrikaner identity as

Rustenberg, deep in what white would-be separatists had designated as Boerestat, unreservedly adopted the black, French-speaking Ivorians as fellow Africans and roared them on against Scotland, France and Tonga. The Ivorians had half-backs, Frederic Dupont and Athanase Dali, who might have helped France, but Dali, their captain, was injured against Scotland and they took an 89–0 hammering, with Gavin Hastings scoring 44 points. Their tournament ended with genuine tragedy as wing Max Brito, a fearless tackler, was left paralysed when injured bringing a Tongan down.

Their fate at Scotland's hands further underlined the growing gap, emphasised since 1991 by giving five points for a try, between the increasingly trained athletes of the major rugby nations and those disadvantaged either by physique or lack of resources. New Zealand, with characteristic ruthlessness, ran up 145 points against Japan – debutant Simon Culhane topping Hastings' record with 45.

This was not even New Zealand's strongest team. Conspicuously absent against Japan was wing Jonah Lomu, who had already redefined rugby physics by proving that you could be 6 ft 6 in., weigh 250 lb and have a sprinter's speed. The sort of weapon that inspires proliferation treaties, Lomu, a quietly spoken Tongan raised far too close for comfort to the gang warfare of South Auckland, became the immediate star of the competition. When he performed that oldest of touring-player rituals – finding a local girlfriend – it was front- and back-page news, a landmark in the development of rugby-player-as-celebrity.

The All Blacks had much going for them – Wilson's brilliance on the other wing, Durban-born Andrew Mehrtens bringing pace, creativity and judgement to the number 10 shirt, free-spirited open-side Josh Kronfeld displaying a homing instinct for the next support opportunity, angular, fresh-faced Ian Jones dominating the lineouts and skipper Sean Fitzpatrick, possibly the most competitive human alive, in constant dialogue with the referees. All were overshadowed by the prodigious Lomu. How to stop him without an elephant gun became the radio topic of choice. Welsh wing Wayne Proctor, outweighed by 90 lb, had to mark him: 'I got close to try and tackle him before he got going – and discovered that he could sidestep as well! Not exactly your conventional winger, is he?'

From early on, a South Africa v. New Zealand final seemed almost predestined. Even a blow to the Springboks like Hendricks' suspension following an epic brawl against Canada became great good fortune when tournament rules allowed them to replace him with the fit-again Chester Williams, whose four quarter-final tries against Samoa proved him as valuable a player as he was a symbol. At the same stage, England, who came to South Africa fresh from a player revolt provoked when the RFU attempted to sack captain Carling for calling its committee '57 old farts' and then stumbled unconvincingly through pool matches against Argentina, Italy and Samoa, eliminated Australia. Andrew's winning drop-goal was rewarded within days in the Queen's Birthday Honours.

In the Durban semi-final, South Africa had to overcome both previously unimpressive France and a biblical deluge that suited only Andrews, a water polo player. Abdelatif Benazzi, France's magnificent Moroccan flanker/lock, nearly derailed them in the dying moments. New Zealand took their place in the final by very different methods 24 hours later, amid the crystal sunshine of Cape Town. Carling, who made a lucrative living lecturing businessmen on the lessons to be learnt from top-class sport and had just published a book called *The Way to Win*, was shown exactly how. Tries in the first four minutes by Lomu, smashing through three would-be tacklers, and Kronfeld, as ever perfectly placed, ended the contest before it started. Number 8 forward Zinzan Brooke landed an almost whimsical drop-goal, and final tallies of four tries for Lomu and 45–29 to New Zealand represented an easing up, although some England supporters felt their humiliation was not completed until wing Tony Underwood, younger brother of Rory and first of Lomu's would-be tacklers, appeared self-mockingly in a pizza advert along with the giant New Zealander. Carling fell some way short of losing graciously when he called Lomu a freak and looked forward to his going away.

The week before the final was dominated by debates about how the Springboks could stop Lomu – France and England's excruciating third-place clash was no competition – until the night before. Then the leaders of the South African, New Zealand and Australian rugby unions called a joint press conference where they announced a ten-year deal with media magnate Rupert Murdoch worth $550 million.

This would pay for an annual Tri Nations championship, with home and away clashes between the three, and a Super 12 competition for provincial teams, replacing the Pacific 10 tournament. Their abandonment of Fiji, Samoa and Tonga – excluded after playing in the Pacific 10 – was a detail beside the wider implications for the game, even if the leaders of the three unions, who had formed a joint body known as SANZAR, denied with straight faces that it meant the end of amateurism.

Before that issue was confronted, there was a final to play. Ellis Park emulated Eden Park 14 years earlier in being buzzed by a low-flying aircraft, only this time it was official – a South African Airways jumbo with 'Good Luck Bokke' painted on its wings that briefly filled the sky above the stands. An unaccompanied choir gave an exquisite rendition of 'Nkosi Sikelel' iAfrika', the African tune joined in incongruous matrimony with the raspingly martial 'Die Stem' to form South Africa's new hybrid anthem. South Africa's bright new flag was more in evidence than the subdued old one. Mandela, accustomed to making an impact with brightly patterned shirts, surpassed himself with a Springbok number 6 jersey identical to that worn by captain Francois Pienaar. This displayed both Mandela's endorsement of the team via his unparalleled knack for political theatre and a personal rapport that would outlive the obvious short-term public advantages to both. The only false note was the stadium authorities whipping up the crowd during breaks in play with pro-Springbok music – in particular, Leon Schuster's 'Hier Komme die Bokke' – still in 1995 something of a breach of propriety.

South Africa solved the Lomu conundrum by a swarming midfield defence that bottled up those inside him. Many doubted that Pienaar was a truly top-class back rower. Ruben Kruger, the other flanker, had been the best forward in the competition. On this day, though, Pienaar was a great player, performing as if fulfilling personal and national destiny. Amid ratcheting tension, the game went into extra time, and Joel Stransky's drop-goal sealed South Africa's 15–12 win. The political symbolism of the presentation could only perhaps have been improved if, of the two men in the green number 6 shirts, the black man had been the youthful athlete and the Afrikaner the elderly politician. Amid the emotion of victory, Pienaar had the presence of mind to remind a television interviewer that there had not been 60,000 South Africans – roughly the number in the stadium – supporting his team, but 43 million, the whole population. The famously competitive Sean Fitzpatrick was a model of graciousness in defeat, refusing to make anything of the illnesses which had mysteriously afflicted his team. It was possible, seeing dancers on the streets of the Johannesburg inner suburb of Hillbrow, to believe in rugby's ability to break down barriers. Before this happy illusion set in, Louis Luyt set about re-erecting them. A fertiliser millionaire who reminded Derek Wyatt of a cross between Marlon Brando's *Godfather* and media magnate Robert Maxwell, Luyt treated the end-of-tournament dinner to a speech of spectacular crassness, claiming that the 1987 and 1991 World Cups had only turned out as they had because of South Africa's absence. The New Zealand, France and England teams walked out – All Black flanker Mike Brewer pausing to offer Luyt a brief estimation of his charm and intelligence.

Not the least remarkable aspect of Luyt's belittling of New Zealand's and Australia's victories was that he was working with them in a struggle for control of the top-class game. The creation of SANZAR and its associated competitions was a response to two threats. The television contract with Murdoch neutralised one – preventing Murdoch's own rugby league Super League, launched in March 1995, from going aggressively after top union players. The other, the World Rugby Corporation (WRC) fronted by former Wallabies prop and IRB member Ross Turnbull, proved harder to beat. An expanded rerun of David Lord's concept, the WRC aimed to create 30 franchises worldwide, each with a squad of 30 players, and an annual programme of 352 matches. By early August, they had 407 signatures, including the majority of the World Cup squads of all the leading nations except England and Ireland, on provisional contracts. The NZRFU, offering the All Blacks more than £100,000 per year per man, received a straight no from Fitzpatrick. Brewer had said to NZRFU official Rob Fisher, 'I hope you enjoy the last meeting of the IRB.' The battle, its detail brilliantly recounted in Peter Fitzsimons's *The Rugby War*, eventually centred on the allegiance of top players from the three southern giants, in particular the South Africans. Amid a whirl of offer and counteroffer, one man stood out, Australian scrum-half Steve Merrick, who declared, 'I've done everything I've ever dreamed of in the last four weeks' and refused to sign for either side.

The established order won because, as former All Black Jock Hobbs pointed out in persuading the current squad back into the NZRFU corner, it had the money guaranteed and the WRC did not. The WRC had high hopes of persuading Kerry Packer into another battle with Murdoch. Packer is reported to have called rugby 'a stupid game played by a bunch of fucking poofters'. He made a small initial commitment but, with battles already under way for rugby league and racing, had no stomach for a third front. The established game also had the advantages of heritage and shared memory. As Fitzsimons wrote in an open letter to Wallabies captain Phil Kearns, he had a choice between 'honour, glory, the Wallaby jersey and enormous riches guaranteed' and 'dissension, civil war, enormous bitterness, pissing on the Wallaby jersey and only the possibility of slightly more riches'. Springbok coach Kitch Christie asked his players to sign up to their union 'for the team, for the country, for yourselves and for what you've already achieved'. Kronfeld and Wilson, echoing Kirk and Kirwan nine years earlier, broke with their teammates to sign with the NZRFU. Pienaar, WRC's recruiting agent in South Africa, wavered.

By mid-August, the WRC threat was effectively finished. The IRB met again in Paris on 26 August 1995. The outcome of the meeting was not assured, even if the NSWRU had declared amateurism dead as early as 10 April and the three southern unions could hardly have remained within an amateur game after their Murdoch deal. Pugh argued that 'Whether or not we promote it, the game will be openly professional within a very short space of time. If we do not participate in, and direct and control, that change, the IRB and the unions as we know them may no longer be running the game.' Amateurism was redundant. The meeting accepted Pugh's logic, although Nick Farr-Jones noted that delegates 'looked like they had just come out of their own funeral'. It was one hundred years, less only three days, since the Huddersfield meeting that had created rugby league.

# CHAPTER FOURTEEN

# Journey without Maps

'May you live in interesting times'

Chinese curse

'We had salary-capping. It was called amateurism'

Peter Wheeler (1997)

Adjustment to open professionalism was easier for the southern nations. They had wanted the changes, so suffered none of the psychological dislocation afflicting some European unions. Existing practices were closer to a fully professional model. The Murdoch deal and the subsequent battle for allegiance meant that they had the money, and top players were already contracted to their unions.

This was not wholly good news for players, however well rewarded. They immediately lost what former England player and coach Dick Greenwood termed 'the inalienable right of the amateur to play like an idiot'. Murray Kidd, Ireland's coach from New Zealand, said, 'Paying people more means you have more control. You can be more demanding. Although it won't guarantee results, it has to be a good thing.' Jason Little was told that, because of his contract with the Australian Rugby Union, he could not go and play abroad.

Little was needed for the Tri Nations and Super 12, both launched in 1996. The progenitors of SANZAR had called their competitions 'the Perfect Rugby Product' and Super 12 in particular was made for television. Donald McRae called it 'rugby's brutal equivalent of one-day cricket – held, preferably, under floodlights and with the full razzmatazz of an open-air pop concert'. Free-flowing games produced basketball-like scorelines: Auckland Blues 56, New South Wales Waratahs 44. The 26 matches played by the Blues in winning the first two tournaments, and establishing a pattern of New Zealand dominance, produced an average of 66 points each. The All Blacks established parallel control in the Tri Nations, winning all eight matches in the first two seasons and looking even more formidable in Britain in 1997, beginning with an 81–3 demolition of Llanelli. After Ireland, who had done nothing particularly wrong, were beaten 63–15, their coach Brian Ashton said, 'They are relentless, powerful men, very dynamic. They put us on the back foot. Their ball retention is superb. They are constantly going forward, which makes it easy for support players to knock off anyone trying to interfere with the ball. They are the best side in the world, the best I have ever seen.'

Only England, who forced the All Blacks to come from behind for a 26–26 draw at Twickenham after losing 25–8 at Old Trafford, could live with them. Taking their cue from coach Hart, the All Blacks were also fluent in the businesslike idiom of the new order. Captain Sean Fitzpatrick said, 'We want to ensure that our product is the best in the world. The basis will be formidable rugby – but we're striving to improve ourselves off the field, from management strategy down to the look of the brand.'

South Africa, though, took over in 1998. While New Zealand dominance continued in the Super 12, Canterbury Crusaders beating the Blues to begin a three-year run of titles, the Springboks dominated the Tri Nations. Their four victories were part of a run of seventeen, equalling the record set by the All Blacks between 1965 and 1969, ended only when a tired team lost its last match of the year to a focused and increasingly competitive England at Twickenham. New Zealand – who had lost Fitzpatrick and Zinzan Brooke to retirement in 1997, and with Michael Jones and granitic prop Olo Browne in their last seasons – found that even great rugby nations can struggle after losing talent and experience. They lost all four matches.

South Africa had not found the intervening period easy. World Cup euphoria evaporated rapidly. Inside two years, the leadership team of Christie, Pienaar and manager Morne du Plessis were gone, and Christie's successor Andre Markgraff had to resign for using apartheid-era racist epithets. One World Cup prize was keeping the Springbok label. Old attitudes too survived. The former national flag was increasingly seen at internationals in 1996 and 1997, even though du Plessis, who had unmatched Springbok credentials as both a former captain (1980) and a son of a captain (1949), said, 'Every time the flag is flown, it is an embarrassment to us.' Mandela's ministers grumbled about the slow growth of non-white participation, with Rian Oberholzer, Luyt's son-in-law and chief executive of the SARFU, admitting in 1997, 'There are highly talented black and coloured players who are not being given a fair show at provincial level.' No black players were picked by Transvaal or Orange Free State in 1997. Finance minister Trevor Manuel, whose credibility with international markets was vital to the new government's economic programmes, admitted that he still supported the All Blacks against the Springboks. In 1998, the SARFU, under government investigation following allegations of maladministration, nepotism and racism, brought a counter-case against the government and subpoenaed Mandela. Tshwete condemned Luyt as 'a white elitist' and on 10 May the SARFU boss was deposed by his executive.

South Africa's playing record was poor, with only two wins, both at home to Australia, in the first two Tri Nations tournaments, and defeat in 1997 by a British Lions team led by Martin Johnson, who resisted the Springboks' one-dimensional bludgeoning to win the series 2–1. The following year was very different. Nick Mallett brought an articulately analytical intelligence to the role of coach, veteran Dick Muir oiled the midfield wheels and number 8 Gary Teichmann led in a manner that showed Pienaar was not indispensable.

Australia came to the 1999 World Cup as the only Tri Nation yet to dominate at test or provincial level. They had still to win more than twice in a single Tri Nations season and lost 61–22 against South Africa in 1997, a result that, in spite of player resistance, cost Greg Smith his job. His successor, Rod Macqueen, another businessman coach, had turned Australia's third force – the Capital Territory Brumbies – into its strongest Super 12 franchise, finalists in 1997. His distinguishing marks included attention to detail, astute management of what would always be, compared with New Zealand or South Africa, limited playing resources – turning full-back Stephen Larkham into an unorthodox yet effective outside-half – and a playing pattern of hit-up after hit-up designed to suck opposing players into defence.

European rugby found it tougher to adjust. Among the innovations of the 1995–96 season, the Heineken European Cup for clubs was profoundly important, even if England's clubs – emulating their soccer counterparts 40 years earlier – stayed out in the first season. The other novelty, cross-code matches with rugby league and players trying both games, was much less durable. The chief lesson of cross-code matches, even if Wigan won the Middlesex Sevens, was the enormous difference between the two, while two-code all-year careers were simply too demanding. After a flurry of Welshmen returning to union roots, inter-code transfers were rare, if sometimes significant.

England had not wanted professionalism and was uneasy with its consequences. Hopes of an orderly transition were dashed once John Hall, owner of Newcastle United FC, bought Gosforth, installed Rob Andrew on a lucrative contract as director of rugby and started offering six-figure salaries. Panic ensued. In early 1996, the market was described as 'Febrile and full of fear. Most players are still up for grabs, prices have not stabilised and everyone is desperately looking for new sources of income.' One difference was clear. Before 1995, conventionally photogenic backs like Carling and Andrew had been the most marketable, but now that money was being spent to build winning teams, nobody was in greater demand than lock Martin Johnson, who re-signed with Leicester.

The RFU did not contract leading players – an omission with more than a decade's worth of consequences. It would have been expensive, and the RFU was carrying a £35 million bank loan for Twickenham's transformation from creaky relic into vast, if somewhat impersonal, modern stadium. The grass roots were already in revolt against professionalism. Conservative MP Malcolm Lord argued, 'Amateurism is the essence of the game. Change that and you destroy something fundamental. The game doesn't want professionalism and can't afford it.' Though contradicting his party's 'bottom line is everything' philosophy of government, Lord's views found an echo among junior clubs aghast at the antics of their senior colleagues who felt change had come without consultation. This revolt took practical shape in early 1996 when the RFU's preferred candidate,

John Jeavons-Fellows, an IRB delegate, was heavily defeated for chair of the union board by Cliff Brittle. For the next two years, the RFU's key committee was split between its chair and most members.

New money bought a spectacular array of imported players. Saracens fielded the most capped player of all time, Philippe Sella, alongside the record points scorer, Michael Lynagh – the latter a particular delight to Saracens ex-league marketing genius Peter Deakin for having a name that fitted the Spanish dance hit 'Macarena'. Before long, they were joined by Pienaar. Saracens left their tiny recreation-ground home at Southgate to share football grounds, first at Enfield then Watford. Deakin knew that marketing relied far more on community schemes than match-day pop music, and Saracens' work in schools rightly earned a high reputation, but everything cost money. Coach Mark Evans, who gave up teaching to go full-time, explained how coaching teams grew: 'In the first year of professional rugby, I did everything – director of rugby, youth development, video analyst, coach. Then Francois Pienaar came on board as coach, then we brought another coach in, and a fitness guy, and so on. Like a lot of professional clubs, the job got bigger and bigger.'

Gates grew rapidly, up 20 per cent across the Premiership in 1997–98, but not nearly as quickly as costs. Saracens' loss of £2.2 million for that season was typical. In the same year, Richmond had an income of £2.1 million but outgoings of £4 million. Richmond's investor was copper trader Ashley Levett. In 1996, he said, 'I'd like to get a return on my £2.5 million and I'd be disappointed if, within five years, Richmond wasn't the top team in the UK and Europe.' In three years, it was dead. In 1998, Levett moved Richmond from the Athletic Ground to share the new football ground at Reading, where caterers accustomed to football fans were thrown when rugby followers all wanted to drink beer – creating enormous queues of bar staff for the few beer engines – and to do so in the bar area rather than in their seats. In 1999, he pulled out in mid-season. Welsh international Allan Bateman said, 'There were 30 professionals out of a job, that he didn't pause a great deal to think about. Adrian Davies was in a rehab centre, working on his knee, trying to get fit, when a phone call came across from one of the administrators saying he was released from Richmond.' The search for a buyer was obstructed by the clubs' collective body, English First Division Rugby (EFDR), which declared that Richmond had forfeited their membership, then claimed a right to buy the club for £1 and finally lodged a bid. Richmond's president Tony Dorman said, 'Our own body is trying to kill us off,' while the receiver declared EFDR's actions 'opportunistic and morally reprehensible'. The reason was that, having supported an extension of the Premiership from 12 to 14 clubs a year earlier, they had decided that 12 was the right number after all. Losing Richmond for good, along with London Scottish, who had merged with London Irish, was seen, disregarding a combined 262 years of history, as a simple way of reducing the numbers. Both clubs reverted to amateur roots in the lower reaches of the Middlesex leagues. Others came close to dissolution. Coventry and Bristol, members of the shortlist for England's most distinguished club, were both in receivership in 1998. Bristol found a new investor, while Coventry reformed as a semi-professional outfit. Rocketing costs were finally arrested in 1999 by the introduction of a salary cap of £1.8 million per club per season.

Money reached well down the leagues. While Brittle's proposal to ban payments below the top two divisions made business sense, it was against the temper of an age impatient with financial regulation, not to mention probably unsustainable in the courts. Former Rosslyn Park and England player Andy Ripley argued in his PhD thesis on professional rugby that payments of £50 in lower divisions had probably been more destabilising than the huge amounts at the top, and his own club opted to stay amateur.

While financial regulation was unfashionable, health and safety were an increasing preoccupation. Few people had more impact on rugby, although it was an unwanted distinction, than Ben Smolden, paralysed during a schoolboy game in 1991. The requirement that only specialists play in the front row, and that scrums are uncontested should sufficient props or hookers not be available, can be traced to the ruling in his favour after several years in the courts.

Bath produced the single greatest English club achievement of this period, ending early French dominance of the Heineken Cup in 1998, but this was a last hurrah for a club as troubled as any other – and publicly so after granting access to a documentary team during the 1997–98 season – by the new order. Hall's money bought his renamed Newcastle club a championship in 1998, but a duopoly of 1996 champions Wasps and Leicester, whose large membership ensured a comparatively painless and stable transition, was emerging.

England too were in transition. Carling, Andrew, Moore and Richards had gone by 1997. There was collateral damage from club v. union strife over funding, league organisation and player release. England players boycotted a squad session in solidarity with clubs in 1997. In 1998, under the Mayfair agreement, clubs accepted release periods for players in return for a system of tripartite contracts and the RFU giving up ideas of regional or provincial competition. England also had their first full-time coach, Clive Woodward, appointed in autumn 1997. A gifted centre, prone to occasional lapses of concentration, Woodward had played in Australia, built a successful business and risen rapidly via Henley, London Irish and Bath to the England job, earning a reputation for quirkiness and attractive rugby. Early selections mixed the inspired – plunged in at full-back, the inexperienced Matt Perry of Bath played superbly – and the bizarre, a hopelessly inexperienced front row capsizing against Australia. Rugby's higher modern profile struck a blow when his chosen captain, the dominating Italian-descended Wasps back rower Lawrence Dallaglio, was deemed famous enough to be worthy of a tabloid 'sting' and forced to resign amid contrived, questionably obtained headlines about drugs on tour.

If England were troubled, Wales were downright miserable. They were more comfortable with professionalism, but in 1995 Alan Pascoe Associates had approached 500 Welsh companies seeking rugby sponsorship and found no takers. Nor were Wales rich in likely investors, although Peter Thomas bought in to Cardiff. Ancient fear of league predators was dispelled, and several prodigals – notably Jonathan Davies and powerful centre Scott Gibbs – welcomed home, but English union clubs were a far greater worry. Richmond in particular showed a taste for Welsh talent. The WRU spent £650,000 to keep 19 players from crossing the Severn Bridge in 1997. In the same year, it spent another £1.5 million on buying Stradey Park to clear Llanelli's debts.

Relations with clubs were tense. Cardiff were keener to find a way into England's Premiership than play in Wales. In 1998–99, they and a rather reluctant Swansea seceded for a year to play friendlies against English clubs. A Welsh hankering for a British league testified to what was lost when cross-border matches ended and to the impact of supporting professionalism on Wales's limited wealth and population. This made Wales supplicant to English clubs and the RFU. They were prepared to deal, but never on terms that Wales found acceptable. Meanwhile, Wales's own search for the right set-up produced desperate short-term expedients, such as the mid-season decision in 1997 to cut the following season's Premiership from twelve to eight clubs. With zero notice, Dunvant, who had won as many games as they had lost, went from mid-table comfort to relegation.

The national team struggled. Promise inspired by the imaginative coaching of Kevin Bowring, returning league talent such as centres Scott Gibbs and Allan Bateman, the whippet-like brilliance of scrum-half Robert Howley and the gamin deceptiveness of outside-half Arwel Thomas was short-lived. A grim weekend in 1998 when Wales conceded 60 points at Twickenham and France scored 51 at Murrayfield inspired talk that the Five Nations was finished. English voices with short memories hankered after dumping the Celts and entering into closer relationships with the southern trio. Considerable national pride – and, some argued, financial common sense, with a £250,000 salary offered – was swallowed in going after Auckland coach Graham Henry as Bowring's successor. Henry, a teacher, brought immediate short-term success and a taste for importation, using Newport's former All Black Shane Howarth and Neath-based Kiwi Brett Sinkinson alongside established Welsh players like hooker Garin Jenkins and Pontypridd's hugely prolific ginger-topped goal-kicking outside-half Neil Jenkins, on his way to being the first player to score 1,000 points in internationals. Henry's local repute grew so rapidly that there were two-hour queues for book signings. Clive Rowlands joked that if Henry and Gareth Edwards walked down opposite sides of a Cardiff street, people would cross to shake hands with Henry. His reputation peaked at the end of the 1999 Five Nations, the last competition before Italy made it six. With the National Stadium undergoing hugely expensive transformation into the Millennium Stadium, Wales were playing home games at Wembley. At home, yet on English soil, a late Scott Gibbs try and typically nerveless Jenkins conversion beat England, who had dominated the match, 32–31 and robbed them of Triple Crown, Grand Slam and championship.

The title fell, remarkably, to Scotland, who had found transition even tougher. The country's mix of small-town and former-pupil – even if open – clubs had no realistic chance of sustaining professionalism, while big-spenders Newcastle were uncomfortably close. The natural vehicle for professional rugby was the four established districts, but poor results and poorer finances led in 1998 to contraction into two professional 'super districts', Edinburgh and Glasgow, that proved spectacularly unpopular with the clubs, particularly in the Borders. National-team fortunes oscillated wildly – a championship bid in 1996 thwarted by English strangulation following a recall for arch-asphyxiator Dean Richards was followed by two consecutive seasons where only Ireland were beaten, then the remarkable triumph of 1999.

One element was the mercurial genius of Townsend, who scored in all four matches in 1999. Another was the exploitation of that increasingly accessible resource, the New Zealander of Scottish descent. Otago centre John Leslie, son of All Black Andrew, scored within ten seconds – roughly the time between his arrival in Scotland and his inclusion in representative teams – of his 1999 Five Nations debut against Wales. His Scotland debut, along with brother Martin, a high-class flanker, had occurred 11 days after he arrived from Japan. Both Leslies and another kilted Kiwi, full-back Glen Metcalfe, were outstanding in Scotland's final match in Paris, decided by an extraordinary burst of five tries in eighteen minutes that acquired extra significance twenty-four hours later when England stumbled at Wembley.

France's drop to bottom place, a severe recession after consecutive Grand Slams, saved Ireland from a fourth consecutive wooden spoon. During the '90s, Ireland won more often – four out of four – in Cardiff than at Lansdowne Road, three from twenty matches. Yet Ireland contributed three forwards to the Lions pack that subdued the Springboks in 1997, including charismatic multi-skilled hooker Keith Wood, son of 1959 Lions prop Gordon Wood, whose headlong commitment both recalled his youth as a gifted hurler and brought new verisimilitude to going bald-headed for something. Keith Wood displayed distinct independent-mindedness by defying IRFU preferences in order to play for Harlequins, still more by falling out with the union over intellectual property rights, a concept new to most rugby fans. First capped in 1994, he waited five years (during which Italy beat Ireland twice) to play in an Irish victory over an established nation. There was, though, hope for Ireland in some fine performances by age-group and provincial teams. Ulster were first to make a European impact, riding an extraordinary wave of emotion, culminating with Lansdowne Road roaring them on in the final against Colomiers, to take the 1999 Heineken Cup.

France found initial transition easiest – although by 1997 its clubs were worrying about the spending of their English counterparts. International wing Philippe St-Andre said, 'We are being left behind, and before long players will start looking to their pocket book rather than their quality of life.' Before long, he matched action to words by leaving Montferrand for Gloucester.

Still, French clubs dominated the first two years of the Heineken Cup, which was won in 1996 by a Toulouse team that also put together a run of four consecutive national titles, then in 1997 by Brive, who devastated Leicester with dazzling virtuosity not equalled in any final since. By 1998, a new force, or alternatively an extremely old one, had arisen. French rugby retro chic took the form of Stade Français, not so much revived as exhumed from the Third Division by media magnate Max Guazzini. Built on decidedly earthy foundations, with coach Bernard Laporte importing the notoriously physical Bègles-Bordeaux front row, but with Dominguez to supply both subtlety and metronomic goal-kicking at outside-half, the bought-in juggernaut claimed a first title for 90 years in 1998.

At national level, there were back to back Grand Slams in 1997 and 1998 built on the power of props Christian Califano and Franck Tournaire, Olivier Magne's speed and anticipation on the flank, the prodigious all-round forward skills of Abdelatif Benazzi and the loose-limbed elegance of wing Emile Ntamack. The second slam was clinched at Wembley in 1998 by a 51–0 victory over Wales that, if anything, slightly understated their superiority, as the diminutive, darting Thomas Castaignede gave a definitive display of attacking outside-half play. But 1999 brought a sudden and mystifying decline.

Bottom place in the championship was followed by a miserable Pacific tour. Its low point was a toss-up between losing to Tonga and conceding 54 points to the All Blacks.

It was France's fourth southern trip in as many off-seasons. Professional rugby fell rapidly into a touring pattern, with the Five Nations heading south at the end of their seasons in May and June – France slightly later because of its Championship final – while the southern trio went to Europe in November. The term 'tour', with its implication of discursiveness, had become a misnomer. Visits were three to four weeks long at most, and, with rare exceptions, only internationals were played. Part of the appeal of quadrennial British and Irish Lions tours was that they still included state or provincial teams and veered slightly off the international beaten track. The balance of international careers changed. England's most frequent international opponents were not home rivals but South Africa and Australia, met at least once, sometimes twice, a year. Appearance records grew spectacularly as matches proliferated. Gareth Edwards took just under eleven years to accumulate fifty-three Welsh caps, all but eight in Five Nations games. Starting in 1996, Robert Howley reached fifty-three caps in a little over half that time, five years and nine months, with thirty of those matches outside the championship. Wales's first four meetings with South Africa were stretched over forty-five years. Between 1994 and 1998, they met four times in forty-three months.

The driving force was maximising income. International matches are the surest way to make money, through the gate and from the other paymaster, television. Murdoch's cash funded professionalism in the southern hemisphere and in England as well, as the RFU broke unilaterally from previous Five Nations agreements in 1996 to conclude a deal worth £87.5 million with Murdoch's BSkyB television. Other unions were furious. RFU treasurer Colin Herridge would recall, 'We were harangued to a degree that I could not believe. I've sat in acrimonious board meetings before, but this was a different level altogether.'

Vernon Pugh's anger as chair of the home unions television negotiating committee redoubled when Sky offered Wales £40 million, twice as much as Scotland and Ireland: 'There's no way we'll abandon them [Scotland and Ireland], because to do so would be to abandon ourselves.' Amid allegations of ill faith on both sides, England were briefly thrown out of the Five Nations and reinstated only because the other unions realised expulsion would be self-destructive. England's argument, echoing the IRB imbroglio of a century earlier, was that having more clubs and most of the TV audience should give them a larger slice of the money. Unilateralism was borne out of desperation at carrying its £35 million Twickenham loan while trying to assist indebted clubs.

Television money came with strings. There were questions in Parliament when New Zealanders realised that only subscribers to Murdoch's channels would see All Black matches live. The importance of the Australian market to those channels also meant tests were increasingly played at night rather than in the afternoon. This suited nobody but television, but its money funded professional rugby in New Zealand.

Touring teams were often tired and/or depleted. This was evident in the summer of 1998. Top British and Irish players went on an exhausting Lions tour in 1997. Then came another tiring home season – Dallaglio played 42 matches. Numerous players were injured, or took their only chance of rest before the 1999 World Cup. England, minus twelve first-choice players, went on a lunatic tour designed to maximise both air miles and fatigue, with four tests in Australia, New Zealand and South Africa in consecutive weekends. Wales, weak in any case, took a virtual second-string to South Africa. The British nations conceded 402 points, scoring only 72 in losing 9 tests. Wales lost 96–13 to South Africa, while England fell 76–0 to Australia and by 64–22 in New Zealand. Union coffers were replenished, television schedules filled. The problem was that the answer to the pressures of professionalism never seemed to vary: more matches and to hell with the players.

These problems, though, paled alongside those of the second tier of nations. By 1997, Canadian player Gareth Rees was warning that 'the World Cup, far from embracing the world, is likely to be a farce', due to the imbalance of resources. For the Pacific islands, professionalism was a mixed blessing. It was never quite true that Samoa existed entirely on money sent home from England to his mum by former All Black Inga Tuigamala, but remittances from 200 professionals playing abroad made a considerable difference to a Third World island. For individuals, there were opportunities inconceivable at home. For this reason, Samoan Rugby Union schools officer Laki Apelu said in 1999 that they could not advise young players to reject scholarships from New Zealand schools – a practice begun by Graham Henry at Kelston High School, Auckland – or professional contracts. Yet it meant losing their best talent, with some inevitably opting for the greater rewards that go with being an All Black or Wallaby. It is worth saying, though, that New Zealand's relationship with the islands has never quite been the sack and pillage portrayed in some British quarters. The Kiwi team has Samoan and Fijian rugby players for the same reason that England fields Jamaican soccer players, because of population movements independent of sport. New Zealand was, however, complicit in depriving the islands of the likeliest means of resistance when they were excluded from the Super 12 competiton. Bryan Williams said at the time: 'The rugby world is supposed to be like a big family – we all help each other out. This quite obviously hasn't happened here. If rugby is a big family, then this is child abuse. Western Samoa rugby simply has to be included in the Super 12 tournament, or the cream of our international players will be taken away and rugby in Western Samoa will become obsolete.'

One difficulty was that Rupert Murdoch was never going to sell many satellite-television subscriptions to the impoverished folk of Apia, Suva or Nuku'alofa. There seems little evidence, though, that the three big unions made the slightest attempt to protect the islands. Their problems were exacerbated when a planned Pacific Rim championship incorporating the islands, USA, Canada, Japan, Hong Kong and Argentina was aborted for want of the necessary $2 million sponsorship.

The consequences were summed up by another former All Black, Brad Johnstone. As coach of Fiji, he was criticised in parliament by MP Bill Cavubati after a 34–9 defeat by France in 1988. The MP's son, also Bill, a 318 lb prop, had been on the bench. Johnstone said: 'You've got to remember we were up against professionals. We cannot compare ourselves with the material, structures and the level of competition they enjoy. One French player earns more than we contracted the whole team for. We are still 20 years behind these big rugby-playing nations in terms of structure, finance and material, and still our players are doing their best.'

One peculiar Fijian difficulty was that several of their players had feet too large for sizes offered by their kit suppliers and needed expensive custom-made boots. There were some compensations in the burgeoning Sevens circuit, turned into a worldwide competition by the IRB from 1999–2000. Nobody ever played better sevens than Fiji's Waisale Serevi, but even here there would be disappointments for Fiji as New Zealand took the Commonwealth Games titles in 2002 and 2006, while England became the dominant force in Hong Kong. Moving to Italy after 1999, Johnstone could contrast the £10 million budget he enjoyed with the £100,000 or so that the IRB and sponsors had provided for the Fijians.

The Italians enjoyed a purple patch in the mid-1990s that helped them, finally, to make an unanswerable case for inclusion in the Five Nations championship from 2000. Between 1995 and 1998, they beat Ireland three times and also claimed victories over Scotland and a French team little different to the one that had just won a Grand Slam in 1997. All three meetings with Wales were lost by single-figure margins, and England were very nearly embarrassed in a World Cup qualifier at Huddersfield, happy to win 23–15. Dominguez and Alessandro Troncon provided high-class continuity at half-back, Ivan Francescato added dash wherever he turned up amongst the backs, while Massimo Giovanelli and Mauro Bergamasco, first capped in 1998, were back rowers whom any of the Five Nations would have welcomed. Unfortunately, by 1999, an exceptional team was past its best, as Italy lost all four matches they played against Five Nations opposition and went down at home to Fiji. Francescato died, tragically young, at the start of the year. There was also a warning of the caprices of rich owners when Silvio Berlusconi pulled out of the historic Milan club, which closed in 1998. John Kirwan, who had married an Italian and played there for several years, said it was 'like Auckland being shut up and the key being thrown away'.

By this time, Italy had a clear ascendancy over Romania, who were still struggling against poverty and the loss of players abroad. Of nineteen players based in France, only six were available for the World Cup. To qualify, they held off the fast improving Georgians, who faced similar issues. New Zealand coach Ross Meurant found that the Georgian national team had only two practice balls when he went in 1997 to advise the Under-19 squad but discovered the local gift for improvisation by asking for tackle bags. Three were presented the following morning: 'They were of denim material, obviously stitched together on a domestic sewing machine and stuffed with rubber.' Another coach's wife had sat up half the night making them.

Georgia fell at the repechage stage introduced in the 1999 qualifiers, losing an intriguing clash of cultures with Tonga. The extension of the number of finalists to 20 did enable some first-time qualifiers. Uruguay's years of progress were rewarded, Namibia's experience in 1995 was an insurance against complacency on this occasion, and Spain, fielding a menacing-sounding back row including players whose names translated as 'Kill' (Mata) and 'Bad Bert' (Alberto Malo), also came through. Malo, a combative red-haired flanker whose Santboiana club was the cradle of modern Spanish rugby, was to earn 74 caps and an admiring biography in Catalan. Preparing to face the professionals of South Africa and Scotland, coach Alfonso Feijoo explained how the other half lived. He reckoned to spend 100 days a year, most funded from his own pocket, on rugby business, while sponsorship was being sought for his players: 'They need to work; they lose money while they are away from their jobs. Of course, they'll come for nothing, because they want to play for Spain.'

Japan maintained their record of always qualifying, their player base underpinned by a nationwide schools competition involving 1,200 teams. Training methods encouraged discipline rather than initiative – the 'run pass', with players running the length of the field for an hour or more exchanging passes, was all but universal – but the traditionalist coach Yamaguchi at Fushimi Technical High School had inspired a television series based on his battle to beat delinquency with rugby practice.

The international elite's game had changed. Allowing tactical substitutions further increased the importance of coaches and undoubtedly aided nations with greater strength in depth. Allowing lineout jumpers to be supported – lifting was still forbidden, but the distinction often appeared semantic – had the knock-on effect of greatly reducing kicking for touch. Because the team throwing in was now highly likely to win possession, the touch-kick was no longer the invariable percentage option. Many mourned the loss of the pure lineout jumper, although Australia's John Eales was just as proficient as under previous rules. The lineout briefly became almost as predictable as the scrum, with defending teams not contesting possession. But by the time the World Cup came around, Llanelli in Welsh domestic rugby and Australia at international level had begun to contest the opposing throw, often to great effect.

The 1999 tournament had echoes of 1991. Wales were nominal hosts, but to win the votes needed for the nomination they were forced to spread the tournament across all five nations – diluting its effect. Wales staged only nine out of forty-one matches, with both semi-finals at Twickenham.

Wales lost to Samoa again but still won their group to reach the quarter-finals because the islanders had come unstuck against Argentina. The Pumas fielded the usual formidable pack and an outside-half Gonzalo Quesada, whose goal-kicking routine included a pause so long it looked as though he had changed his mind. In a competition with an extraordinarily high standard of goal-kicking – 82 per cent of conversions were landed, up from 58 per cent in 1987, and the Canadian Gareth Rees landed all 19 of his kicks – Quesada led the scorers with 102 points, including 23 in the 28–24 play-off win over Ireland that took Argentina into the quarter-finals. There they met France – recuperating from their ghost of tournaments past, a lucky referee-error-aided group-stage win over Fiji – and pushed them hard before exiting 47–26.

It was a good tournament for the River Plate. There were pre-tournament prognostications of three-figure scores against Uruguay and Spain by Scotland and South Africa. Instead, this proved to be the only pool where nobody reached 50 points in a match. Only persistent press questioning about a Uruguayan rugby team who 27 years earlier survived an air crash, eating the bodies of dead teammates – inspiration for the film *Alive* – ruffled them. They felt, quite reasonably, that their own story, a country with a few hundred adult players reaching the World Cup, was worthy of attention. Their captain, Ormachaea, was older than the accompanying president of the Uruguayan Rugby Union, Andres Sanguinetti, whose other distinction was that his older half-brother was president of Uruguay. Cohesion based on eighteen players from Carrasco Polo and forward strength born of consistent contact with Argentina told in the one match they could hope to win, against Spain at Galashiels, where the venerable Ormachaea, in his twentieth year as an international player, scored the final try. Namibia were less successful, although nobody matched the euphony of a teamsheet beginning Van Wyk, Van Dyk, Van Rensberg and Van der Merwe.

In further echoes of 1991, England lost at home to New Zealand. Lomu, recovered from his first bout with kidney disease, scored a thunderous long-range try. Disappointed England coach Clive Woodward greeted a cataclysmic-sounding backstage crash during his post-match conference with the words 'that's Jonah getting out of the shower'. In the quarter-final in Paris, England were mown down by an extraordinary barrage of drop-goals from Springbok outside-half Jannie de Beer. His five in thirty-one minutes were more than anyone had landed in an entire international, more probably than anyone in serious rugby since Albert Goldthorpe, destined to become an early league star, kicked five for Hunslet against Kendal in 1891.

True to Wales's luck as host, the most compelling action came in semi-final weekend at Twickenham. De Beer kicked 21 more points for South Africa against Australia, a heavyweight contest with echoes of Ali v. Frazier as the quicker, lighter Australians battled the powerful Bokke. His sixth penalty, eight minutes into injury time, would be remembered as one of the great kicks had South Africa won. He was 40 metres out, wide on the right amid swirling wind and rain, knowing a miss would end his nation's tenure as holder. He landed it, but South Africa were undone in extra time by a long, skiddy drop-goal from Larkham, who had never dropped one before.

That drama was comprehensively outdone the following day. Previous form suggested that France could play much better than in their previous matches and still lose heavily to New Zealand, and that is what was happening until ten minutes after half-time. Lomu, the shark's fin of his haircut grimly appropriate as defenders cleared his path, had scored two tries and the All Blacks were leading 24–10. Two drop-goals for France by Christophe Lamaison looked like mere punctuation but instead signalled the greatest French uprising since 1789, 33 points in 27 minutes leaving the All Blacks a bemused ruin. Like their predecessors facing Obolensky on the same ground 63 years before, the All Blacks were undone by the unpredictable and unaccountable.

More predictably, the final was a crashing anticlimax. France played like the team their record proclaimed – a mediocre outfit who had caught light in a bottle for that semi-final half-hour. It was a bad day for republics – while France lost, Australia's referendum voted to keep the monarchy, allowing the Queen a moment of satisfaction as she presented the trophy to John Eales, known to have voted against her. This was Eales's apotheosis – the third great gift of Australia's Italian community to rugby, a quietly self-deprecating man in succession to his rumbustious predecessors Cerutti and Campese. He responded to a magazine questionnaire by suggesting that Woody Allen would play him in a film, admitting that his most embarrassing moment was when a friend doctored his answerphone message to have him claiming to be the finest rugby player since the war. His friend had a point. Eales was one of those players who redefines the possibilities of a position, an absurdly accomplished lock who not only dominated the lineout but made corner-flagging tackles and emerged from the bottom of rucks to calmly land place-kicks. Most extraordinary of all was that playing a position associated with the physically uncompromising, he was not only never involved in an untoward incident, but none of the notoriously tough individuals who had played against him – he had first faced Martin Johnson in a youth international in New Zealand more than a decade before – appears ever to have thought it worthwhile trying to provoke him.

A fourth consecutive southern hemisphere win reflected the greater athleticism of their game. Former international referee Corris Thomas, the IRB's chief analyst, rejected suggestions that the Tri Nations had a different pattern of play, arguing that the real difference was in the extra 10 per cent of time that the ball was in play in Tri Nations, compared with Five Nations, matches.

Australia's ascendancy was maintained for two more years, with victories in the Tri Nations of 2000 and 2001 and over the 2001 British and Irish Lions, defeated 2–1 in an excruciatingly close finish after the Lions had taken the first test. Macqueen gave way to Eddie Jones after the Lions tour, while Eales continued to the end of the 2001 Tri Nations, lifting the trophy after the All Blacks were beaten in the closing moments of match and tournament. The Capital Territory Brumbies broke New Zealand's Super 12 stranglehold in 2001, when South Africa and Australia monopolised the semi-final places. There were signs at least of a serious broadening of Australia's base. Sixty per cent of New South Wales's Under-21 team came from outside the public schools, while one multiracial high school had devised a haka beginning 'Tonga! Samoa! Lebanon!'. The 2001 Super 12 result proved, though, to be an aberration. By 2002, New Zealand were back on top in both tournaments. The World Cup semi-final defeat in 1999 had provoked a backlash against the business idiom associated with Hart, who had resigned, and a hankering for older verities. The All Blacks had nevertheless struggled under Hart's personable successor Wayne Smith, replaced in 2001 by John Mitchell, a Waikato number 8 who had belonged to Clive Woodward's England set-up. New Zealand also discovered that semi-final defeats were not the only way to lose World Cups. It was deprived of co-host status for the 2003 tournament in a row over demands for 'clean stadiums' with no conflicting advertising or sponsorship agreements. The repercussions rumbled into 2002 as the Eichelbaum Report on the fiasco dominated the New Zealand media even in general election week and provoked a clear-out of officials, replaced by a new executive led by Jock Hobbs.

Mitchell showed little respect for totemic stars, discarding Wilson and the brilliant attacking full-back Christian Cullen. On his first tour, Britain and Ireland in 2001, he took a young side picked on form rather than reputation, Richie McCaw showing himself an open-side of the highest quality and Aaron Mauger a second-five in the classic mould. Mitchell's reliance on the Canterbury team who reclaimed control of the Super 12 in 2002, their third win in four years, created a stir when Chris Laidlaw, in a thoughtful newspaper column turned into a media storm by crude presentation and sensationalist reporting, pointed out that this represented a re-whitening of the All Blacks after several years in which islander representation had been growing inexorably. This was an echo of schools rugby, where islanders dominated Auckland competitions and the 1999 New Zealand Schools squad included eleven Samoans, five Tongans, four Maoris and six Pakehas. Warwick Roger pointed to a mild gentrification effect – first-generation Samoans had gravitated to boxing, but their more middle-class sons were playing rugby.

In South Africa, black players like centre Gcobani Bobo and scrum-half Enrico Januarie, both of the Johannesburg-based Golden Cats, were making the breakthrough to representative level in previously all-white provinces. South Africa's difficulty was turnover of coaches – eight in a decade from readmission – and inability to win at both Super 12 and Tri Nations level, with four consecutive last places for the Springboks and only one Super 12 finalist between the 1999 and 2003 World Cups. Perhaps the most striking evidence of South African decline was All Black scrum-half Justin Marshall, who played in and won more tests against the Springboks than anyone in history, suggesting during the 2003 World Cup that his generation and those younger increasingly regarded Australia as the great enemy. A miserable end-of-season tour in 2002 had done nothing to lift spirits. A 30–10 defeat by France might have been acceptable. To lose 21–6 to Scotland, who were struggling in the lower half of the Six Nations, then by a staggering 53–3 to England in a match disfigured by an early Springbok sending off and accusations of violent and reckless play, certainly was not.

The only extenuation was that England looked capable of beating anyone. English rugby was still not at complete peace. While Brittle was defeated in 1998, his Reform Group had recaptured the RFU chairmanship in 2001. Big clubs hankered after a gated community, with no relegation and only desirable, moneyed aspirants admitted to the Premiership. This preference for plutocracy over merit was expressed in 2002 when Rotherham, who had fought their way up seven divisions in a dozen years to win a Premiership place in 2001, were relegated but promptly won promotion again, only to be denied the place their on-field performances had earned on a technicality.

The clubs stabilised financially – the average Premiership crowd rose by more than half, from 5,507 to 8,438 between 1999 and 2003 – and took control in Europe. Northampton's Heineken Cup win in 2000 was followed by Leicester's in 2001 and 2002 – the 2001 win particularly impressive since it was obtained in Paris, next door to the home ground of opponents Stade Français. Still more indicative of English strength was that the second-string European Challenge, initially a French monopoly, was also won by English clubs in these years.

Research in 2003 produced findings to delight the marketing managers, confirming long-held assumptions that rugby had a more prosperous following than even newly gentrified football. Premiership rugby fans were 61 per cent professional and managerial, with 57 per cent earning more than £30,000 per year – more than half of Harlequins' fans were on £40,000 or more. Only Gloucester had a profile anywhere near football's. Twenty-one per cent of fans were female.

The grass roots were more worrying. Another report showed that the percentage of people declaring themselves interested in rugby union had dropped from 24 to 18 per cent in seven years. Britain's long working hours, reducing available leisure, were partly to blame but did not by themselves explain rugby's problems. A particular worry was declining participation, with one in nine players giving up the game over two years. One hope for the RFU, which had commissioned the research, was that a successful World Cup might renew enthusiasm.

Player release continued to create tension, but differences were smoothed over for 15 months leading up to the 2003 World Cup. Woodward, retained after the disappointment of the 1999 campaign, had constructed a large specialist back-up team – including defence and kicking coaches with league backgrounds – at great expense. With Twickenham paid for and packed out for almost any opposition and the club game stabilised, the RFU, which made a £7 million profit in 2002, could afford it. Richard Pool-Jones, a French-based player who ran a successful printing business, said, 'England rugby is the most professional environment I've been in, not just in sport, but in any domain. It is highly motivated and has given me some excellent ideas for my own business career. The attention to detail means everything is intelligently done.'

Woodward was constructing a team to match, although it lacked the steamroller quality of the 1990s which had made it successful in Europe. The 1990s England teams, though, had lacked variety and initiative, struggling against opponents they could not physically dominate, so had limited success against the southern hemisphere. Woodward's great achievement was to change England's mindset, much as soccer coach Arsène Wenger had done with previously defence-fixated Arsenal. He encouraged players to think for themselves and replace risk-aversion with calculated risk-taking. Veteran prop Jason Leonard said, 'He's very good at challenging preconceptions and making you think about the way you do things.' Certainly he was fortunate in the depth and quality of his squad, and there were strokes of good fortune within it. In spite of leading the Lions in 1997, Martin Johnson might never have captained England but for Dallaglio's media mishap in 1998, but now he led by intimidating example. Injuries to others propelled full-back Josh Lewsey into the team in 2003. Other successes, however, were Woodward's. Where previous coaches saw flanker Neil Back's limited stature, Woodward saw an immense talent whose speed, intelligence and anticipation were the perfect back-row complement to Dallaglio and the consistent, understated Richard Hill. He encouraged the signing of Jason Robinson, a sublime broken-field runner with ball-bearings where others have joints, from Wigan rugby league. He had also capped outside-half Jonny Wilkinson as an 18 year old with 58 minutes of senior rugby experience. Wilkinson, by 2003 the world's youngest veteran and England's record points scorer, was a study in the transformation of rugby lives. Two generations earlier, an academically competent Home Counties public schoolboy would have gravitated to Oxford or Cambridge and played three varsity matches. In the 1970s, he might have gone to Loughborough. Instead, Wilkinson went from school in Hampshire to a professional contract at Newcastle, coached by Rob Andrew, England's outside-half for most of the previous decade. Wilkinson lacked the flamboyance of many great outside-halfs or the blinding pace of a Jonathan Davies. He had, though, a metronomically accurate goal-kicking style honed by hours of daily practice, a firm grasp of midfield geometry and, most importantly of all, judgement under pressure. His points-scoring made him the most marketable figure in the game's wealthiest national market, and by 2003 he had overtaken Jonah Lomu, sidelined again by an increasingly desperate kidney condition, as the world's richest rugby player.

From 2000 on, England won seven consecutive matches against the southern giants, one against New Zealand and three each over the others. They had, though, developed a recurring problem with the home nations. From 1999, last-day defeats by Wales, Scotland and Ireland cost England Grand Slams in consecutive years. The 2003 Six Nations season saw the final-day Grand Slam bogey slaughtered. Ireland had also won all four matches and were at home. They did not play badly, but were demolished 42–6. The one remaining gap on England's record was not to have won tests in Australasia. That too was ticked off by a 15–13 victory over New Zealand – who would shortly afterwards completely dominate the Tri Nations – in Wellington that included one period when sin-binnings reduced the England pack to six men, then a hugely dominant 25–14 win in Melbourne. There was little doubt who went to the World Cup ranked number one.

The order of precedence in their wake in Europe had been reshuffled. France pruned its First Division, which had 40 teams and a top-16 play-off as recently as 1997, down to 16 teams with 4 in the play-offs in 2002. Those clubs had lost early European dominance. Coach Bernard Laporte's national team was inconsistent as he sought a synthesis between the festive and the efficient, developing something of a complex about the new Stade de France, which was constructed for the 1998 soccer World Cup. A Grand Slam in 2002 with a newly, superbly complementary back row of Magne, the immensively destructive Serge Betsen and athletic Basque number 8 Imanol Harinordoquy, along with the extremely intelligent scrum-half Fabien Galthie reclaiming the captaincy from Fabien Pelous, a powerful Toulouse lock whose looks suggested eligibility for Easter Island, promised well, but in 2003 France had dropped back to third.

Scotland declined rapidly from its 1999 peak, losing its opening match the following season to Six Nations debutants Italy, who went on to lose their next 14 championship matches. Mobile ball-handling prop Tom Smith was the only Scottish first choice in the 2001 Lions team, and the districts continued to struggle both for support and European success. Italy's 15th championship match after beating Scotland was against Wales, whose seasons resembled the old joke about the Soviet harvest: worse than last year, better than next. Wales were defeated and went on to lose all five Six Nations matches in 2003. Wales too had stadium problems, although the curse of the Millennium Stadium was its weight of associated debt. There was also scandal when imports Howarth and Sinkinson turned out not to be qualified following an investigation in 2000 that led to a tightening of procedures and a ruling that, in future, nobody would be allowed to play for more than one country. Consistent Heineken Cup failure by Welsh clubs, Llanelli apart, doomed them at the highest level. Fifty years on from when Cardiff could beat the All Blacks, and Swansea draw with them, the clubs, after years of wrangling, were downgraded to semi-professional status from 2003–04, replaced by five regional teams in the Celtic League, which since 2001 had incorporated Wales's clubs along with Ireland's provinces and Scotland's districts.

It was no fluke that Leinster and Munster were the league's first two champions. Ireland's revival was a timely riposte to those who argued that Celts were no longer competitive. While the English-based Wood and Leinster centre Brian O'Driscoll, a dazzling runner with extraordinary hands, were the stars, Ireland's rise coincided with that of the Munster provincial team. Munster were narrowly defeated in the Heineken Cup finals of 2000 and 2002 as their pursuit of the European trophy became the competition's defining romantic narrative, accompanied by an invading army of thousands of fans with immense capacities for alcohol and enjoyment and an ingrained sportsmanship that meant opposition goal-kicks, however controversial the award, took place amid sepulchral silence. History, so often troublesome to Ireland, for once did it a favour. Four provinces were about the right concentration of talent at sub-national level, and identities long predating any form of organised sport meant that fans cared about them. Only England won more matches than Ireland's 14 between 2000 and 2003, but neither national team nor provinces could yet make the final step from contender to champion.

Elsewhere in Europe, Romania's misery was underlined by a 134–0 beating at Twickenham in 2002. A highly promising Russian qualifying campaign (which sent Ireland across seven time zones to play in Krasnoyàrsk) was aborted when an investigation of Russia's South African recruits led to disqualification. Russia's demise meant that Georgia, who had already beaten them in the qualifiers, were the only debutants at the 2003 tournament. They were now serious challengers to Romania as Europe's leader outside the Six Nations, winning the European Nations Cup, a competition for the leading six Continental nations, in 2001, but losing out to Romania a year later. Membership of the Council of Europe meant that Georgians could play in France, and this was consequently the base for 18 of the 25-man squad who went to Ireland for a World Cup qualifier in 2002. Not all was well, though. French coach Georges Saurel pointed out that it was the first time they had played an established nation since the last World Cup qualifiers. Echoing George Simpkins' unanswered plea on behalf of Fiji in 1987, he said, 'We need games like this more often. We will only progress by playing.'

Ninety-two teams had entered, against sixty-eight four years earlier, but the final qualifiers had a familiar ring. Uruguay, which had proudly opened a new, dedicated national training centre in 2000, squeezed narrowly past the USA and Chile to join Canada in qualifying from the Americas. Samoa, offering dire warnings about its ability to do so again unless it received serious help, qualified alongside Fiji, while Tonga once again came via the repechage route, flattening Korea 194–0 over two legs, along with the USA. Namibia tied 43–43 with Tunisia over two legs but qualified on try count, while the Tunisians fell in the repechage. Malta called up Ray Watts, the 45-year-old hooker for Nantyfflon seconds in South Wales, qualified via his mother, to play against Moldova in Chisinau.

Australia, aware that it lacked a mass rugby following, worked hard at selling the tournament, building on expertise from the 2000 Sydney Olympics. Volunteers were recruited en masse. More than 200 marketing and promotion staff were taken on, compared with three in 1999. The strategy of engaging Australians with teams worked brilliantly. Townsville in Queensland is one of the Australian towns that was bombed during the Second World War, yet its rugby fans were so enamoured of the Japanese that the invariably popular Fijians – population less than 1 per cent of Japan's and a per capita GNP of about one-twelfth – found themselves, in one of those geopolitical inversions in which rugby specialises, cast as giant against a much-loved underdog. It even worked in Sydney, which sees enough top sport even without an Olympics to be blasé. Georgia shirts became a popular fashion item. Georgia v. Uruguay attracted more than 30,000 spectators and noise levels worthy of a packed Millennium Stadium. The one fault was television-driven scheduling, which discriminated systematically against the non-established nations, most of all those capable of creating a shock.

Tonga and Italy were rightly aggrieved about playing Wales on less rest than their better-established opponent. All eight 'foundation nations' progressed, although Argentina lost only 17–16 to Ireland, who had earlier come similarly close to upsetting Australia in Melbourne after O'Driscoll scored an extraordinary try, apparently via a hole in the space-time continuum. Fiji, whose backs bore comparison with any in the tournament even after the astonishingly quick Rupeni Caucaunibuca was suspended, led Scotland for much of their meeting before losing 22–20. At the other end of the scale, scheduling Australia v. Namibia at Adelaide Cricket Ground ensured a scoreboard capable of displaying 142–0 without difficulty. At least Namibia had some of the most versatile players – Rudi van Vuuren had played World Cup cricket earlier in the year, taking five England wickets, while Schalk van der Merwe's fearlessness on the flank reflected a day job as an animal tamer reputed to have once head-butted a lion. The Namibians were rivalled as the tournament's renaissance men only by Georgian captain Ilia Zeguinidze, an international lawyer who spoke five languages.

France and New Zealand made the early running. The All Blacks' only serious challenges on the way to the semi-finals came from an electrifyingly bloodthirsty Tongan haka and a Wales team who suddenly relocated national traditions of flair and invention to lead for much of an extraordinary pool-stage finale before going down 53–37. France had been smoothly menacing, with Laporte's synthesis seemingly close to consummation, their back row omnipresent and invincible while Frédéric Michalak, protected by Galthie's intelligence at scrum-half and Yannick Jauzion's physical presence at centre, dazzled at outside-half. Australia progressed without impressing. England scuffled and struggled, seriously troubled by first South Africa then Samoa in the group stages before being outscored three tries to one in the quarter-final by Wales, who

271

threatened to overrun them before the half-time introduction of veteran South African-born centre Mike Catt had injected stability and a little imagination.

Yet the scufflers prevailed over the stylists in the semi-finals. Australian control and purpose were evident from the opening moments against the All Blacks. Dreadlocked flanker George Smith and blond Phil Waugh controlled the breakdown, centre Stirling Mortlock repeatedly broke All Black defensive lines and gloriously unpredictable New Zealand outside-half Carlos Spencer was nullified. Twenty-four hours later, amid a deluge, England did much the same job on France, with Hill and Back winning the battles of inches while Michalak was harried to distraction. The boot of Wilkinson, who scored 24 points to follow his 23 against Wales, did the rest.

The week before the final was unedifying, as English and Australian papers, aided by a time difference that allowed them to report the latest insults from the other side and think up their own, indulged in intercontinental slanging. The hammering of England for reliance on the boot and poor weather ignored both the nature of Australia's well-deserved victory over South Africa four years earlier and the inconvenient fact that Sydney has exactly twice London's rainfall.

It was not immediately obvious which was the home team the following Sunday at Sydney's Olympic Stadium. With Australia's large expatriate English population swelled by a huge temporary influx, white shirts were almost as common as gold. The match itself recalled the grimly tense struggle eight years earlier at Ellis Park. England were stronger, but their edge was nullified both by some idiosyncratic refereeing of the scrum and Australia's ingrained will to resist. Each scored a try through an ex-league wing, England's Jason Robinson replying to Australia's Lote Tuqiri. Australia's Elton Flatley landed an equalising injury-time penalty that, if not as technically demanding as de Beer's Twickenham shot four years earlier, was, because of its apparent ease, even more of a test of nerve. As at Ellis Park, a drop-kick settled it, but in favour of the visitors rather than the hosts. Johnson won a lineout, scrum-half Matt Dawson – a great player on the big occasions – scrambled vital extra metres and Wilkinson calmly landed the goal. A few minutes later, Johnson – at last somebody who looked like a rugby player after the four unfeasibly presentable young men who had preceded him – lifted the trophy.

The world, it seemed, turned upside down. John Mitchell, who, like Hart four years earlier, lost his job for a semi-final defeat after seasons of brilliance, questioned whether the fluidity of Super 12 rugby was the right preparation for the physical demands of the international game.

When the next World Cup kicked off in France in September 2007, it seemed that a more conventional orbit had been resumed. England had regressed, with four consecutive poor seasons. Club v. country warfare had resumed, claiming a hugely significant victim when Woodward resigned less than a year after the World Cup. His successor, Andy Robinson, was sacked late in 2006, and veteran Brian Ashton – England's fourth successive ex-Bath appointment – took them to the World Cup. Johnson retired from international rugby immediately after the 2003 victory. Wilkinson, struck by a succession of injuries, did not play for England again until 2007, although the fame to which his winning kick propelled him meant he commanded far more column inches and income than anyone who did. A survey in 2005 estimated his personal fortune at £8 million, making him one of the richest British sportsmen outside soccer's gilded youth. He would, there is little doubt, have swapped much of it for renewed fitness. Less noticed, but just as importantly, Hill played little more international rugby. Prop Trevor Woodman was forced to retire, and others lost form – the inevitable fate, perhaps, of achievers who have achieved. The exception to the general malaise was the sevens squad coached by Mike Friday, whose 2004 victory in Hong Kong, completing a hat-trick, was followed by another in 2006. At club level, Wasps won two Heineken Cups and three consecutive Premierships – each time beating the team who had topped the table in play-offs that are yet to gain full acceptance – with a lightning quick, high-risk defensive formation that subverted usual assumptions as opponents found that the longer they retained possession, the more vulnerable they were. Wasps were the only English finalists between 2002 and 2006 as France resumed their default role as Europe's dominant force, but the London side faced Leicester in the 2007 final.

The direction of cross-channel club apprehension shifted as salary-capped English clubs complained of the superior spending power of clubs like Toulouse, who won the All-French Heineken Cup finals of 2003 and 2005, and Stade Français and Biarritz, both of whom fell short due to over-caution in Europe but had the compensation of back-to-back national titles. At national level, Laporte's synthesis seemed to recede from sight. A Grand Slam in 2004 and championships in 2006 and 2007 – the latter the first Six Nations title won when not paying full attention, as Laporte shuffled his squad in preparation for the World Cup – reflected others' failings as much as French excellence. Laporte's extensive advertising portfolio and other business activities also excited attention, not all of it positive, but this did not dissuade new French president Nicolas Sarkozy from naming him as sports minister – the appointment to take effect at the end of the World Cup – after his election in mid-2007.

France's best performances came in the second half of the season in which they did not win the championship, 2005. That, to general amazement, was Wales's year – a first Grand Slam for 27 years delivered by dash, forwards who passed where those of other nations ran into contact and perma-tanned centre Gavin Henson supplying a touch of rock star (plus a girlfriend with aspirations in that direction) along with crucial penalty- and drop-goals. More predictably, it fell apart amid injuries and in-fighting in 2006, as Mike Ruddock emulated the last two coaches to win anything for Wales – Tony Gray in 1988 and Alan Davies six years later – by losing his job within a year. While all national coaching jobs damage their failures, Wales's remains unique in also devouring its successes. Nor were the underpinnings of the national team too secure. Whatever their failings, the clubs had never failed to get at least one team into the Heineken play-offs. The new regions did that in two out of three seasons, losing one of their number when the Celtic Warriors were closed down after one season, disenfranchising Wales's most consistent nursery for talent, Bridgend, and the community that had best supported club rugby over the previous decade, Pontypridd.

Scotland suffered similar problems. In the summer of 2006, all three professional teams were jeopardised by the Scottish Rugby Union's financial problems, which led to the axing of the Border franchise in 2007. And this was without the compensation provided by Wales's one year of national success, although the appointment of the lucid Frank Hadden as coach and victories over France and England at Murrayfield in 2006 broke the pattern of depression at top level.

Italy too showed signs of competitiveness – in spite of another wooden spoon – in 2006 and saw them fulfilled in 2007 when Scotland, devastated by three early tries, and Wales were beaten. Players like lock Marco Bortolami, precocious number 8 Sergio Parisse and the dashing Bergamasco brothers would challenge for selection in any team.

Ireland continued to offer a model of consistency, which, however, still included an unhappy tendency to have one bad day – generally against France – per campaign. Triple Crowns in 2004, 2006 and 2007 reflected ascendancy over other home unions. England were beaten four times in a row, culminating in a 43–13 hammering in 2007. Ireland had gone into the championship with high expectations after an autumn programme including conclusive defeats of Australia, demolished in a first half of brilliant wet-weather rugby, and South Africa. Lansdowne Road was under reconstruction, so England were played at Croke Park, home of the Gaelic Athletic Association. The vote by the GAA to allow 'garrison games' like rugby to be played there for the first time not only saved the Irish team from a spell in exile but marked a significant moment in the nation's coming to terms with its complex and bloody past. Croke Park is not only a sports stadium but a nationalist shrine following the death of Tipperary Gaelic football captain Michael Hogan – commemorated in the naming of one stand – and 13 spectators at the hands of British security forces in 1920. The atmosphere for the visit of England and in particular the pre-match playing of 'God Save the Queen' was inevitably charged. Ireland played as though avenging an ancestral curse, while England's performance had the air of an extended apology. Unfortunately, two weeks earlier, Ireland had entertained France at Croke Park and conceded two tries in the first few minutes and another in the final second to lose a match they had largely dominated. So championships remained elusive. The same was true of the provinces until May 2006, when Munster's passion for the Heineken Cup was at last requited by victory over

Biarritz at an exultant Millennium Stadium – an uplifting, hugely popular triumph highlighted by a bizarrely postmodern moment 20 minutes from time when the stadium screens showed O'Connell Street in Limerick packed with fans, producing simultaneous roars of encouragement from street and stadium.

British and Irish limitations had been painfully evident on the 2005 Lions tour of New Zealand. This reaffirmed why Lions tours are so valued, taking top-class rugby to off-the-test-track communities like New Plymouth, Invercargill and Palmerston North, but also showed how difficult the task facing the tourists has become. Clive Woodward replicated the military-expedition aspects of his England days with 30 support staff but was ultimately brought down by injuries, ill-considered selection and the quality of the opposition. Failure, partly attributable to a belief that the men who had delivered for him in 2003 could do so two years on, damaged his reputation but should not detract from his remarkable achievement two years earlier. To simultaneously meld the styles of four national teams – increasingly entrenched by the club-like qualities of test squads – find your best XV plus replacements and ensure that every player gets a fair go in the space of a few matches is a formidable challenge. It was evident that players still regard Lions selection as a supreme honour, while New Zealand were delighted to entertain them. New Zealand, with Danny Carter irresistible at outside-half and McCaw demonstrating that he plays his position better than anyone else in the world plays theirs, were gestating another powerful team.

New Zealand's successful organisation of the tour did no harm to its chances of being chosen as host for the 2011 World Cup. This was secured against all expectation ahead of Japan in October 2005. New Zealand ran a high-risk campaign, warning that the competition would grow beyond its capabilities by 2015 and 2019, begging questions of its infrastructure now and creating a hostage to fortune should it need to bid again. The decision ensured that the World Cup will be played once more in the country where, more than any other, rugby remains a central preoccupation. It can be argued that it has a broader base than before, as women's rugby develops. Unlike their male counterparts, the Black Ferns have been as proficient at World Cups as elsewhere, winning the tournaments of 1998 in the Netherlands – where their lowest score was 44 points – and 2002 in Spain, completing their hat-trick in Canada in September 2006. Their most experienced player, Anna Richards, reckons to have lost only twice in more than 100 international matches and was made a member of the new national Order of Merit in 2005, the year in which a tribute to her was the main article in the *New Zealand Rugby Almanack*.

Choosing Japan as the host would have offered a rare chance to both encourage a developing nation and maximise commercial return. Former prime minister Yoshiro Mori accused the established nations of 'passing the ball around among their friends'. Other nations had still greater reason to feel excluded. The addition of two teams to the Super 12 and the extension of the Tri Nations in 2006 offered an opportunity to make good the wrong done to the Pacific islands back in 1995. The combined islands' Pacific Warriors team, who made such a vibrant debut in 2004, giving the Tri Nations serious contests on consecutive weekends, could have been added to the Super 12 franchise, and Argentina could have been rescued from its isolation as the most significant rugby nation with no regular competition by adding it to the Tri Nations. Neither was done, as extra South African and Australian franchises were added and the Tri Nations extended and unbalanced by the addition of a third round of fixtures.

The IRB took action in 2005, announcing increased targeted funding for second-rank nations, in particular improving facilities and management for elite players in the islands, and new tournaments, including a Pacific Nations Cup. If it was predictable that the Junior All Blacks would win the first two editions in 2006 and 2007, it at least supplied and supported competition for the islands and Japan. What remained to be seen was whether the IRB's initiatives would significantly close the gap between the rest and the top eight, or if former Australian coach Eddie Jones – who spoke with some authority as former national coach in Japan – was right when he argued that the nations ranked from nine to sixteen would not get any better by playing each other. How much difference membership of the lucrative Tri Nations could make to Argentina became clear when the UAR went into receivership in mid-2006. Its team, though, remained good enough to beat that year's Welsh touring team twice, then follow up in the autumn with a defeat of

England at Twickenham. There were suggestions that, with the squad largely based in France and Britain, it might make sense to bid for a place in the Six Nations.

In Europe, Romania regained second-rank primacy, beating chief rivals Georgia and Portugal in the final rounds of a European Nations Cup played over two seasons to pip Georgia on points difference. Portugal's rise, winning the tournament in 2003, had been too late for the qualifiers for that year's World Cup. Their concern was that an outstanding cohort might have passed a best good enough to worry Fiji in late 2005, before the contest for places in the 2007 competition began in earnest. Consigned to the repechages, they beat Morocco and – to some surprise – Uruguay, to claim the last place available.

Morocco had once again come second in Africa to Namibia. The Namibians had not, however, had it all their own way in the qualifiers. In the penultimate stage, they lost their matches away to both Kenya and Tunisia, emerging from a three-team group in which every match was won by the home team only on the strength of hammering the Kenyans in Windhoek. Their victims were upwardly mobile on the sevens circuit, and both were in 2007 admitted to the core group of teams who contest every event. Kenya, who reached the semi-finals of the 2007 Adelaide Sevens, beating England before falling to eventual winners Samoa, were a study in the evolution of African rugby. The Kenyan game was long cast in the image of its Nondescripts club, so called when founded in 1923 because of its multiplicity of (white) national origins. As late as 1993, a touring squad photograph includes only two black faces among twenty-six players. Historian Michael Mundia Kamau dates the beginnings of transformation from the foundation in 1977 of Mean Machine RFC at the University of Nairobi. Students remain the vital element – Teddy Omondi, a professional player in France with Racing Club reckoned in 2007 that they account for 60 per cent of current players – but ethnicity has changed, with Africans now the overwhelming majority.

One consequence of four-year World Cup cycles is that everything is seen in the context of its bearing on the next tournament – a focus which grows steadily narrower as the cycle nears its end. In 2003–7, the All Blacks, not for the first time, provided the central preoccupation. After a brief interregnum in 2004 when South Africa took the Tri Nations on points difference when every match was a home win, and the ACT Brumbies won the Super 12, New Zealand resumed its dominance of the southern hemisphere. Three consecutive Tri Nations titles were won, with eleven wins in fourteen matches, and the Canterbury Crusaders regained the Super 12 in 2005 before winning the first Super 14 a year later. For New Zealanders, the fear, and the rest of the world's hope, was that the definitive rugby nation was stuck in a cycle of its own, once again peaking between World Cups. The paradox was that the greater their success between tournaments – the demolition of the 2005 Lions and their domination of the 2006 Tri Nations being cases in point – the more acute those fears grew.

Only Portugal's repechage-final elimination of Uruguay prevented the same 20 teams that had played the 2003 World Cup reassembling four years later in France. Pre-tournament, there were widespread fears of a series of massacres, with smaller nations unable to cope with the ever greater strength and pace of professional teams, and there was talk of reducing the number of competitors from 20 to 16 to avoid such mismatches and the possible risk to amateur players under such circumstances. Most experts saw New Zealand and France as the likeliest finalists, with South Africa the main challengers. Little was made, not least because the two competitions had been no guide at all to World Cup form in either 1999 or 2003, of the fact that the Heineken Cup final had been all-English and the Super 14 all-South African, with North Transvaal Blue Bulls beating Natal Sharks 20–19 to become the first champions from the Republic.

For the third World Cup running, Argentina provided the opening-match opposition for the hosts. If the idea was that they were good enough to provide a decent match without quite upsetting the established order, it was rapidly proved out of date. Fielding a team full of players entirely comfortable with French conditions – most played in the Top 14 championship, and there were five from Paris, more than in France's team – and with an excellent record against their adversaries, with four wins in their last five meetings, including taking their all-time ground record in Marseilles, Argentina won more conclusively than a 17–12 scoreline suggested. Defeat unleashed ferocious criticism of Laporte, attacked not only for some odd selections and substitutions but for the more serious crime of putting his political ambitions in front of coaching priorities. Before the match, he had full-back Clément Poitrenaud read the team the letter written by French Resistance martyr Guy Môquet before his execution in 1941. The problem was not just the possibility that this undoubtedly moving document might have upset France's players but that the letter had become closely associated with President Sarkozy, Laporte's future boss, who had ordained that it be read in every French school on the anniversary of Môquet's death.

Argentina's victory launched two trends: that this World Cup would be anything but predictable and that, initially at least, the Six Nations would struggle. Over the next few days, England stumbled to victory over the USA, Wales looked in serious trouble for 50 minutes against Canada, and Ireland beat Namibia by only 32–17 rather than the deluge widely predicted. The Irish were still less convincing against Georgia, who fielded what was widely described as a shadow team after being compelled to play only four days after facing the Argentinians. Shadow or not, they scared Ireland witless, with the only issue after a spectacular interception try by Georgi Shkinin whether the Irish would hang on for any kind of win. It took a couple of blown Georgian lineouts at crucial moments to ensure that they did, by 14–10.

New Zealand, Australia and South Africa, meanwhile, moved in untroubled fashion through their pool matches. The next big north v. south clash saw the Springboks demolish England 36–0, with an outstanding performance by scrum-half Fourie du Preez, who created their three tries. The south, it appeared, had moved firmly ahead again – playing with greater imagination, pace and power, particularly at the breakdown, where the Springboks won nine turnovers to England's one.

The issue, it seemed, was no longer whether any of the Six Nations could launch a serious challenge for the trophy – the idea of a successful English defence now seemed laughable – but if they could hold off the second-tier nations showing serious signs of renewed vigour. Among these, Tonga, only a few weeks after a 50–3 hammering by Samoa, reversed the established Pacific order by winning 19–15 when they met in Montpellier. Built around an outstanding back row featuring the spectacular bouffant hairstyle of number 8 Finau Maka and the driving power of open-side Nili Latu, the Tongans had become immensely popular in their host community of Clapiers by forgoing all official invitation-only Rugby World Cup functions to ensure that every event they attended was open to locals. Victory over Samoa was followed by throwing a serious scare into a South African shadow team, who squeezed through 30–25 only after using their heavyweight benchwarmers and seeing a last-second bounce go their way.

If Fiji had looked less impressive, they had been involved in two breathtaking finishes. Again cast, for the only time in four years, as the overdogs in their clash with Japan, they had to withstand an extraordinary four-minute post-hooter assault as the Japanese desperately tried to reverse a 35–31 deficit. After-match scenes were notable for hundreds of Toulouse children chanting 'Japon, Japon' and waiting for autographs while Rugby World Cup officials tried to persuade Fijian players more interested in socialising with the locals to enter the media area for interviews. Against Canada, they were again hanging on with a single-score lead as the Canadians drove towards their line, only for the ball to go loose and full-back Kameli Ratuvou to score a long-range try. Portugal did concede 108 points to New Zealand but were delighted to claim a try themselves, were never embarrassed and proceeded to give Italy and Romania serious matches. Open-side and captain João Uva and outside-half Duarte Cardoso Pinto were particularly outstanding, and Romania were able to claim a 14–10 victory only through the application of muscle and the second-half appearance of their superb hooker Marius Tincu.

The final weekend saw a series of eliminators to join South Africa, New Zealand and Australia in the last eight. England, who had regrouped with a self-critical team meeting following the South African fiasco and made numerous changes, beat Tonga 36–20 after an early scare when dangerous centre Sukanaivalu Hufanga gave the islanders the lead. Ireland, who had earlier lost perhaps the worst match in the tournament to France, had to win conclusively against Argentina and, in spite of scoring two good tries, were never really close. The most disappointing of any of the 20 campaigns concluded with a deserved 30–15 win for the Argentinians, with number 8 Gonzalo Longo Elía producing his best performance in an outstanding tournament. Scotland were heavily indebted to the boot of wing Chris Paterson – who would finish the competition with a 100 per cent record from 19 kicks at goal – for an 18–16 win over Italy.

The second tier had had its shining moment earlier the same day as Fiji continued Wales's eight-year cycle – following the Samoans of 1991 and 1999 – of World Cup embarrassments by islanders, ejecting them 38–34 in Nantes. After an extraordinary first-half explosion of tries had taken them to a 25–3 lead, with centre Seru Rabeni, wing Vilimoni Delasau and flanker Akapusi Qera running amok, Fiji fell behind, then regained both lead and control only for an interception try by Martyn Williams to seem to have destroyed their hopes. The Fijian reaction recalled that of the 1991 Australians at their moment of crisis in Dublin. They kicked off, regained possession and drove their way steadily to the Welsh line where prop Graham Dewes was awarded the try after a long, excruciatingly tense review by the video referee. What was striking was that Fiji won not only by playing the brilliant sevens-style rugby for which they are famed but through superiority in the more prosaic virtues – tactical nous, conserving their own possession and kicking sensibly – they are generally assumed to lack. The eclipse of Nantes was Wales's final reckoning for the overthrow of Ruddock 18 months earlier and led in turn to the sacking of his successor, Gareth Jenkins.

Three explanations suggest themselves for the greatly improved performances of the second- and third-tier nations. One is that the IRB's High Performance programme, aimed at making a difference by 2011, was having a quicker impact than anyone had expected. Another is that while lacking domestic professional set-ups of their own, most of these teams had at least a core of players being paid to perform abroad. All but three of Georgia's thirty-man squad were playing in France, including a solid bloc of tight-five forwards employed in the Top 14. The last is that while pre-World Cup training camps were a hugely beneficial novelty for players from these countries, allowing them to work on the collective techniques so important in rugby and to bond as teammates, they represented the tedium of more-of-the-same for players from more established nations. The French squad's nickname of 'Marcatraz' for their Marcoussis training base was only half in jest.

The week between the pool stages and quarter-finals was filled with speculation that all three remaining northern hemisphere teams – France, England and Scotland – might be eliminated. It did not turn out that way. Where the 2003 World Cup had turned inside out at the semi-final stage, the 2007 edition did so on a single day in the quarters. England eliminated Australia 12–10 in Marseilles with a game plan of extreme simplicity – win the scrums, hit hard at the breakdown, occupy territory and let the boot of Wilkinson do the rest. They were rarely in danger of scoring a try but put an unbreakable stranglehold on the Australians.

Later that evening in Cardiff – one of the matches played there to fulfil commitments agreed when Wales staged the tournament in 1999 – New Zealand's nightmare rose up again to smite them. They led France by 13 points just before half-time but steadily lost their grip thereafter, in spite of enjoying 77 per cent of possession across the 80 minutes. France fought back to 13–13 while New Zealand were a man down following the sin-binning of Luke McAlister. Daniel Carter was forced off with an injury and although Rodney So'oialo restored the All Black lead, a moment of brilliance from replacement outside-half Frédéric Michalak, making a break then pivoting in the tackle to provide a perfect pass for Yannick Jauzion, swung it back in France's favour. Trailing by only two points, New Zealand drove deep into French territory but lacked the simple nous needed to drop a match-winning goal. They departed amid much muttering about English referee Wayne Barnes, who had admittedly missed a forward pass in the build-up to Jauzion's score. IRB refereeing chief Paddy O'Brien, a New Zealander, told journalists that after reviewing the match he calculated that Barnes had made more than 600 decisions, only a handful even questionable. When a home-based referee produced a not dissimilar conclusion for the *New Zealand Herald*, the NZRU refereeing chief's reaction was to promise that he would be hunted down and disciplined.

A little more predictability was restored in the other two matches, but not before Fiji, trailing 20–6 to South Africa and with Rabeni in the sin bin, had scored two tries while a man short to level at 20–20. Had lock Ifereimi Rawaqa not, in a moment recalling Koroduadua's fateful knock-on in 1987, been tackled at the line by South African wing J.P. Pietersen or another Fijian not knocked on following a five-yard scrum, Fiji's momentum might have taken them on to the greatest shock yet. Instead, the South Africans calmly regrouped, tightened the game and ended with a 37–20 win. Argentina's expected victory over Scotland was momentous – the first time the eight foundation unions' monopoly on semi-final places had been broken – but dull. It was notable that while the other three winners had, with good reason, celebrated as though they had won a final, the South Africans had remained quietly in one corner of the field. In part, this was to allow the Fijians a long-drawn-out and ecstatically received lap of honour around the Marseilles Vélodrome, but it also suggested a team who felt they had achieved nothing yet.

France, restored to home soil, were widely expected to beat England in the first semi-final. They had done so twice in warm-up games, could match England physically and had much more creativity. That was the theory, anyway. The reality, completing a progress to the final that had even England's players using words like 'surreal' and 'parallel universe', was that France succumbed to England's great strength – the ability to make other teams play exactly the way they wanted. Josh Lewsey scored a first-minute try after a kick ahead broke viciously to bemuse Damien Traille, an experienced centre turned by Laporte into a novice full-back, and while France recovered to take the lead, they played with a complete lack of imagination or enterprise. England hung on and stole a 14–9 win with a Wilkinson penalty and drop-goal in the last ten minutes. In the other match, South Africa finally ended Argentina's progress, scoring three first-half tries after errors as the Pumas tried to force the game and finishing 37–13 victors after panther-like wing Bryan Habana had claimed his second try of the match and eighth, matching Lomu's record set in 1999, of the tournament.

The eve of the final saw two momentous developments. A Frenchman, Bernard Lapasset, was elected president of the IRB – final full acceptance, less than 30 years after becoming members, into the concert of rugby nations, recognition also for his role as chief organiser of an outstanding tournament, with huge crowds and magnificent atmosphere at every French venue. Then came the first worthwhile third-place match in 20 years as Argentina reprised their opening-day win over France, this time by an overwhelming 34–10 as they ran like stereotypical Frenchmen to overwhelm the disappointing hosts. The third score, launched by a break from full-back Ignacio Corleto, continued by a massive pass from their prodigious outside-half Juan Martín Hernández and completed by wing Federico Martín Aramburu, was perhaps the best of the entire tournament.

By comparison, the final was an anticlimax. There were believed to be around 50,000 English fans in Paris, most watching in bars or on big screens around the French capital. They had little to cheer. After suckering previous opponents into playing their own game, England encountered one that was happy to play it – and could do so better than they did. Lock Victor Matfield dominated the lineout, there was hardly an attacking movement worthy of the name and, amid an almost complete lack of the tension usually associated with tight, low-scoring matches, South Africa won 15–6, five penalty goals to two. South African captain John Smit received the trophy from President Sarkozy, Britain's Scottish premier Gordon Brown had the mortification of being both introduced as 'Prime Minister of England' and booed by their fans, and South Africa's President Thabo Mbeki joined joyfully in the team's celebrations.

The 2007 World Cup could claim success in terms of crowds – an average of 47,000 – a projected profit of £90 million and an unpredictability that answered one of the most potent criticisms of tournaments. There is little doubt that it was won by the best team. If there were worries, one was the extent to which the later stages were dominated by defensive percentage play, with the pick-and-go and up-and-under repeated ad nauseam by teams unwilling or in some cases unable to try anything more imaginative. At the same time, it was worth heeding the words of Eddie Jones, the former Australian coach who worked as a technical assistant to the Springboks and pointed out, 'World Cups are about winning, and you don't get points for beautiful rugby.' It was a point rather missed in New Zealand, where complaints about dull rugby, aimed particularly at England, ignored the fact that the 'never mind the style, look at the scoreboard' approach of Phil Vickery's team made them the tournament's heirs to the All Blacks of the Meads-Don Clarke era. As Jones pointed out when asked about possible rule changes, 'One of the great things about rugby is that, more than any other game, everything is linked to everything else. If you change one thing, there's a danger of causing problems elsewhere.'

It was ever thus, and as the game embarks on another four-year cycle culminating in New Zealand in 2011, with the All Blacks doubtless facing still greater pressures as they aim to end their World Cup jinx on home soil, it is unlikely to change. And would we really want it to?

# CHAPTER FIFTEEN

# Going Forward

'There is no summation. After an account of what has been,
there is only anticipation of the future'

Dai Smith and Gareth Williams, *Fields of Praise* (1980)

'Of the two chief varieties [of football], Rugby and Association,
it is hardly to be doubted that, outside the United Kingdom at
all events, the chances of complete supremacy are in favour of
the former'

Dave Gallaher and Billy Stead, *The Complete Rugby
Footballer in the New Zealand System* (1906)

There is a good reason why Gallaher and Stead's prognostications
for football codes proved so inaccurate. Their experience was
confined to the Empire. They were not to know that over the next
century British possessions, former and current, would be almost
the only points of resistance to soccer's worldwide hegemony
among the football codes. In part, these pockets of resistance
arose because, in spite of soccer's British origins, other codes had
become firmly established in those countries – New Zealand and
South Africa dedicating themselves to rugby, Canada and the USA
taking to their own varieties of football and Australia doing both.
As the Scottish historian Bill Murray has argued, based not only on
his academic research but on his first-hand experience as a soccer
player in Australia, it is extremely hard for one code of football to
displace another that is firmly established.

Still, it is salutary to see that such sagacious observers of rugby
could have been so wrong. The extent of change over recent
years induces wariness in looking forward. The temptation is to
predict the infinite continuation of current trends, but one lesson

287

of history is that, whatever happens, unchanging continuation will not.

One popular prediction should, though, continue to be wrong. There is no reason why the two rugby codes should not continue to exist side by side. Union may be larger, richer and shorn of former ideological hang-ups, but league will survive as long as people want to play and watch it. Rugby league folk are a disputatious lot – Dave Hadfield and Tony Collins both point to a cultural similarity with the political left – but the one thing they all agree on is not wanting either union or a hybrid. Nor is it in television's interests to devise a hybrid. The specialist channels who increasingly fund sport need a range of products to sell subscriptions. Reducing the number of products, alienating aficionados, makes no sense.

It is also safe to predict that television will continue to matter. Its influence has grown disproportionately in the transition to open professionalism, its money a precondition of that transformation. Experience of other sports shows that television money remains just as essential under mature professionalism. There is a price for this. When the BBC was paying £9,000 per match in the 1970s, its influence was marginal. Now that it is paying roughly £1 million per match, it calls the tune. Hence the Six Nations scheduling that meant England for four years running had the advantage of playing the last match on the final Saturday.

This is part of a wider pattern. Professionalism is expensive. It favours the rich and the numerous. The three largest economies among the top eight rugby nations are Australia, France and England. That they also account for five out of six World Cup finalists since 1999 is not a coincidence – it is much easier to find the money necessary for the salaries of players, coaches, advisers and analysts, for up-to-date gym equipment, computer programmes and, for that matter, new stadiums in those societies than in smaller or poorer nations.

This does not make it impossible for those nations to compete, but they have to be smart in exploiting their more limited resources. New Zealand has clear advantages in its national passion for the game, making it the choice of the athletic and ball-playing elite, and the transfusion of talent via migration from the Pacific islands. South Africa's long-term prospects will be redoubled if rugby can make a real impact among its non-white peoples. Wales's experience over the last 30 years – remember that, as recently as 1973, the perceptive Chris Laidlaw argued that the game there was more deep-rooted and likely to survive better than in New Zealand – shows what can happen when trends are against you and resources are not well managed.

It is a quarter of a century since Stephen Jones, looking forward 20 years, wrote, 'I am prepared to bet that no one single member of the 1981 IRB is consistently beaten by a team outside the present board, even though Argentina and Romania may have their successes.' You could say he lost his bet. Samoa beat Wales three times consecutively, twice at Cardiff in world cups, in the 1990s.

Writing immediately after the 2007 World Cup, it is clear that serious ground has been gained. It was no fluke that Argentina should have finished third or that this is now their world ranking, merely the continuation of several years in which they have been more than a match for many established nations, particularly Scotland and France. Fiji's victory over Wales was one for intelligence and control as well as attacking brilliance. We are back to the point in the early 1990s when developing nations like Canada, Italy and Samoa could give the best of the foundation unions a serious match.

Yet Jones's essential point is proven. Rugby's sheer complexity and range of specialist skills, both individual and collective, always were a barrier to its adoption and growth. It takes much more time and specialised expertise to teach young people the essentials of rucking than it would to instruct them in becoming an effective soccer defence. Professionalism has deepened the problem. Where developing nations have professional players, they struggle to get them released and lack the professional back-up teams of the established nations.

Salvation is unlikely to come from the established nations. It is not in the short-term playing or commercial interests of New Zealand that Samoa should start competing for its best players, or of any of the more vulnerable members of the top eight that Argentina should get the resources it needs to displace one of them from that level, although it would do none of them any harm to think beyond the selfish and the short term. It is, though, in everybody's longer-term interest that there should be a wider range of credible opponents and that it should not be possible to predict with reasonable certainty the quarter-finalists in the 2015 World Cup. Unpredictable as the 2007 tournament was, the only truly surprising quarter-finalist was Fiji.

When the common good demands what individuals cannot or will not deliver, state (in international rugby terms, IRB) intervention is called for. Hence the belated but nonetheless welcome High Performance package of development assistance and funding for new competitions unveiled by the IRB in 2005. That this seems to have started paying dividends in 2007, one World Cup earlier than expected, should be a spur to further action rather than self-congratulation. This is a matter not only of pump-priming investment but of ensuring that second-tier countries get regular, serious international fixtures and of re-examining the rules on player qualification so that small countries do not lose individuals who pass briefly through the systems of larger nations.

None of this is easy. Rugby is a game of minorities and small nations – France's south-west is the largest geographic agglomeration for whom it is the defining sport – but, among second-rank nations, Samoa (population 175,000), Fiji (905,000) and Tonga (115,000) are so small and poor as to be seriously handicapped. Japan can and should stage a World Cup very soon, but simple physical limitations restrict the chances of its rugby team performing as well as its soccer team did in 2002. In the USA and Canada, rugby is boxed in by the indigenous varieties of football, although the US game would be transformed if even a small proportion of the gifted college footballers who do not turn professional could be persuaded to switch codes. Argentina and Romania's handicap is slightly different – they are large enough to be serious soccer nations, so rugby captures only a minority of the athletic elite. Argentina will lose to retirement the magnificent thirty-something generation – players like scrum-half Agustin Pichot, hooker Mario Ledesma and Longo Elía – who have taken it to its current heights and can only hope the cohorts rising to support the likes of Juan Martín Hernández and Marcos Ayerza will be half as good. It also has to find a way around the mismatch between its own location in the southern hemisphere and that of its leading players in the north, meaning that membership of the Tri Nations would impose an unfeasibly long season on those players while that of the Six Nations would do little to develop Argentinian – as opposed to Spanish, or wherever they were based – rugby. It was still, though, encouraging to read that television interests in the southern hemisphere – often a drag on development, with their preference for the established and the moneyed – were sufficiently impressed by Argentina's World Cup performance to be keen to put pressure on the SANZAR unions to bring them into the Tri Nations.

The best medium-term bet for a breakthrough may well be lurking in the third tier. Georgia's population of five million means it is too small to be seriously competitive in soccer, but it is ample for a rugby nation. Huge crowds for significant international matches suggest that rugby could provide effective self-expression for a young nation state. Georgia also has an identity that long predates independence and physical heritage expressed through wrestling and the rugby-like folk game of *lelo*. Their performances in the World Cup in 2007, particularly in nearly beating Ireland, further underlined this potential. Against that are poverty and political uncertainty, but well-targeted IRB investments and contact by leading nations might pay serious dividends. If senior teams cannot go, tours to Romania, Russia and Georgia should be the ideal way for testing how young players cope with the demanding and the unfamiliar.

A further issue here is whether or nor rugby should push for a place in the Olympics. While it has enough political issues without enmeshing itself in the five-ring circus, the argument in favour is the extent to which Olympic status releases funding in many countries. It is as well, perhaps, that not being an Olympic sport fatally hampered rugby's development in the German Democratic Republic, but it would be a loss to rugby's long-term health if a country like Mexico, an associate member of the IRB in 2004 and a debutant on the world stage at the 2005 Los Angeles Sevens, was held back. There is enough stop-start in Mexico's history to make that a worry, but more than enough vivacity in a small but highly committed rugby community to believe that it – and every other associate or full member – has something serious to offer the game.

Legislating for rugby will continue to be as complex and frustrating as traffic management. The current points system has been in force for 16 years, but any further revaluation of the try risks reducing the deterrent effect of penalties. As the athleticism of players reduces time and space, one possibility – given the expense of extending or widening pitches in existing stadiums – is reducing teams to 14 or 13 players. Any benefits, though, would have to be weighed against the loss of specialised roles that help give the game its variety, of destabilised scrummages and, in the professional game, of job losses.

Two challenges specific to the elite game loom. One is the never-ending pressure on top players. That the RFU and the Players Union commissioned serious academic research on burnout is excellent. That their players – and everybody else's, except perhaps Ireland's – in the northern hemisphere continue to be subject to programmes whose inevitable consequence was an injured XV on the sidelines of the 2006 Six Nations who were probably stronger than any of the competing teams, is not. We are also about to see the first wave of retirements by players who have known nothing but professionalism, with the likely vocational retraining needs that implies. There is a vital role here for players' unions in every country that has professional rugby.

Most predictable of all is that rugby will continue to be played for money by a privileged few but for enjoyment by many more, both male and female. It has long been thus in soccer, rugby league and cricket, the money paid to Steve Bloomer or Wayne Rooney, Billy Batten or Sean Long, W.G. Grace or Freddie Flintoff making no difference to the multitudes who played for the sheer pleasure of it or who paid to watch. It was rugby's mistake – often voiced by journalists or administrators who were themselves being paid for their role in the game – to believe that it did. Elite players always were highly motivated achievers, paid or not. When Victorian gentlemen argued over interpretations, Gallaher and Stead catalogued the means by which tries were scored, Wakefield invented corner-flagging and Muller slaughtered midfield backs, the aim was the same: winning. Professionalism has been a bumpy ride but has cleansed the game of hypocrisy and much foul play. Freed of the cant associated with amateurism, it is evident that it is the game itself – that exasperating compound of beauty and violence, elegance and complexity, gentlemanliness and hooliganism – that matters.

# Bibliography

Adair, Daryl and Wray Vamplew, *Sport in Australian History*, Oxford UP, Melbourne, 1997

Auckland RFU, *100 Years of Auckland Rugby*, Auckland RFU, Auckland, 1983

Barnes, Stuart, *Rugby's New Age Travellers*, Mainstream, Edinburgh, 1997

Barrow, Graeme, *All Blacks versus Springboks*, Heinemann, Auckland, 1981

    *Up Front: The Story of the All Black Scrum*, Kingswood, London, 1985

Baskerville, A.H., *Modern Rugby Football: The New Zealand Method*, Gordon and Gotch, London, 1907

Batchelor, Denzil, *Days without Sunset*, Eyre and Spottiswoode, London, 1949

Beanland, V.A.S., *Great Games and the Great Players: Some Thoughts and Recollections of a Sports Journalist*, W.H. Allen, London, 1945

Belich, James, *Paradise Reforged*, Penguin, Auckland, 2001

Billot, John, *The All Blacks in Wales*, Ron Jones, Ferndale, 1972

Birley, Derek, *Land of Sport and Glory: Sport and British Society, 1887–1910*, Manchester UP, Manchester, 1995

    *Playing the Game: Sport and British Society, 1910–45*, Manchester UP, Manchester, 1996

    *Sport and the Making of Britain*, Manchester UP, Manchester, 1993

Black, David and John Nauright, *Rugby and the South African Nation:*

*Sport, Cultures, Politics and Power in the Old and New South Africas*, Manchester UP, Manchester, 1993

Bodis, Jean-Pierre, *Histoire Mondiale du Rugby*, Privat, Toulouse, 1987

    *Le Rugby d'Irlande*, Maison des Sciences et de l'Homme de l'Aquitaine, Bordeaux, 1993

    *Le Rugby Sud-Africain*, Karthala, Paris, 1995

Booley, Abdurahman, *Forgotten Heroes: History of Black Rugby*, 1892–1992, Manu Booley, Cape Town, 1998

Booth, Douglas and Colin Tatz, *One Eyed: A View of Australian Sport*, Allen and Unwin, St Leonard's, Australia, 2000

Brittenden, Dick, *Give 'em the Axe: The First Hundred Years of the Christchurch Football Club*, The Club, Christchurch, 1963

Campomar, Gonzalo Etcheverry and Luis Ignacio Ubille Schamarit, *El Rugby en Uruguay*, Union de Rugby del Uruguay, Montevideo, 2001

Carling, Will, *The Way to Win: Strategies for Success in Business and Sport*, Warner Books, London, 1996

Chester, Rod and Neville MacMillan, *Centenary: 100 Years of All Black Rugby*, Blandford Press, Poole, 1984

Collins, Tony, *Rugby's Great Split: Class, Culture and the Origins of Rugby League Football*, Frank Cass, London, 1998

    *Rugby League in Twentieth Century Britain*, Routledge, London, 2006

Collins, W.J.T., *Rugby Recollections*, R.H. John, Newport (Gwent), 1948

Dallaglio, Lawrence (with Chris Jones), *Dallaglio on Rugby: Know the Modern Game*, Hodder, London, 1998

Danzig, Allison, *History of American Football*, Prentice Hall, Englewood Cliffs, New Jersey, 1956

Davies, Gerald, *The History of the Rugby Union World Cup*, Sanctuary, London, 2003

Delaney, Trevor, *Rugby Disunion: A Two-Part History of the Formation of the Northern Union*, Trevor Delaney, Keighley, 1993

Deutscher Rugby Verband, *100 Jahre Deutscher Rugby Verband*, DRV, 2000

Diehm, Ian, *Red! Red! Red!: The Story of Queensland Rugby*, Playright, Caringbah, Australia, 1997

Difford, Ivor, *The History of South African Football*, Speciality Press, Wynberg, 1933

Dine, Philip, *French Rugby Football: A Cultural History*, Berg, Oxford, 2001

Dobson, Paul, *Thirty Super Springboks*, Human and Rousseau, Cape Town, 1995

Douglas, Derek, *The Thistle: A Chronicle of Scottish Rugby*, Mainstream, Edinburgh, 1997

Duckham, David, *Dai for England: The Autobiography of David Duckham*, Pelham, London, 1980

Dunning, Eric and Kenneth Sheard, *Barbarians, Gentlemen and Players: A Sociological Study of the Development of Rugby Football*, Martin Robertson, Oxford, 1979

Edinburgh Academical Football Club, *Centenary History*, 1958

Ellison, Thomas, *The Art of Rugby Football*, Geddis and Blomfield, Wellington, 1902

Escot, Richard, *Rugby Pro*, Histoires Secrètes, Solar, France, 1996

Eyre, Ernest and Selwyn Speight, *C'mon Shore*, North Shore RFC, Auckland, 1973

Eyton, Thomas (ed.), *Rugby Football (Past and Present) and the Tour of the Native Team*, William Hart, Palmerston North, 1896

Fagan, Sean, *The Rugby Rebellion*, RL 1908, Sydney, 2005

Fitzsimons, Peter, *Fitzsimons on Rugby*, Allen and Unwin, Sydney, 1999
    *The Rugby War*, Harper Sport, Sydney, 1996

Fletcher, Thomas (ed.), *School Football*, NZRFU, Wellington, 1934

Frith, David, *My Dear Victorious Stod*, David Frith, New Malden, 1970

Gadney, Cyril, *The History of the Laws of Rugby Union Football, 1949–72*, RFU, London, 1973

Gallaher, Dave and Billy Stead, *The Complete Rugby Footballer in the New Zealand System*, Methuen, London, 1906

Garrard, W.G., *Canterbury Rugby Union Football*, Canterbury RFU, Christchurch, 1929

Gent, Dai, *Rugby Football*, Eyre and Spottiswoode, London, 1932

Godwin, Terry and Chris Rhys, *The Guinness Book of Rugby Facts and Feats*, Guinness Superlatives, London, 1981

Green, Michael, *The Art of Coarse Rugby, or Any Number Can Play*, Stanley Paul, London, 1960

Greenwood, J.E., *A Cap for Boots*, Hutchison Benham, London, 1977

Griffiths, John, *Phoenix International Book of Rugby Records*, Phoenix House, London, 1987

Grundlingh, Albert, Andre Odendaal and Burridge Spies, *Beyond the Tryline*, Ravan, Johannesburg, 1995

Haden, Andy, *Boots 'n' All*, Blandford Press, Poole, 1984

Hands, David, *The Five Nations Story*, Tempus, Stroud, 2000

Harding, Rowe, *Rugby: Reminiscences and Opinions*, Pilot Press, London, 1929

Hickie, Thomas, *A Sense of Union: A History of Sydney University RFC*, Playright, Sydney, 1998

 *They Ran with the Ball*, Longman, Sydney, 1993

Holt, Richard, *Sport and the British: A Modern History*, Oxford UP, Oxford, 1989

 *Sport and Society in Modern France*, Macmillan, London, 1981

Holt, Richard and Tony Mason, *Sport in Britain*, 1945–2000, Blackwell, Oxford, 2000

Howell, Max and Lingyu Xie, *Wallaby Greats*, Rugby Publishing, Auckland, 1997

Howitt, Bob, *New Zealand Rugby Greats* (vols. 1, 2 and 3), Hodder, Moa, Beckett, Auckland, 1997

Howitt, Bob and Diane Haworth, *Rugby Nomads*, Harper Sports, Auckland, 2002

Huggins, Mike, *The Victorians and Sport*, Hambledon and London, London, 2004

International Rugby Board, *Minutes, 1886–2002*

Jenkins, John, *A Rugby Compendium: An Authoritative Guide to the Literature of Rugby Union*, British Library, London, 1998

Jenkins, John, Duncan Pierce and Timothy Auty, *Who's Who of Welsh International Rugby Players*, Bridge, Wrexham, 1991

Jiggens, Clifford, *Sammy: The Sporting Life of S.M.J. Woods*, Sansom, Bristol, 1997

Jones, Stephen, *Endless Winter*, Mainstream, Edinburgh, 1993

 *Midnight Rugby*, Headline, London, 2000

 *On My Knees*, Mainstream, Edinburgh, 2004

Keating, Frank, *The Great Number 10s*, Corgi, London, 1999

Keohane, Mark, *Chester*, Don Nelson, Cape Town, 2002

Kilburn, J.M., *In Search of Rugby Football*, Arthur Barker, London, 1938

Kirk, David, *Black and Blue*, Hodder, Moa, Beckett, 1997

Lacouture, Jean, *Voyous et Gentlemen*, Gallimard, Paris, 1993

Laidlaw, Chris, *Mud in Your Eye*, A.H. and A.W. Reed, Wellington, 1973

Lalanne, Denis, *The Great Fight of the French XV*, A.H. and A.W. Reed, Wellington, 1960

    *La Mêlée Fantastique*, A.H. and A.W. Reed, Wellington, 1962

Leonard, Jason (with Alison Kervin), *Jason Leonard: The Autobiography*, Collins Willow, London, 2001

Lowerson, John, *Sport and the English Middle Classes*, 1870–1914, Manchester UP, Manchester, 1993

McGee, Greg, *Foreskin's Lament*, Victoria Press, Wellington, 1981

McKenzie, Norman, *On with the Game*, A.H. and A.W. Reed, Wellington, 1962

McLean, Terry, *The All Blacks*, Sidgwick and Jackson, London, 1991

    *Bob Stuart's All Blacks*, A.H. and A.W. Reed, Wellington, 1954

    *Great Days in New Zealand Rugby*, A.H. and A.W. Reed, Wellington, 1959

    *Red Dragons of Rugby*, A.H. and A.W. Reed, Wellington, 1969

    *Willie Away*, Herbert Jenkins, London, 1964

McRae, Donald, *Winter Colours: Changing Seasons in World Rugby*, Mainstream, Edinburgh, 1998

Macrory, Jennifer, *Running with the Ball: The Birth of Rugby Football*, Collins Willow, London, 1991

Magoun, Francis Peabody, *History of Football from the Beginning to 1971*, Bochum-Langendreer, Cologne, 1938

Malin, Ian, *Mud, Blood and Money: English Rugby Union Goes Professional*, Mainstream, Edinburgh, 1997

Marshall, Revd Frank (ed.), *Football: The Rugby Union Game*, Cassell, London, 1892

Maschwitz, Eduardo (ed.), *1899–1999: 100 Años Unión Argentina de Rugby*, Manrique, Zago, Buenos Aires, 1999

Mason, Nick, *Football! The Story of All the World's Favourite Game*, Temple Smith, London, 1974

Massie, Allan, *A Portrait of Scottish Rugby*, Polygon, Edinburgh, 1984

Morgan, Cliff (ed.), *Rugby: The Great Ones*, Pelham, London, 1970

Morgan, Paul, *A History of Rugby*, Sutton Publishing, Stroud, 2003

Morgan, W. John and Gerald Davies, *Sidesteps*, Hodder and Stoughton, London, 1985

Morgan, W. John and Geoffrey Nicholson, *Report on Rugby*, Sportsmans Book Club, Newton Abbot, 1959

Mori Research Report, *Making an Impact*, London, 2003

Mourie, Graham (with Ron Palenski), *Graham Mourie, Captain*, Moa, Auckland, 1982

Nauright, John and Timothy Chandler (eds.), *Making Men: Rugby and Masculine Identity*, Frank Cass, London, 1996

    *Making the Rugby World: Race, Gender, Commerce*, Frank Cass, London, 1999

Nepia, George and Terry McLean, *I, George Nepia*, A.H. and A.W. Reed, Wellington, 1963

Nicholls, Gwyn, *The Modern Rugby Game and How To Play It*, Health and Strength Ltd, London, 1908

Nicholson, Geoffrey, Cliff Morgan and David Frost (eds.), *Touchdown and other Moves in the Game*, RFU, 1971

Nish, Alison, 'The Development of Rugby Football in Japan, 1874–1966', MA thesis, Sheffield University, Sheffield, 1996

Owen, O.L, *The History of the Rugby Football Union*, RFU/Playfair Books, London, 1955

Palenski, Ron, *The Jersey*, Hodder, Moa, Beckett, 2001

Parker, A.C., *Giants of South African Rugby*, A.H. and A.W. Reed, Wellington, 1956

    *The Springboks*, Cassell, Wellington, 1970

Parry-Jones, David, *Prince Gwyn: Gwyn Nicholls and the First Golden Era of Welsh Rugby*, Seren, Bridgend, 1999

    *The Gwilliam Seasons: John Gwilliam and the Second Golden Era of Welsh Rugby*, Seren, Bridgend, 2002

Phillips, R.J., *The Story of Scottish Rugby*, T.N. Foulis, London, 1925

Pollard, Jack, *Australian Rugby Union*, Angus and Robertson, Sydney, 1984

Potter, Alex and Georges Duthen, *The Rise of French Rugby*, A.H. and A.W. Reed, Wellington, 1961

Poulton, Edward Bagnall, *The Life of Ronald Poulton*, Sidgwick and Jackson, London, 1919

# BIBLIOGRAPHY

Premier Rugby National Fan Survey, *Summary Report*, 2003

Reason, John, *Six of the Best*, John Reason, London, 2004

Reason, John and Carwyn James, *The World of Rugby: A History of Rugby Football*, BBC, London, 1979

Reisman, David, *Individualism Reconsidered*, Free Press, Glencoe, Illinois, 1954

RFU Museum, *Gone but not Forgotten: Rugby's War Dead*, exhibition graphic, 2003

Rhys, Chris, *Guinness Rugby Union Fact Book*, Guinness, London, 1992

Richards, Huw, *Dragons and All Blacks: Wales v. New Zealand – 1953 and a Century of Rivalry*, Mainstream, Edinburgh, 2004

Richards, Huw, Peter Stead and Gareth Williams (eds.), *Heart and Soul: The Character of Welsh Rugby*, U of Wales Press, Cardiff, 1998

> *More Heart and Soul: The Character of Welsh Rugby*, U of Wales Press, Cardiff, 1999

Roger, Warwick, *Old Heroes: The 1956 Springbok Tour and the Lives Beyond*, Hodder and Stoughton, London, 1991

Royds, Admiral Sir Percy, *The History of the Laws of Rugby Football*, RFU, London, 1949

Ryan, Greg, *The Contest for Rugby Supremacy: Accounting for the 1905 All Blacks*, Canterbury UP, Christchurch, 2005

> *Forerunners of the All Blacks*, Canterbury UP, Christchurch, 1993

Ryan, Greg (ed.), *Tackling Rugby Myths*, Otago UP, Dunedin, 2005

Schwartzmann, Helen (ed.), *Play and Culture*, Leisure Press, West Point, New York, 1980

Sellar, Walter and Robert Yeatman, *1066 and All That*, Methuen, London, 1998

Sewell, E.H.D., *Rugby: The Man's Game*, Hollis and Carter, London, 1950

> *Rugby Football Today*, John Murray, London, 1931
> *Rugby Football Up to Date*, Hodder and Stoughton, London, 1921

Smith, David and Gareth Williams, *Fields of Praise: The Official History of the Welsh Rugby Union, 1881–1981*, U of Wales P (on behalf of the WRU), Cardiff, 1980

Smith, Sean, *The Union Game: A Rugby History*, BBC, London, 1999

Stedman, Laura, *Women's Rugby: A Work in Progress*, exhibition graphics, RFU Museum, 2006

Stewart, J.J., *Rugby: Developments in the Field of Play*, Massey University, Palmerston North, 1997

Sturrock, Douglas, 'A History of Rugby Football in Canada', MA thesis, University of Alberta, Alberta, 1971

Thomas, Clem, *The History of the British Lions*, Mainstream, Edinburgh, 1996

Thomas, Watcyn, *Rugby-Playing Man*, Pelham, London, 1977

Thomson, A.A., *Rugger My Pleasure*, Museum Press, London, 1955

Thorburn, Sandy, *The History of Scottish Rugby*, Johnston and Bacon, London, 1980

Tillinac, Denis, *Rugby Blues*, La Table Ronde, Paris, 1993

Tillman, H., *Great Games of New Zealand Rugby*, Lancaster Press, Christchurch, 1957

Tugwell, Dick, *Champions in Conflict: The Bath Rugby Revolution*, Robson, London, 1998

Turley, Alan, *They Gave Us Rugby*, Nelson College, Nelson, 1996

Vamplew, Wray, *Pay Up and Play the Game: Professional Sport in Britain, 1875–1914*, Cambridge UP, Cambridge, 1988

Vamplew, Wray and Brian Stoddart (eds.), *Sport in Australia: A Social History*, Cambridge UP, Cambridge, 1994

Van Esbeck, Edmund, *The Story of Irish Rugby*, Stanley Paul, London, 1986

Volpe, Francisco and Valerio Vecchiarelli, *2000 Italia in Meta*, GSEditrice, Rome, 2000

Wakefield, Wavell and Howard Marshall, *Rugger*, Longman, London, 1930

Wakelam, H.B.T. (ed.), *The Game Goes On: A Symposium on Rugby Football*, Arthur Barker, London, 1936

Watts Moses, Eric, *History of the International Rugby Football Board*, IRFB, London, 1960

> *History of the International Rugby Football Board: Supplement No. 1, 1961–72*, IRFB, London, 1972

Williams, Bleddyn, *Rugger, My Life*, Stanley Paul, London, 1956

Williams, Gareth, *1905 and All That: Essays on Rugby Football, Sport and Welsh Society*, Gomer, Llandysul, 1991

Williams, Graham, *The Code War*, Yore, Harefield, 1994

# BIBLIOGRAPHY

Williams, Graham, Peter Lush and David Hinchliffe, *Rugby's Berlin Wall*, London League Publications, London, 2005

Woodward, Clive, *Winning!*, Hodder and Stoughton, London, 2004

Wyatt, Derek, *Rugby Disunion: The Making of Three World Cups*, Gollancz, London, 1995

Wyatt, Derek and Colin Herridge, *The Rugby Revolution*, Metro, London, 2003

Wynne-Thomas, Peter, *Give Me Arthur*, Arthur Barker, London, 1985

Young, Percy, *A History of British Football*, Stanley Paul, London, 1968

Zavos, Spiro, *After the Final Whistle*, Fourth Estate, Wellington, 1979
   *The Gold and the Black*, Allen and Unwin, Sydney, 1995
   *The Golden Wallabies*, Penguin, Ringwood, 2000
   *Ka Mate! Ka Mate!: New Zealand's Conquest of British Rugby*, Viking, Auckland, 1998
   *Winters of Revenge*, Viking, Auckland, 1997

Zavos, Spiro and Gordon Bray, *Two Mighty Tribes*, Penguin, Albany, 2003

## Articles

Allen, Dean, 'Beating them at their Own Game: Rugby, the Anglo-Boer War and Afrikaner Nationalism, 1899–1948', *International Journal of the History of Sport*, 2003

Barlow, Stuart, 'Diffusion of Rugby Football in the Industrialized Context of Rochdale, 1868–90: A Conflict of Ethical Values', *International Journal of the History of Sport*, 1993

Blackledge, Paul, 'Rational Capitalist Concerns: William Cail and the Great Rugby Split of 1895', *International Journal of the History of Sport*, 2001

Buchanan, Ian, 'Rugby Football at the Olympic Games', *Journal of Olympic History*, 1997

Crawford, Scott, 'Rugby in Colonial Otago', *International Journal of the History of Sport*, 1985

Grundlingh, Albert, 'Playing for Power?: Rugby, Afrikaner Nationalism and Masculinity in South Africa, 1900–1970', *International Journal of the History of Sport*, 1994

Hibbins, Gillian, 'Origins of Australian Rules Football', *International Journal of the History of Sport*, 1989

Hollyman, John, 'Rugby Union Football in Spain', *Vida Hispanica*, 1993

Horton, Peter, 'Dominant Ideologies and their Role in the Establishment of Rugby Union Football in Victorian Queensland', *International Journal of the History of Sport*, 1994

'Padang or Paddock: A Comparative View of Colonial Sport in Two Imperial Territories', *International Journal of the History of Sport*, 1997

'Rugby in Queensland', *International Journal of the History of Sport*, 1992

Kamau, Michael Mundia, 'A Review of Kenyan Rugby', unpublished, 2000, held in RFU Library, Twickenham

Kossuth, Robert, 'Transition and Assimilation: English Rugby and Canadian Football in Halifax, Nova Scotia, 1930–55', *Football Studies*, 1999

Little, Charles, 'Travelling Away to Play at "Home": New Zealand Footballers in Britain, 1888–1905', conference paper, 2005

Merrett, Christopher, 'In Nothing Else are the Deprivers so Deprived: South African Sport, Apartheid and Foreign Relations, 1945–71', *International Journal of the History of Sport*, 1996

Park, Roberta, 'From Football to Rugby and Back, 1906–19', *International Journal of the History of Sport*, 1984

'Mended or Ended: Football Injuries and the British and American Medical Press, 1870–1910', *International Journal of the History of Sport*, 2001

Sharp, M.P., 'The Control of Cricket and Rugby in Sydney, 1890–1912', *International Journal of the History of Sport*, 1988

Smith, Adrian, 'An Oval Ball and a Broken City: Coventry, its People and its Rugby Team', *International Journal of the History of Sport*, 1999

'Civil War in England: The Clubs, the RFU and the Impact of Professionalism on Rugby Union, 1995–99', *Journal of Contemporary History*, 2000

Thomson, Rex, 'Rugby at the University of Otago: Humble Beginnings for New Zealand's Premier Club', *International Journal of the History of Sport*, 1997

Tranter, Neil, 'The First Football Club?', *International Journal of the History of Sport*, 1993

    'Organised Sport in Nineteenth Century Scotland', *International Journal of the History of Sport*, 1990

Van der Merwe, Floris, 'Sport and Games in Boer Prisoner of War Camps during the Anglo-Boer War, 1899–1902', *International Journal of the History of Sport*, 1992

Vincent, Geoff, 'Practical Imperialism: The Anglo-Welsh Tour of New Zealand, 1908', *International Journal of the History of Sport*, 1998

**Periodicals and Annuals**

*The Football Annual* (Auckland)
*The Football Annual* (London)
*Football Handbook*
*Guide Français et International du Rugby*
*International Rugby Yearbook*
*The New Zealand Rugby Annual*
*The New Zealand Rugby Football Annual*
*Oval World*
*Playfair Rugby Football Annual*
*Rothman's Rugby Yearbook*
*Rugby Almanack of New Zealand*
*Rugby Annual for Wales*
*Rugby Digest*
*Rugby International*
*Rugby News*
*Rugby World*
*Rugger*
*SA Rugby Annual*
*Wisden Rugby Almanack*

**Websites**

All Blacks: www.allblacks.com
Amateur Athletic Foundation of Los Angeles: www.aafla.org
New Zealand Rugby Museum: www.rugbymuseum.co.nz
Rugby Football Union: www.rfu.com
Scrum.com: www.scrum.com
Teivovo (Fijian Rugby): www.teivovo.com

# Index

# INDEX

# INDEX

# INDEX

315

# INDEX